STRANGE RUNNING TALES

WHEN ULTRARUNNING WAS A REALITY SHOW

STRANGE RUNNING TALES

WHEN ULTRARUNNING WAS A REALITY SHOW

Davy Crockett

Utah Ultras LLC

Ultrarunning History Series

1. Frank Hart: The First Black Ultrarunning Star
2. Grand Canyon Rim to Rim History
3. Strange Running Tales: When Ultrarunning was a Reality Show

Front cover: "The Scene at Two O'clock This Morning – Rowell Making His 432d Mile: The Pedestrian Contest at Gilmore's Garden (Madison Square Garden)". *The Daily Graphic: An Illustrated Evening Newspaper*, New York, Saturday March 15, 1879

Copyright © 2023 by Utah Ultras LLC

All rights reserved. No portion of this book may be reproduced in any form without written permission from the author, except as permitted by U.S. copyright law. Images included are in the public domain unless otherwise designated.

Second Printing - Paperback

ISBN – 9798390048375

Ultrarunninghistory.com

Contents

The Barclay Match – 1,000 Miles in 1,000 Hours 1
The Barclay Match Craze 9
Shots Fired During Barclay Match 21
The Strange Indiana Walking Wonder 27
Hallucinations and Cranky Runners 37
Runner Misbehavior 45
Sickness and Death 53
Race Disruptions 65
Steve Brodie – New York Newsboy 79
Fraud, Theft, and Nuisance 97
The Murder of Alice Robison 109
Love Scandals 129
Corruption and Bribes 147
Richard Lacouse - Scoundrel 163
Arrests 181
George Noremac and Murder 195
The Strange and Tragic 219
Sources 235
About the Author 245
Index 247

"Instead of being like the ball match or even the horse race, the pedestrian contest becomes a trial of physical powers, like the prize-fight, in which the agony of the participants forms the chief attraction to the public." Buffalo Morning Express (New York), September 29, 1879

Introduction

Many people have the mistaken belief that the sport of ultrarunning (running competitively beyond the marathon length) is a new sport that emerged in the 1970s in America. They are then surprised to learn the truth, that running or walking ultra-distances competitively has existed for hundreds of years all over the world.

For centuries, many indigenous Americans were outstanding long-distance runners who could run ultra-distances. They used their talents in important roles to carry messages and news to distant communities. In 1680, coordinated message runners dispatched from Taos Pueblo, in present-day New Mexico, to Hopi Villages in present-day Arizona, nearly 400 miles away, using their talents to coordinate a successful, simultaneous, revolt involving 70 villages against their Spanish oppressors. Competitive races were held among the Hopi and Tarahumara in Mexico for centuries, traveling distances well over 100 miles.

Among Europeans, it should not be surprising that men who became physically fit wished to test their endurance by proving that they could walk or run incredible distances during defined periods of time. These competitions first emerged as "journey walks" between cities on rugged dirt roads in all weather.

FOSTER POWELL.

A British long-distance walker, **Foster Powell** (1734-1793) started a focus on walking/running for six days and is recognized as the "Father of the Six-Day Race." In 1773, Powell caused a great stir when he walked and ran about 400 miles from London to York and back in less than six days. "Walking" in those very early days was a general term. These pioneer ultrarunners of the late 1700s and early 1800s actually performed a "jog-trot," or a mixture of walking and running. There was no emphasis yet on "fair heel-toe" walking.

Powell established a six day standard that would be remembered for decades. Nearly all six-day attempts in the decades that followed pointed their efforts to Powell's previous accomplishments. Dozens attempted to match or improve on his feat. By 1779, Powell was the first long-distance runner who was referred to as a "pedestrian" performing that art of "pedestrianism." That term took hold in England and eventually referenced competitions on foot for all distances, even sprints.

"Pedestrianism" came into the American public eye when **Edward Payson Weston** (1839-1929) of Providence, Rhode Island, made several attempts in 1874 to walk 500 miles in six days. **P. T. Barnum** (1810-1891), of circus fame, had the brilliant idea to move such attempts indoors for vast audiences to watch, in his massive Hippodrome in New York City. In 1875, Barnum put on the first six-day race in history, won by Weston with 431 miles. In these races, the winner was the athlete who reached the furthest distance within six days.

EDWARD PAYSON WESTON

During the late 1870s, this new reality show of indoor six-day races exploded across America. People of all classes became fascinated by the competition, drama, and human tragedy that could be witnessed during these events. Organizers held more than 400 six-day races in America and Great Britain during the 19th century. Spectators would usually pay 25 cents per day to enter smoke-filled arenas and city halls to cheer and wager on their favorite runner. In only a few years, pedestrianism became the number one spectator sport in America. During about three decades, millions of enthusiastic onlookers would watch walkers and runners circle indoor tracks for days, secretly hoping to witness suffering, fainting, and even fistfights like modern-day hockey matches. Indeed, pedestrianism was like the modern-day reality shows that addict television viewers today.

Strange Running Tales: When Ultrarunning was a Reality Show

Hundreds of athletes, men and women of all races and cultures flocked to be participants in the sport hoping to achieve fame and fortune. Some could win millions of dollars in today's value. Most of them trained hard, but others were only seeking opportunities for fast money, sometimes through dishonest means. Critics of the sport were many. Some called their efforts unnatural, just attempts to "win the empty applause of a thoughtless mob."

As with many professional sports, pedestrianism had a high impact on the families of the athletes. Husbands or wives would be away for days, weeks, and even months in their quest to win fortunes. Their hearts would often drift away from their more important family responsibilities. Sometimes spouses would take part by handling/crewing their loved-one, but often they were not supportive of this type of occupation. Once, during a six-day race in New York City, a wife belittled her husband for doing so poorly and moving so slowly. She went out on the track and showed him she could beat him on a lap, embarrassed him, and made him give up the race and return home.

The sport of ultrarunning during the 19th century was truly filled with tales of strange tales that are unthinkable and shocking to us today. This book will highlight the most bizarre, shocking, funny, and head-scratching stories that took place in ultrarunning, mostly during a 30-year period that began about 1875. These fascinating stories were discovered by scouring thousands of newspaper articles published in the era with amazing details. They were often front-page stories in the *New York Times, Boston Globe, Chicago Times, San Francisco Examiner*, and other widely read newspapers. The drama-filled stories were serious best sellers, resulting in Extras being printed during races and telegrams sent worldwide.

Many of these stories are "outliers," not representative of most of the events and athletes that took part. Most of the ultrarunners were outstanding citizens who later served in noble professions. But with no serious regulations and oversight, the free-wheeling, wager-driven, drug-filled sport was a melting pot of activity that attracted some of the worst characters and behavior of the period. Sad tragedy resulted and even some deaths.

CHAPTER ONE

The Barclay Match – 1,000 Miles in 1,000 Hours

Richard Manks attempting a Barclay Match

Could a person walk or run 1,000 miles in 1,000 hours, doing a mile in each and every hour for nearly 42 days? That was the strange question that surfaced in 1809 in England. Such a crazy challenge would involve enduring sleep deprivation and altering sleep patterns dramatically. Over the years, hundreds of men and women would take up the challenge that became known as the Barclay Match. In a way, these matches were similar endurance activities to the bizarre dance marathons/walkathons of the 1930s that required participants to be on their feet every hour. They also had similarities to the modern "Last Man Standing" events that require a certain number of miles to be run each hour. Nineteenth-century critics of these 1,000-mile events called them "cruel exhibitions of self-torture that had no point except to win the empty applause of a thoughtless mob and put a few pounds into the pockets of the walkers. There is nothing to learn from such exhibitions save they are positively injurious, physically and morally." But others thought the matches gave "convincing proof that man is scarcely acquainted with his own capacity and powers."

These "1,000 miles in 1,000 hours" events captivated the world, were cheered in person by tens of thousands of people, were wagered with the equivalent of millions of today's value in dollars, and launched the long-distance sport of "pedestrianism" into the public eye. It was first thought that this 1,000-mile feat was an impossibility, and it was called a "Herculean" effort. But during a 100-year period, there were more than 300 attempts at this curious challenge, and more than half were successes. How did this all begin?

Captain Robert Barclay

Robert Barclay Allardice (1779-1854), or "Captain Barclay," of Ury, Scotland, was born to a Scottish family. His father had been a member of Parliament and owned extensive estates. When Barclay was fifteen years old, he won 100 guineas wager walking heal-toe six miles in one hour, which at that time was considered a significant accomplishment. When he was twenty years old, he covered 150 miles in two days, and in 1801, in very hot weather, he walked 300 miles in five days. Also, that year he walked/ran 110 miles in 19:27 in a muddy park. He served as an officer in the army and thus received the title of "Captain."

Captain Barclay

Barclay was clearly onto something that could make him good money and huge fame. In September 1808, he considered accepting a challenge of walking 1,000 miles in 1,000 consecutive hours for 1,000 guineas, which was an enormous fortune at that time. (Worth about $175,000 in today's value). He first conducted a secret test at his estate in Scotland. Instead of testing himself, he had one of his tenant farmers walk one mile every hour for eight days. Barclay accepted the 1,000 miles in 1,000 hours challenge.

Others had attempted this before, but no one went longer than 30 days. For example, in 1772, a tailor began a walk on a large wager to walk 1,000 miles in 1,000 hours on "a spot of ground marked out for the purpose near Tyburn Turnpike" in London. It is believed that he was unsuccessful. A pedestrian named Jones sought to walk every hour for a month but quit in less than three weeks. Various problems, such as lack of sleep and swollen legs, caused them to fail.

1,000 Miles in 1,000 Consecutive Hours

Captain Barclay

Months passed and Barclay's challenge was finally put together to be performed on open land near Newmarket, England. They laid out a half-mile course for him to walk back and forth in a straight line over smooth land. Tent camps were constructed at each end for recorders and assistants.

Barclay began the monotonous six-week task just after midnight on June 1, 1809. Seven gas lamps on poles 100 yards apart were lit each evening like streetlamps. He would generally start each mile about fifteen minutes before the finish of the first hour and then do the next mile at the top of the second hour. In that way, he could take about a 90-minute rest before heading out again for the next two miles. Over the first three nights, he overslept by a few minutes and had to speed up his pace significantly to finish an entire mile before the hour ended.

He dressed in a "jacket and breeches, and woolen stockings. His shoes appeared to be very large, and a handkerchief hung loosely about his neck." He would usually have two men walk on each side of him, day and night.

After every mile, they signed their names into a logbook, describing the weather and how he was feeling.

On his first day, his slowest mile was 16 minutes, and the average mile was 15:15. "He paced along at a sort of lounging gait without any apparent extraordinary exertions, scarcely raising his feet two inches above the ground." He ate his first breakfast at 5 a.m. when he dined on roast fowl with bread and butter and drank a pint of strong ale and two cups of tea. For the first few days, he didn't go to bed between walking stretches, and just reclined on a sofa or did a little strolling in Newmarket outside the course.

By the eighth day, Barclay had walked about 135 miles. Word spread through the towns about his unusual challenge, turning it into a reality show for their time. Onlookers from all over came in their horse carriages and were curious to see if he was exhausted. He was not, and appeared to be happy, and in good health. His sleeping patterns adapted. At night, he could fall asleep instantly and arise at the right time with no trouble.

However, the longer he went, the more afflictions arose. At times, he was greatly bothered by the dust. On day ten, he grew very tired because of the high wind and rain. On the 12th day, he rested often, and slept well, but complained about pain in his neck and shoulders. On the 13th day, his calf muscles were seizing up and were very painful every time he started a new mile.

Barclay ate four meals a day, about every six hours. His diet usually comprised cold beefsteaks and mutton chops for 5-6 pounds of meat each day. He also ate some vegetables and would drink about two bottles of port wine. For every mile, he added a few bonus yards so that no one could

First Day.—June 1st, 1809.

Hour	Min. past	Seconds	Time per Mile	State of the Weather.
N. 12	2	14	12	Rainy.
1	¼	15	14½	Fair but cloudy.
2	42	57	15	Do. do.
3	¼	14½	14	Do. do.
4	42	56	14	Windy and stormy.
5	¼	14	13½	Do. do.
6	40	55	15	Windy and sunshine.
7	¼	14½	14	Do. do.
8	41	55½	14¼	Very hot.
9	¼	14¼	14	Do. do.
10	41	55½	14½	Windy and hot.
11	¼	15	14½	Cool and pleasant.
D. 12	42½	57	14¼	Windy and hot.
1	¼	15	14½	Windy and dusty.
2	41¼	56	14¼	Hot, windy, and dusty.
3	¼	14½	14	Do. do.
4	42½	56	13½	Do. do.
5	¼	14½	14	Do. do.
6	39	55	16	Stormy.
7	¼	14½	14	Moderate.
8	29	45	16	Cool and pleasant.
9	¼	15	14½	Do. do.
10	41	55½	14½	Dark and cloudy.
11	¼	14	13½	Dark with rain.
N. 12	43	56	13	Clear moon-light, and fair.

make a charge that he wasn't covering the distance. After a couple of weeks, his mile times slowed from about 15-minute miles to 21-minute miles.

The owner of the nearby "Horse and Jocky Pub" saw a great business opportunity. On the 16th day, he invited Barclay to move to new lodgings near the pub, with a new course laid out on the Norwich Road. The change was agreeable to him, and he felt more comfortable. His food could be cooked outside. It was also huge for the pub, because the spectators watched Barclay's progress as they drank and ate.

For some reason, Barclay's muscles were in great pain around 3 a.m. each morning. On the 19th morning, he had difficulty walking and would need to lie down frequently to sleep. The next day, they soaked his legs and feet in vinegar, which took away the soreness. The weather was consistent for the first 20 days, with some rain nearly every day. After that, heat became the enemy, which hardened up the road. They used a "water cart" once a day to soften up the road and pound down the dust.

Increasingly larger crowds came to watch the grueling spectacle. It wasn't just a sporting event; it was also a social event. They held picnics and ran races among themselves. Not everyone wanted him to succeed, especially those who were betting against him. Things got very dangerous for Barclay. Some antagonists broke the gas lamps put out for the night with rocks or shot them with muskets. Barclay carried pistols on his waist belt and arranged for a bodyguard, **John Gully** (1783-1863), a former boxing champion.

John Gully

On the 23rd day, Barclay had a terrible toothache, and he became feverish. It took two days for the tooth to calm down. On day 25, he had a hard time starting his miles. His attendants used remedies such as oil and camphor to rub down his painful muscles. The pain progressed down to his ankles and his legs became swollen. When heavy rain fell, he had to wear a heavier coat and his mile times increased to 36:30.

On the 26th day, Barclay fell into a deep sleep, and it was apparent he was still asleep as he began his 607th mile. His attendant, **William Cross**, had to beat him on the shoulders with a walking stick in order to wake him up in time to complete his mile within the hour. His mile times slowed to well over 30 minutes, making it too hard to get any rest. He soon had so much pain he kept crying out and "walked in a shuffling manner." It was said, "His courage was unconquerable." With a week to go, he had doubts if he could continue because of spasms in his legs. But with only a few days left, he was very confident about succeeding. It was reported, "He declared he would die on the road rather than give in."

Captain Barclay

Forty-second Day.—July 12.

Hour.		Started min. past.	Returned min. past.	Time per Mile.	State of the Weather.
M.	1	½	24½	24	Cool and pleasant.
	2	35	55	20	Do. do.
	3	½	25	24½	Do. do.
	4	34	56½	22½	Do. do.
	5	½	21	20½	Do. do.
	6	35	56	21	Do. with sunshine.
	7	7	28	21	Do. do.
	8	35	55½	20½	Warm, with do.
	9	½	22	21½	Hot, do.
	10	34	55	21	Very hot, and do.
	11	½	22	21½	Do. do.
D.	12	35	55	20	Do. do.
	1	½	21	20½	Do. do.
	2	30	52	22	Do. do.
	3	15	37	22	Hot, but pleasant.

During the last two days of his long journey, he was in good spirits and completed his miles in shorter times than he had for many days. The weather was better, and he walked many hours without his large coat. The crowds of people during the concluding days were "unprecedented." No lodgings could be found anywhere in the Newmarket area. They roped off Barclay's walking area to keep it clear because the course became so crowded.

On the afternoon of the 42nd day, he finished his last mile "with perfect ease and great spirits, amidst an immense concourse of spectators." The crowd went wild. His bodyguard led the masses in three "rousing cheers."

When reporters asked him what he planned to do now that it was over, he said he looked forward to taking a long, good sleep. But he said he would need to be awakened about three times during the night to transition into longer sleep. Right after finishing, he went and took a warm bath as the bells of Newmarket rang loudly. He won an enormous sum of about 16,000 guineas. All bets exceeded 100,000 guineas or about $8 million in today's value.

During the six weeks of walking, he lost about 32 pounds, weighing 154 pounds at the finish. Altogether, his moving time on the course was 12 days, 8 hours for the 1,000 miles in 41.7 days.

Captain Barclay had proven it could be done. The fame of his accomplishment spread like wildfire. He made history, and some later called Barclay the "Father of Pedestrianism."

Robert Barclay Allardice

CHAPTER TWO

The Barclay Match Craze

Initial Unsuccessful Copycat Attempts

Barclay's success, especially financially, caused a 1,000-mile craze to erupt instantly in 1809, as others tried to duplicate his accomplishment. It became known as a "Barclay Match." Within a week of Barclay's finish, the first copycat was **Mr. Howe**, "a stout, athletic man." He took up the challenge in Somerset, England, for 300 guineas. The odds were 10-1 against him. He walked over some land by his home at Cliffe Common. After twelve days, he was still walking, but "it was expected every hour that he would give in." Howe quit after the 15th day and lost 200 guineas. It was reported that "his health was much injured."

Another man, in Ireland, weighing 280 pounds, took on a wager to accomplish the Barclay Match "to walk over a thousand miles in a thousand successive hours." The betting odds were 50-1 against him. A report included, "The portly personage who was to be the

> The young Scottish Clergyman, who undertook to read six chapters of the Bible every hour for 1000 successive hours, and pursued his ridiculous task thirteen days and nights, has fallen into a profound sleep or trance, from which he has never yet awoke, although it is evident he still lives. *Lon. Pap.*

A variation in 1809

hero in this extraordinary scene waddled forth to the racecourse. All eyes were eagerly fixed upon him and just as they thought he was about to start, he pulled out of his pocket a sheet of paper on which was written the words, 'A Thousand Miles in a Thousand Successive Hours.' He laid it on the ground, and then deliberately walked over it, to the astonishment and chagrin of the deluded beholders. A universal murmur was immediately set up at this hoax and many swore that they would not be 'walked over' in that kind of manner, but demanded their stakes be returned. It being the opinion of the umpires, however, that the wager was fairly won, the winner immediately pocketed the money and walked off."

Others attempted the challenge but failed. In 1811, A **Mr. Blackie** of Somershire, England, made the attempt but had to quit after 23 days because of terrible swollen legs. He had lost nearly 50 pounds during his try. Others quit because of injured feet and pulled hamstrings. The newspapers seemed to delight in all these failures, making Captain Barclay's fame grow even more.

First Successful Copycat Barkley Match

In 1811, success was reached! It was reported that **Thomas Standen**, age 60, of Salehurst, England, successfully completed the Barkley Match at Newmarket, and extended it to 1,100 miles in 1,100 hours. The event did not receive wide coverage or crowds. Why 1,100 miles? Many pedestrians wanted to "one-up" Barclay. They could not do it faster, but they could go further, and attempt variations that required their rest times to be shorter, and more frequent, pushing the limits of sleep deprivation.

Josiah Eaton - 1,100 Miles in 1,100 Hours

Josiah Eaton

In 1815, **Josiah Eaton**, age 46, was a baker from Woodford, Northamptonshire, England. He was a small man, only 5'2". He announced he would attempt the Barclay Match but add more to it, and walk 1,100 miles in 1,100 hours, not realizing that Standen had already accomplished this extended feat four years before.

Eaton walked at Blackheath, England. The magistrates in Blackheath had been cracking down on such attempts that involved heavy gambling. To make sure they did not disrupt things, he announced he would not receive any money for his efforts. There was a lot of skepticism about whether he or anyone could duplicate or exceed what Barclay had accomplished. It was said, "Captain Barclay was not only a man of great constitutional power, but he also knew how to train, whereas Eaton did not appear to possess the former, neither had he adopted the latter."

Eaton started on November 10, 1815, near the "Hare and Billet Pub" on a quarter-mile course with two small red flags marking each end. He wore a white hat, blue coat, and striped waistcoat and slept in the pub. "A great concourse of persons assembled towards evening." Like Barclay, he walked one mile at the end of the hour and another mile at the beginning of the next hour, giving him about 90 minutes of rest between his walking efforts.

Blackheath

As Eaton went along well, unsubstantiated rumors emerged that he wasn't walking at night. To counter this, Eaton made a statement, "I will, for 100 guineas, give up the distance now performed, and begin again with the assertion of such malicious falsehood, if he will enter the lists against me."

After ten days, a poem was published in the newspaper:

Since tramping now is all the rage
Some hundred daily take the stage
The walking man to greet on;
And oft impatient of delay,
From meals unfinished run away,
To Blackheath, there, to Eat-on
Why Eaton walks, it is not known very well,
'Tis for Pedestrian glory some have said;
But other folks with much more reason tell,
This is the way the baker makes his bread!

Eaton accomplished the Barclay Match plus 100 more miles on December 26, 1815. The *Gentleman's Magazine* wrote, "The extraordinary task of pedestrianism, which has just been completed by Josiah Eaton, has not only exceeded all former experiments of this nature, but given convincing proof that man is scarcely acquainted with his own capacity and powers."

Within two weeks, he discovered that someone else had already accomplished 1,100 miles in 1,100 hours, and Eaton was disappointed. Because Eaton did not receive money for all his effort, he remained a poor baker. Within a month, he was in debtor's prison for not being able to pay a debt.

1,100 Miles in 1,100 Hours at the Top of Each Hour

Eaton was obsessed and must have stewed over his wasted effort that did not set a new record. After release from prison, Eaton organized another 1,100 x 1,100 walk, again at Blackheath, starting on June 10, 1816. This time he was required to start each mile at the top of the hour, which would be much harder, only getting about 45 minutes' consecutive rest. Also, all his miles were required to be walked within 20 minutes. The betting odds were "greatly against him."

Early on, Eaton had feet problems and then had swollen legs, but he was in good spirits, and he soon adapted his sleep patterns to cat naps. He could quickly fall asleep and his attendants easily awakened him. With about 75 miles to go, Eaton injured his ankle, which forced him to use two walking sticks for a while. The last mile finally arrived. It was reported, "Eaton in performing the last mile, was attempted to be thrown three times by some supposed hirelings of his opponents." The interference failed. He successfully completed 1,100 miles in 1,100 hours on July 20, 1816, in front of an "immense crowd" after nearly 46 days of walking every hour. "At the conclusion of his performance, the air rang with acclamations, and partaking of some refreshment."

2,000 Half Miles in 2,000 Half Hours (1 Mile Each Hour)

Eaton continued to attempt even stranger variations of the Barclay Match. Later, in 1816, Eaton's friends accepted a wager of 500 guineas that he could walk 2,000 half miles in 2,000 successive half hours. This would involve only getting about 22 minutes of rest each half hour, requiring an outrageous sleep pattern for nearly 42 days.

Eaton started on October 23, 1816, walking on a course about three miles from Croydon, England, on the Brixton Causeway. He walked on a quarter mile out-and-back path near a private home where he took his rests. Umpires were always on hand to witness the effort.

Brixton Causeway

Within a couple days, Mr. **Petty Sessions** was trying to get magistrates to stop the match because of the inconvenience it was causing locally from the crowds coming to watch. Within ten days, the newspaper was calling Eaton the "Sleep Walker." An observer wrote, "he frequently takes a few winks during walking, and only requires, it is said, a gentle shake from his attendant to render him awake to what he has to perform." By the time he was halfway, skepticism had mostly gone away, and betting was in his favor.

Eaton had been promised money from several men if he succeeded, but as he neared the finish, he discovered they would not follow through. He was told that the primary backer had died and that the bet was void. Eaton realized that no serious bet had been made.

As he was getting close to reaching the 2,000 half miles, he issued a shocking statement, "I feel myself fully competent to complete the task I have undertaken, of walking 2,000 half miles in 2,000 successive half hours, which would have been finished on the 5th of December at noon; but being deceived by the gentlemen who should have supported me, I am determined not to complete the task. I therefore hereby give notice, I shall walk only until 11:00 on Thursday, December 5, 1816, being only 1,998 half miles, and recommend all parties to consider their bets to be null and void." He stopped as he promised with one mile to go, walking his last half mile freshly in

Josiah Eaton

8:30. He claimed he did not receive even a shilling from the pub owner. In all, he only received 25 guineas, which didn't come close to covering his expenses. Despite the halt, his 1998 x 1998 half-mile effort was declared, "the greatest pedestrian feat ever performed."

4,032 Quarter Miles in 4,032 Quarter Hours (1 Mile Each Hour)

Next, it became truly strange. In 1818, Eaton started an attempt to walk a quarter mile every 15 minutes for six weeks (1,008 miles in 4,032 quarter miles) at Stowmarket, Suffolk, England. He began his outrageous attempt across from the "Pot of Flowers Inn" on May 11, 1818. After each quarter mile, he would ring a bell. Wet weather affected his endeavor early on, making him very tired and lame, but he recovered and soon bets were close to even money.

It was reported, "He falls asleep immediately on throwing himself on his bed, which is placed in a hut at the end of his ground and awakes at the slightest touch or call." Hot weather arrived and caused problems, but he

continued to push forward. Eaton was successful and finished on June 30, 1818. They paraded him through the streets of Stowmarket in front of a crowd of 2,000 people who loved the reality show.

1,500 Miles, 1.5 Miles Each Hour

The next variation increased the mileage per hour. In September 1816, **N. B. Barnet**, age 72, started a 1,500-mile attempt in 32 days on a course at the "Mitre Tavern," Lower Tooting, Surry, England. He was successful, with 45 minutes to spare. Along the way he achieved 1,000 miles by doing 1.5 miles every hour, starting at the first of every hour.

A report included, "For the last five or six miles he was accompanied by a large concourse of persons, male and female, on horseback and on foot, who were anxious to witness of his pedestrian power. At the end of the last mile, he was received with shouts of applause by his friends at the Mitre; and after he had refreshed himself, they seated him in a triumphal car and bore him in grand procession through Lower and Upper Tooting, the village musicians, two fiddlers and a tambourine player, accompanying him in his progress with the very appropriate air, 'See The Conquering Hero comes.'"

1,200 Miles in 1,200 Hours (1 Mile Each Hour)

Robert Skipper worked as an "ostler" (took care of horses) at an Inn in Norwich, England and had also served in the army for about 15 years. In 1822 he took on an extended Barclay Match to walk 1,200 Miles in 1,200 Hours. His feat was accomplished near Papermills Turnpike, Cambridge, England. After finishing, he immediately for fun, walked six miles within the next hour.

Robert Skipper

1,000 Miles in 2,000 half hours (2 Miles Each Hour)

A few months later, also in 1822, Skipper was back at it, this time to do 1,000 miles in 2,000 half hours. He began on Sept 25, 1822, next to cricket grounds, Prussia Gardens, on a turnpike road going from Newmarket to Norwich. It was reported, "He is going on well at present, and excites great attention. He performs his task on the public road, half a mile out and half a mile in."

He was successful. Thousands were on hand to witness the finish, including many Dukes and Lords. When he finally could sleep solid for five hours after finishing, it made him pretty ill because his body couldn't adjust fast to continuous sleep. He did not come away rich because no bets were involved. He only collected rewards from generous supporters.

1,750 Miles in 1,000 Hours

Battersea Fields

In August 1938, **Charles Harris**, a 14-year pedestrian veteran, walked 1,500 miles in 1,000 hours (1.5 miles each hour) in Finchley, England. A couple months later, he attempted another 42 days of walking to go 1,750 miles in 1,000 hours (1.75 miles each hour) at Battersea Fields in London. His method was to walk 3.5 miles each session, which he would begin a about 38 minutes past the hour, giving him 22 minutes before starting the next 1.75 miles at the top of the hour. This would give him about 1:15 continuous rest every two hours. On weekends, large numbers of spectators came to witness.

At 1,464 miles Harris was still in good spirits but it was reported his "physical energies were beginning to fail. He no longer walked with a firm and vigorous step." During the rain, he caught a severe cold and was coughing violently. He had terrible sores and blisters on his feet and was limping.

During his last weekend, Battersea Fields, along the Thames River, was packed with about 6,000 people trying to get a glimpse of Harris walking. He successfully completed the feat on December 3, 1838, and received "warm congratulations" and his friend paraded him around on a chair led by flags and a band playing music.

1852 Barclay Match Frenzy

In the early 1850s, **Richard Manks**, "the Warwickshire Antelope" and **James Searles**, "The Wonder" from Leeds, England, were rivals and tried to outdo each other, accomplishing variations of the Barclay Match. They both achieved 1,750 miles in 1,750 hours. The publicity they achieved started a frenzy of Barclay Matches in 1852, accomplished by about ten men.

On September 20, 1852, Searles began the unthinkable, 2,000 miles in 2,000 half hours on a round track that involved seven laps to a mile near the Pineapple Inn, at Toxteth Park in Liverpool, England. During the first week, it was reported, "One astonishing feature in connection with the pedestrian is that he rises from his bed at the fixed time without requiring any person to rouse him and starts on his journey apparently quite refreshed."

Toxteth Park

As the finishing days approached, a badly sore knee bothered Searles, but he was still pushing forward. He said he would finish if he had to walk on crutches. He complained of dizziness during the night but recovered during the days. One night, a man wanted to see if Searles was really still walking. The doubter climbed to the top of a railing surrounding the grounds and fell over into a pond. Searles, walking at the time, heard the splash in the dark and rushed to help the man get out of the pond. He won over his skeptical spy who said Searles was "the cleverest man in Europe."

He finished on November 1, 1852, and had lost nearly 30 pounds along the way. It was said, "The match may be considered one of the most extraordinary ever recorded in the annals of pedestrianism." That evening, at a benefit held for him where he danced a clog hornpipe.

The public started to get rather skeptical in if these matches were being conducted fairly. It was written, "Deception has been often practiced by persons engaging to accomplish the distance in the time named, and, with the collusion of others, the cheat may be easily played off." Some indeed were charades to attract spectators that were charged entrance to watch the walker performed in enclosed areas. Some walkers in these enclosed areas had been accused of stopping during the nights.

Woman Barclayists

Woman also attempted and achieved the Barclay Match, perhaps more often than men. But their achievements were rarely covered widely as compared to the men. Many English venues prohibited women from doing walking events and they conducted most of them in more private settings. It has been estimated that there were nearly 120 women who attempted, completed, or claimed to have completed a Barclay Match of some flavor between 1809 and 1908.

Emma Sharp

Emma Sharp, age 30, accomplished one of the most widely covered walk by a woman, of Bowling, England, who started her walk on September 17, 1864, at Bradford, England near a pub, "The Quarry Gap Hotel." She was sensible and dressed like a man. It was written that "almost the only indication of her sex is in her large drooping straw hat, which was ornamented with a white feather and other feminine adornments." She carried a stick in her right hand.

Sharp, used a roped-off 120-yard course and walked a mile at the end of an hour and another at the top of the next hour. For the two miles, she would walk 14 laps + 80 yards to and from her room. Unlike other attempts by women, thousands came out to watch and made bets. Early on she suffered from swollen ankles, but they became stronger as she went along.

Shady characters attempted to stop her. They attacked her with chloroform, threw burning embers at her, attempted to drug her food, and tried to trip her. During the final days, eighteen police officers disguised as civilians watched over her and attempted to catch these criminals. One friend walked in front of her with a loaded rifle at night. Emma finally walked the last two days carrying a pistol, which many times she would fire in the air as a warning.

Sharp, finished successfully her 1,000 x 1,000 on October 29, 1864, in front of thousands of spectators. A band played, and they roasted an ox in her honor. Her husband had been embarrassed by her man-like efforts and stayed out of public view. But once he realized how much money she won, he quit his job and started his own business.

The Barclay Match in America

The Barclay Match eventually made its way to America in 1842. **Captain Thomas Ellsworth** "the St. Louis Pedestrian" accomplished the first known American Barclay Match near Boston, at the one-mile Cambridge Trotting Course near Porter's hotel.

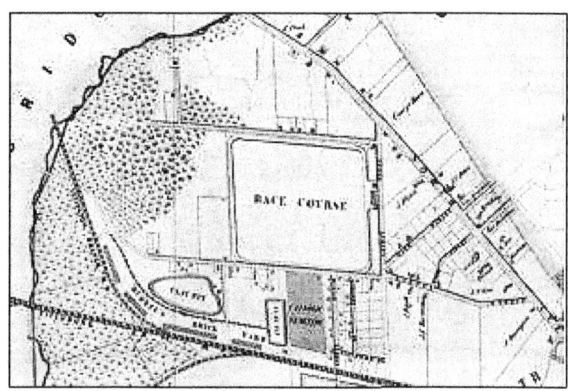
Cambridge Trotting Course

In 1843, Ellsworth competed against a **Mr. Fogg** in a 1,000 x 1,000 contest on a course at Chelsea, Massachusetts. Ellsworth finished. He attempted it again in May 1845, in New Orleans, Louisiana, on the "Eclipse Course." Three men were hired as watchers and had to swear in front of a judge with threats of perjury charges that they would report on his success or failure. Ellsworth went on to finish his third successful 1000 x 1000. For the fourth time, he went the distance in 1851 at St. Louis, Missouri. In 1855, he did it again for the 5th time in Sacramento, California. He became the most prolific Barclay Match walker in American history.

4,000 Quarter Miles in 4,000 Periods of 10 Minutes (1,000 Miles in 667 Hours)

William Gale

In 1877 **William Gale**, age 52 of England, twice accomplished the most terrible sleep-deprived Barkley Match, going 1,000 miles in 667 hours, by doing a quarter mile every ten minutes. He did this twice in 1877, once at the Canton Hotel Grounds at Cardiff, England and another time in the Agricultural Hall in London.

But by the second week, his sleep patterns had adjusted and he could sleep comfortably for about four-five minutes between his walks. He would fall asleep at once in a sitting position and would wake up instantly on being touched. For each 24-hour period, he slept about a total of 3-4 hours. Sometimes he didn't know where he was. He thought he was out in the country in a farmyard. He could only recognize the dark line of the track before him. More than 10,000 people came to watch him reach his 1,000th mile. He walked his last quarter mile in 2:04.

There was harsh criticism in the newspapers about his accomplishment. "Gale's walk of 1,000 miles was a disgusting as well as a cruel exhibition of self-torture. He accomplished his task and may claim the barren honour of having done more than any other pedestrian, but no one would be surprised to hear that the unnatural strain which he put upon himself had brought him to a premature grave. For four weeks, this man has been walking with an interval every ten minutes of five- or six-minutes' rest. Toward the end of his weary and bootless tramp, he had to walk in a semi-somnolent state, and on one occasion he stood still, fast asleep. He had to be continually roused and urged on. He has walked his 4,000 quarter-miles in 4,000 successive ten minutes, but what does it amount to? At the best, he has won the empty applause of a thoughtless mob and put a few pounds into his pocket. There is nothing to learn from such exhibitions save they are positively injurious, physically and morally."

CHAPTER THREE

Shots Fired During Barclay Match

On March 3, 1879, at the Fifth Regiment Armory in New York City, during **Peter Van Ness'** attempt to walk 2,000 half-miles in 2,000 consecutive half-hours, one of the most shocking events in ultrarunning history took place. Van Ness, sleep deprived, drunk, and in intense pain, got hold of a gun and shot his trainer, **Joseph Burgoine**, in the arm, and next took a shot at his manager, **Simon Levy**, grazing his silk hat. Panic resulted among the spectators. It could have resulted in mass murder. How could this be?

Peter Van Ness

Peter Lewis Van Ness (1853-1900) was from Brooklyn, New York. He began his famed professional pedestrian career in 1876 when he started to walk six-day matches against women, reaching 450 miles. He was about six-feet tall and plodded along in a "rakish style" and a strange gait, wearing striped stockings up to his knees. He had walked in several six-day races and had success in 50-mile races.

On January 27, 1879, Van Ness, age 25, started his 2,000 half miles in 2,000 half hours competition in New York City against **Edward Belden** (1856-1926), age 22, of Milwaukee, Wisconsin. The venue was in the old Fifth Regiment Armory in lower Manhattan, at Hester and Elizabeth Streets. The wagering stakes between the two were huge, $500 ($5,800 value today). Belden was trying

View from Armory, many street peddlers

to cover the 2,000 half miles in consecutive 20-minute segments. A track of sawdust and loam was created in the Armory's drill room with eleven laps to the mile.

The 1,000 Mile Match Begins

Everything started out well during the first week. Both men started to complain of calloused heels and Van Ness suffered from headaches. But both looked well and didn't show signs of exhaustion. "Van Ness walks with a free and easy movement of his whole body, keeping a sharp eye on his opponent and laughing and talking with friends in the room. His walk is strongly suggestive of a hungry man on his way to dinner."

Belden wore velvet trunks, red socks and a light-colored vest covered with medals. After a couple of weeks, he hit his knee against one of the stakes along the ring and they feared that he would have to quit. "A speedy application of liniment relieved the pain and kept down the swelling so that the effects of the blow soon wore off." Van Ness was very nervous and cross, and "frequently had difficulties with his trainer when 'time' was called, and he had to appear on the track." The dismal hall had strong odors of stale cigar smoke and beer. A small Italian orchestra played tunes on a harp, violin, and flute.

After 20 days, Belden was a mess. "His feet were a mass of blisters, and it was almost impossible to wake him up." The stress put on both men, physically and mentally, was incredible. On Feb 23rd, after 28 days, Belden was successful in his grueling task and reached his 1,000 miles. "After finishing his journey, he retired to his room, donned citizens' clothes, returned to the track and walked three half miles." Van Ness was at 672 miles and continued. He said that he felt so well that he could continue for six months.

> TRIALS OF ENDURANCE.
> BELDEN AND VAN NESS WALKING—ONE-HALF OF THE FORMER'S TASK DONE—MRS.

Van Ness Parties

On March 3, 1879, after Van Ness had covered about 859 miles in 36 days, everything went bad for Van Ness. Many of his friends from Brooklyn came to watch his performance and, during his rest spells, would join him in his room to drink. "The

Hester Street, where Armory was located

pedestrian joined them in their carousal. He drank freely of port wine and became hilarious." Out on the track in his drunkenness, he entertained about 50 people with "some rapid walking and occasionally peculiar fancy steps, as if he were balancing himself on a giddy trapeze."

A bell rang when he reached his half mile, and he went back to his room to party with his friends. Finally, completely drunk at 8:30 p.m., his handlers forced his friends to leave. For unknown reasons, one of his friends left him with a gift of a revolver which was loaded. Van Ness then fell into a deep sleep.

Shots are Fired

"When the moment came for him to be called to go upon the track, his trainer, **Joseph Burgoine**, undertook the task of getting him out of bed. But Van Ness was sound asleep, and it required physical force to awaken him. He protested against the operation and became violent and abusive." Burgoine was forceful and insisted the Van Ness return to the track. His ankles and legs were badly swollen, and he complained about a burning sensation in his throat and brain.

"He broke away and dodged through a door opposite the dressing room. His trainer, Burgoine and the assistant trainer, **Rafferty**, burst through the door, and were met by the raving pedestrian with a seven-shot revolver in his hand. He had every appearance of a maniac. His eyes glared ferociously, and he was muttering unintelligible words to himself."

"Van Ness excitedly presented a revolver at his trainer's head, snapped the trigger, but it misfired. A second time, he was more successful. The ball passed through Burgoine's arm, just below the elbow. Burgoine fell and shouted, 'I am shot!' Then Van Ness discharged the pistol at his assistant trainer several times in rapid succession, causing a momentary stampede among the audience. The crowd of women and men rushed into the street and intense excitement prevailed." One version of the incident claimed that Van Ness ran out into the building and emptied his pistol at the spectators, but that appeared to be a dramatic embellishment. But the audience heard the shots, and the Italian orchestra dropped their instruments and got down behind the railing.

LEG LUNATICS.

Van Ness, Crazed With Pain and Fatigue,

Shoots His Trainer and Creates a Panic.

Van Ness' manager and financial backer, **Simon Levy** (1840-1902), of Flushing, Long Island, New York, owner of clothing stores, rushed into the room and a bullet "popped his head," putting a hole through his silk hat, but luckily missed his scalp. The final shots only hit walls. "Van Ness struggled desperately with the two men and acted generally as if he were bereft of his reason." After discharging seven shots, someone finally disarmed him with no police intervention. Van Ness then fainted and was comatose.

Woman pedestrian rising star, 17-year-old **Amy Howard**, (1862-1885) of Brooklyn, who had just put on a walking exhibition in the hall, was in the women's dressing room next door. Hearing the shots, the women in the room screamed. A bullet was later found in the wall of that room. "Howard declared that the bullet went almost near enough to her head to scorch her frizzes."

Amy Howard

The Show Must Go On

With so many dollars of wagers on the line, the show must go on. They administered "Hot drops" to the crazy pedestrian, and shortly thereafter Van Ness resumed his task after 9:00 p.m. Most of the spectators, fearing they would be shot, had left the building.

Why wasn't Van Ness hauled off to jail by the police? His trainer, Burgoine, who suffered greatly from the shot to his arm, stayed in the room, and wanted to keep his wounding secret.

> The acme of athletic amusements is reached when a crazed pedestrian draws his little pistol from his pocket and begins to pepper the crowd of spectators. It then becomes as interesting as a bull-fight and almost as dangerous as a game of base-ball.

He especially did not want to involve the police, fearing that they would arrest Van Ness and take him away from the track. There was too much money on the line. But a detailed story about the incident was covered in the newspapers the next day. Burgoine explained that this was not the first time that Van Ness had behaved in a crazed manner, that he had experienced several mad fits during his walk. At one point, in another race, he had even demanded getting a pistol to kill a cat that had been following him on the track.

Marketing Hoax?

The Boston Post speculated, "It is supposed the whole affair was an advertising dodge." Given the printed evidence and conflicting strange versions of the story, it is possible that the Boston Post was correct. But contemporaries seemed to mostly believe the incident was true. The shot in the arm was only a flesh wound. On March 10, 1879, Van Ness successfully completed his 2,000 half miles in about 2,000 half hours. It is pretty clear that he missed at least one-half hour during the incident.

Two weeks later, Van Ness raced against **John Colston** at Eagle Hall in Hoboken, New Jersey. But during the evening he quit, claiming that he received a telegram that his brother, **Schuyler Van Ness,** was dying in Brooklyn. "The visitors of the hall denounced the affair as a fraud." His brother must have recovered because he did not die until 1908. Van Ness did not accomplish any further significant pedestrian accomplishments, and he soon disappeared from the sport. He died of a heart attack in 1900 while playing cards with his family. "Peter Van Ness suddenly fell from his chair and died in a few minutes. He was in the best of health and had been laughing and joking over the game of cards."

CHAPTER FOUR

The Strange Indiana Walking Wonder

John Owen Snyder (1834-1887), a farmer from Millgrove, Indiana, developed a bizarre ultrarunning affliction that caused him to walk or run nearly continually. He would walk at least eighteen hours a day and did it for three years. The mileage claimed, over 60,000 miles, seems to be physically impossible. No one in history has legitimately come close to that mileage in three years. But with multiple detailed investigative reports, thousands of witnesses, and examinations from more than 50 doctors, there is little doubt that the man had a severe, very rare ultra-walking affliction, and perhaps he did walk nearly that far.

Snyder Family in 1880 Census

Snyder was married with five children and lived on a small remote farm a few miles from any town. While working in the harvest fields with his sons on October 24, 1884, a feeling attacked his arms that was terribly painful. He discovered that the relief only came when he did vigorous exercise. He said, "I wanted to use my arms all the time. I had to keep 'em in motion. I chopped wood in the day and at night I would grab a broom and scrub all night."

Walking Begins

In six weeks, the disease shifted to his hips and legs, requiring him to walk to find relief. "I could not stand still. I had to keep moving. I used to go slow at first. I couldn't sit down. My legs would get cold and pain me. Then I got to going pretty fast and then it got me running."

He thought three layers had mysteriously formed on the soles of his feet. He believed that the only way to remove them would be through walking. "He at once took up the line of march in the rear of his dwelling on his farm, walking in a circle." His friends and neighbors tried to get him to stop but failed in their efforts. His doctor tried to convince him that the problem was in his head, not his feet and legs.

Efforts to Cure Snyder

A religious evangelist came one day to cure him. Snyder said, "He went down upon his knees and prayed so long and loud that it made me tired.

He said I had no faith. I told him to go over to a neighbor and cure a poor fellow afflicted with cancer and then call again, and I would have more faith. He never returned."

Early on, they sent him to an asylum, and he continued to walk while under mental care. "When restrained from walking, his feet alternately would lift from the ground. He said that if he would stop walking, his limbs and body would fly into a thousand fragments." He was released from the hospital and declared mentally sane, harmless, but afflicted by a rare brain disease. He continued to walk.

Church in Millgrove, Indiana

Nationwide Publicity

About nine months later, in August 1885, many news stories were published nation-wide about Snyder, over-estimating that he had walked 16,000 miles so far. "He walks around a small ring near his house in all kinds of weather, eating as he walks and stopping only when too tired to go any longer. Then he drops into a chair and sleeps a few hours and immediately resumes his walk. He has not lain down since he was attacked by this peculiar mania."

Farmland near Millgrove, Indiana

CEASELESSLY TRAMPING

An Entirely New Species of Crank Developed in the Hoosier State.

He never seemingly would grow hungry and never asked for food or drink, but took anything given him, all the time continuing his endless round. His two adult sons had to take over the farm work. One day, he put his continuous walking to good use. He steered a horse plowing the field. But when the plow struck a root and became stuck, he let go of the plow handles and continued in a circle around the field himself. His plow paths were always in a continuous circle.

As his continuous walking persisted, he became stronger and could increase his pace and run occasionally. Witnesses could not keep up with him. "The circle in the rear of his residence is beaten as hard as a rock, and not a vestige of grass may be seen. He never removed his clothing, but about 2 a.m. he occupied a chair near his circle and at once would fall asleep."

NEVER TIRES.

John [Snyder, the Perpetual Hoosier Pedestrian, and Some of His Peculiarities.

JOHN OWEN SNYDER, WHO CAN'T STOP WALKING!

In cold weather, he walked inside his small home in a room reserved for his walking. While inside, he felt like a prisoner but would speed up his pace until he "fairly ran about his apartment." He wore broad, heavy-soled shoes, without socks, and the muscles and tendons of his legs were as tense and firm as rawhide. Oddly, he never became sick. His digestion was good and temperature, circulation and respiration normal.

Even more strangely, he seemed to have a gift to foretell coming events. Many events occurred, as he predicted. In 1885, he talked about a great world war that would happen in a few decades, but also predicted that the world would soon end as the sun cooled. "He never jests or laughs, nor whistles, but will talk to all who visit him and is clear and lucid on all points except the cause of his desire to walk. He is of a quiet disposition, unless aroused by some insinuation that he is a crank or monomaniac; then he is someway violent and demonstrative."

After more than a year of this, he believed it would take 50,000 miles to cure him of his malady. But after believing he exceeded that distance, he kept it going.

Hundreds Come to Witness

Hundreds of curious people would visit Snyder on his remote farm each week and watch him walk for hours. They went away mystified but convinced that the bizarre reports were true. A few months later, it was falsely reported that he was walking himself into his grave. "He was in the clutch of death but has resumed walking. Physicians say it is only a question of endurance. Death alone, they say, can relieve him from the iron grip of his mysterious malady."

A WALKING MANIA.

STRANGE STORY OF AN INDIANA FARMER'S HALLUCINATION.

Walking at a Rapid Rate for Eighteen Hours a Day—The Professional Pedestrians Stand No Sort of Show by His Remarkable Record.

A month later, during the cold December of 1886, a reporter described his home, an old three-room log cabin. "In front and on either side of the cabin are narrow foot-paths, worn deep into the earth and made hard almost as rock by constant travel." He went into the house and found Snyder marching around a wood-burning stove. The walker enjoyed telling the story of his sad affliction.

He stated that he had not been able to sit down for a meal with his family in over two years. "A large pan was strapped in front of him, in which is placed his food." He had also perfected the art of sleepwalking. "The many absurd and ridiculous stories that have been put into circulation concerning him afford himself and his family much amusement, as well as a great deal of annoyance."

In two years, he had worn out ten pairs of heavy shoes and twice that number of soles and had walked an estimated 59,000 miles. He had been married for 30 years and two of his adult sons cultivated the farm and provided support for the family. Three daughters helped with duties in the home. He felt confident that he would overcome the disease.

Exhibitions in Museums

In January 1887, Snyder was convinced to put on exhibitions in cities throughout the Midwest attracting thousands to come to see him. As he traveled from city to city, he walked in train cars. His managers secured venues for him to walk day and night. His first visit was to Cincinnati, Ohio, where he walked at a museum in a space 100x50 feet enclosed by a railing.

> He Don't Walk for Prizes;
> He Don't Walk for Fun;
> He Don't Walk for Money.
> He Would if He Could, but
> **He Can't Stop Walking!**
> The Museum will not be closed, but will be open day and night this week. Come at any hour and see that this strange case is just as represented.

> **THE WALKING WONDER.**
> The Case of John Snyder Baffles the Power of the Physicians.

A Doctor Zenner, professor of nervous diseases at Ohio Medical College, observed him for 48 hours. Snyder walked for all but seven of those hours, proving to the doctor that he was not an imposter. But his disease was a mystery.

After two weeks, he next moved on to Chicago by walking in a train's baggage car. He then walked at Kohl & Middleton's Dime Museum for $100 per week. Chicagoans were amazed. "He walks with rather an awkward shuffle, with his hands hanging in a listless way at his side. He walks for the same reason other people breathe, because he is obliged to in order to live."

He started to be called "The Indiana Walking Wonder." He told the people at a Dime Museum, "I can set down sometimes

> **KOHL & MIDDLETON'S SOUTH SIDE DIME MUSEUM,**
> 146, 148, 150, 152 S. Clark-st., near Madison.
> Week beginning Monday, Jan. 17.
> MR. JOHN O. SNYDER,
> The Man Who Can't Stop Walking.
> He Eats and Sleeps While on the Tramp.
> Open all day and night this week.

and sleep a half an hour, but not often, and it isn't pleasant. I have lain down on the bed several times but couldn't stand it. In the last four months,

I have lain down four times. I don't get tired walking. I get tired when I stop." Changing his clothes was a big problem because he was always moving. For three days and nights, his attendants watched for an opportunity when he could stop long enough to change his pants.

THE WALKING WONDER.

He Will Exhibit His Perpetual Pedestrianism, but Will Wear No Monkey Jacket.

In Chicago, they reserved an entire floor of the West Side Museum for his use to walk day and night around a little track. Spittoons were arranged along his route because he was a big tobacco chewer. He kept company there with Princess Ida and a company of performing birds.

His walking pace was observed to be about three miles per hour. "Snyder walked with a shuffling gait, very difficult for an ordinary man to keep step with. He always wore rough shoes, the heavy kind often worn by farmers when plowing. Sometimes he would trot for an hour or two." Many physicians and professors came to observe him and tried to diagnose the illness. No one had ever seen anything like it before. The general opinion was that he was a victim of a nervous disorder.

While in Chicago, the odd feeling went from his legs to the soles of his feet and he had hope that he was finally walking out of it, but the weather changed, and the pain went back up into his legs again. He explained what it felt like. "It is a kind of tickling pain. It goes first up one side of my leg and then down the

Chicago Dime Museum on left

other and feels more like a bug or something crawling up and down your legs more than anything else."

He moved his show on to Indianapolis. More than 10,000 people would come to Eden Musee to watch him walk during a week. He then walked at various fairs in Indiana. But after nine months, he stopped his tour once an impostor started appearing in cities. He put a stop to the fraud and vowed to never appear in public again. His appearances netted him about $12,000 (worth $370,000 in today's value). The fortune allowed him to expand his farm to 50 acres and make his family comfortable.

Eden Musee

Snyder's Final Months of Walking

A few months later in the summer, a correspondent visited Snyder walking on his farm on a hot day in the 90s. "Notwithstanding the excessive heat, Mr. Snyder showed not the slightest evidence of fatigue, as it may seem, was as cool, apparently as an iceberg, no traces of perspiration being visible." Hundreds visited the farm weekly.

During the Fall of 1887, Snyder became ill and started to get steadily weaker. His legs began to swell, making him walk with a limp. "It was a sad scene that met the eye of this reporter. With feeble, tottering steps, and a face upon which was stamped

SNYDER'S 59,000-MILE TRAMP

The Singular Affliction to Which a Blackford County Farmer Is Subject.

A Man Who Is Irresistibly Impelled to Spend His Days and Nights in Walking, and Who Has Covered 59,000 Miles in Two Years.

suffering and melancholy." When asked if he would ever stop walking, he replied, "I am afraid not in this world. In the next, dunno."

He soon became pale and haggard and, at times refused to talk. He was slowly dying. When visited in early November, he said, "I feel I am nearing the end of my journey." A week earlier, he rejoiced when he thought the end had come when he became blind and felt faint, but he revived and continued on. He said he still averaged walking about 20 miles per day. He

CHAPTER FIVE

Hallucinations and Cranky Runners

As the indoor six-day races increased in popularity, spectators noticed that these reality shows featured "cranky or daffy runners" whose minds turned to mush after several days of running with little sleep. They experienced hallucinations, doing crazy things, delighting the thousands of spectators who came hoping to watch a train wreck of runners.

Cranky Runners

It was said that by hour 36 of a six-day race that runners could be expected to do strange things, as exhaustion and sleep deprivation caused

WALKERS ARE GETTING DAFFY.

One Imagines the Race Is Over and Another Counts Each Lap a Full Mile.

hallucinations. It was explained, "The cranky spell is reached, and the contestants furnish no end of amusement. Their tired brains are in a whirl, and it is only to be expected that the men should act like inmates of a 'funny house.'"

THE SCORERS.

For example, during a 1901 six-day race on a small track in the old city hall in Pittsburgh, Pennsylvania, **Martin Fahey** (1857-1937), a Shenandoah miner, went cranky and became violent after 150 miles. He demanded that the scorers credit him with a mile every time he completed a lap, probably 1/15th of a mile. "He claimed that the scorer and spectators had entered into a conspiracy to defraud him, and he was so demonstrative that his trainers found it advisable to take him out of the race." He was soon fast asleep and put on a train for home. "As the news went out from Old City Hall that the men were going insane from the terrible strain of the race, people flocked to the place, expecting to see the men do something violent. The hall was crowded to its capacity by the curious, who one minute sympathized with the men in their apparent suffering and the next minute were moved to laughter by their antics."

Tony Loeslein (1873-1939), a tailor from Erie, Pennsylvania, went cranky after 200 miles, left the track, and went into the crowd. "He asked the spectators to aid him in claiming that his trainers had stolen all his money and clothes. He tried to convince a small group of people that he was a much-abused man, and would have succeeded, had not his trainer arrived on the scene and placed him back on the track, where he continued to run, seemingly well-satisfied."

Missing Runners

Runners would at times go bonkers so badly that they went missing. "One of the leaders suddenly stopped and climbed over the rail and ran into the tent of one of the other contestants. He was missed by his trainers who eventually found him and dragged him out, and in a few minutes was back on the track going around as steadily as ever."

James Dean, of Boston, Massachusetts, one of the brave black runners of the era, was a stenographer from Boston, Massachusetts. During a six-day race held in Pittsburgh's Old City Hall, he suddenly accused his crew of attempting to poison him and then would not accept food from them unless it was first tasted by someone to prove that it wasn't poisoned.

RACE HAS LEFT HIM A MANIAC
William Dean, a Pedestrian, Crazed by Week's Awful Grind.

After he reached 412 miles on the last day, he was in a "daffy" condition, and was taken to the hospital. He then escaped his attendants while in the bathroom, went through an open window, and down a fire escape. "A search was at once instituted and kept up for several hours without finding any trace of the missing racer." He was later found wandering the streets and was taken to the police station. "His clothing

St. Francis Hospital

was covered with blood, the result of a hemorrhage from his nose. He was ragged and covered with dirt. He was wholly irrational and babbled meaninglessly."

Dean's trainer, the former champion of the world, **Frank Hart** (1857-1908), soon arrived and took the "demented man" to St. Francis Hospital. "It is said that Dean was completely broken down from his exertions in the race. He will probably recover after rest and treatment." After another day in the hospital, Dean recovered well and, two months later, was again competing in a six-day race.

Hallucinations

Hallucinations from being exhausted and sleep-deprived occurred frequently. During that same race, **Frank Sheldon,** who had run 241 miles, was given a bottle of ginger ale by his trainer to drink. "While he was gulping down the soft stuff, he yelled out that there was a number of men outside throwing stones through the window at him. Suddenly he threw the bottle through the window, breaking a large pane of glass." Next, he attacked a life-size tin soldier that was part of an advertising display for a department store. "He tore the soldier from his fastening, the crowd laughed, and Sheldon was taken from the track by his trainers." Later Sheldon imagined that every man who spoke to him was his trainer and now and then would call some man in the crowd to come and rub him down. He would walk unsteadily, muttering and moaning to himself, peering hollow-eyed into the crowd.

"BUGS" IN THEIR HEADS.

Hallucinations and Optical Illusions Which Trouble Pedestrians.

THEY SEE MOUNTAINS,

Which They Must Climb—They Walk Ropes and Pass over Slender Bridges.

AT TIMES THE TRACK RISES AND STRIKES THE WALKER.

A common hallucination plagued six-day runners, probably because the runners would look down so long at the track. They often would believe that the track was springing up in front of them. One runner, **Kid West,** of Harrisburg, Pennsylvania, asked for a hammer and nails so he could fix the track that was jumping up toward him. **Stephen Barnes "Old Soldier"** (1846-1916) also imagined that the track was jumping up in his face, so he walked backwards to give his eyes a rest from staring at the track. He then ran into the railing that surrounded the scorer's box. But the collisions seemed to bring him to his senses, and he turned around and started running forwards again.

Charles Harriman (1853-1919), a shoemaker from Massachusetts, also experienced this hallucination. He said, "No part of the track seemed level. I was constantly walking uphill or downhill. In Madison Square Garden, on the north side, there seemed to be a hill so steep that I could hardly climb it. When I turned south, it was just as easy as could be and just like slipping down a toboggan shoot."

These hallucinations intrigued doctors. "The walker imagines that he is walking up and down a hill. No part of the level track is level to him. It is a series of hills and valleys. The phenomenon results from looking intently at the track for a long time. It produces a peculiar effect upon the optic nerve."

Charles Harriman

Sammy Day

Sammy Day (1847-1913), an Englishman from McKees Rocks, Pennsylvania, believed that on day two of a race, that he had won the six-day race and was only continuing to amuse his Pittsburgh friends, singing most of the time.

Tom Beachmont, (1875-1950) of New Hampshire, also imagined he had won the race, and wanted the race management to pay him the first-place prize. His trainer had a lot of trouble keeping him on the track, but toward evening, he was all right again.

George Cartwright (1848-1928), of England, stopped during a six-day race and commented to his trainer, **Henry Seeley**, "'Say, Hank, I just got through the woods back there all right, but I don't know about climbing that mountain there,' and he pointed down the track." Seeley asked if he dodged the trees all right. Cartwright said they were pretty thick. He was encouraged to just follow the runner ahead of him.

George Cartwright

Another runner, **William Nolan** of Denver, Colorado, imagined that someone had changed his shoes while he had slept and had given him a pair with soles so long that he was in danger of tripping himself. He said, "They go all right up the stretches, but I am afraid at the turns." Sleep didn't seem to help get this notion out of his head. When he finally quit the race for good, he still believed that he had strange shoes.

In Madison Square Garden, **Orain Moore** was seen staying very carefully to the center of the track. "His trainer ran up to ask what the matter was. Moore stopped, stretched out his arms and shouted, 'Don't stop me! Can't you see the rope is cut half in two and I'm afraid it will break before I can cross,' and he gazed down at the sawdust as if looking into an abyss hundreds of feet in depth." Harriman observed Moore doing this, "He was walking ahead of me and suddenly threw his hands out, balancing himself carefully, tiptoe for a hundred yards or more and finally with a glad cry passed over the imaginary danger and leap forth on the run once again."

Charles Harriman experienced a similar hallucination. He imagined he was passing over a railroad bridge where the ties were very far apart. "For over an hour, he strode about the track, covering three feet or more at every step, occasionally stopping with his feet close together to collect himself." His trainer could not convince him that the track was solid. Harriman said, "I walked miles behind another man, putting my feet where his had been and all the while firmly convinced that I was walking on railroad ties. Now and then a hallucination would come to me that I was on a high bridge and that I must be careful and not fall through."

Charles Harriman

During another race, a runner started hallucinating that he was "rolling among old logs covered with thousand-legged worms." Another runner suddenly stopped on the track, believing that he could no longer walk. "Upon glancing at his feet, he was shocked to see that they had turned into hickory saplings and the saplings grew with such rapidity that they raised him in the air."

Another troublesome thing was hearing strange sounds, mostly in the early morning hours when things are more silent with few people on the track. "Crackling sounds as of a furious blaze, crashing of timbers and wails as of the human voice are heard and sometimes the sounds are most frightful."

Sleep and Dreams

Fitful dreams always plagued runners in six-day races when they were trying to sleep. A typical dream was that the runner saw his competitors passing him one by one and he could not increase his own speed. **Daniel O'Leary** (1846-1933) would dream of a "phantom" competitor who would follow him like a shadow "with looks of exultation in its eyes. At times, it would bar his way. It would

stand facing him at the curves, making grimaces and contortions."

Antoine Strokel (1851-1940), an Austrian runner, was so sleepy during a race that he simply stopped on the track, laid down and went to sleep, causing other runners to trip over him. When awakened, he "made things lively for a few minutes." To combat sleep deprivation, some runners, such as **James Albert (Cathcart)** (1853-1942) of Philadelphia, Pennsylvania, would carry a sponge soaked with ammonia and put it under their noses.

Waking up a runner was a hazardous task for some of the handlers. It was said that **Tom Cox,** an Irishman, was one of the hardest to deal with after a nap. "He will fight like a tiger. When he is asleep, he looks like a dead man. During one match, his friends held a bogus wake over him."

Antoine Strokel

A female pedestrian, **Ada Anderson** would usually strike her attendants when they tried to wake her up. But like ultrarunners generations after her, she perfected the art of sleepwalking around the track. She was often observed walking laps "with the step of a drunken person" watched carefully by her trainer to make sure she didn't injure herself by running up against a railing. "Then at last, the end would come, when her frame was about to give out, suddenly she would wake up, leap into new life and bound forward around the track with the spring of a deer, her eyes bright and her mind active."

Ada Anderson

Davy Crockett

CHAPTER SIX

Runner Misbehavior

Most of these early runners conducted themselves with honor and dignity. But as some runners would get extremely tired but mentally still firmly focused on massive monetary prizes, they would sometimes do outrageous things to others who were standing in their way. During a 1902 six-day

> **SIX-DAY WALKERS HAVE FIST FIGHT**
> Finnerty and Guerrero Come to Blows and Police Interfere.

two-man relay race in New York City, with several thousand people watching, **Tom Finerty**, an Irish-American, broke into a sprint, taking up a position near the rail.

Gus Guerrero

Gus Guerrero, (also known as Jose de Peralto) a Latino-American from California, was 34 miles ahead in this race. He also took up the fast run, following closely behind Finerty and seemed to try to shove him from his position next to the rail. "The Irishman turned around and struck Guerrero a stunning blow in the face, felling him." Guerrero, who was given the racist nickname by other runners of "The Greaser," jumped up and went after Finerty. They knocked each other down several times in a fight that lasted a few minutes.

"Madison Square Garden was in an uproar as the men were fighting and even the racers halted and joined in the crowd that surrounded the contestants. After

> **SIX-DAY PEDESTRIANS ENGAGE IN A FIGHT**
> Tom Finerty and Gus Guerrero Pummel One Another Until the Police Interfere.

the police broke it up, they all resumed racing, but when Guerrero passed Finerty, he struck the Irishman in the face and another fight started for a few minutes." Both ended up with badly bruised faces. The police threatened to stop the race and evacuate Madison Square Garden if the trouble persisted.

During a 1903 six-day race in Philadelphia, on day four, the race was thrown into turmoil. **John A. Glick** (1869-1929), a weaver from Germantown, Pennsylvania, was struggling to hold onto third place. After he was passed by a runner, he "began to lose control of himself." A native American runner,

JOHN GLICK GOT INTO A FREE FIGHT.

It Happened on the Track at the Go-as-You-Please-Six-Day Race in Philadelphia.

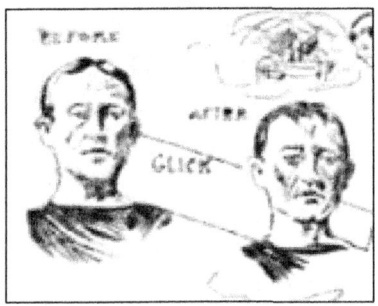

Dean Davis, was next gaining on him fast and the two became involved in a "hot spurt" for a full mile. Finally, Glick gave up going at the furious pace and when Davis went by him, Glick struck him in the back of the neck, knocking him down. Davis got up and retaliated, hitting Glick squarely in the face.

Others, both runners and trainers, joined in the riot. "Several spectators leaped over the railing and followed suit, and an all-round rough house ensued. The other racers were brought to a standstill and there was a general stampede on the part of spectators in other parts of the building to the scene of the fight." The police took control and within a few minutes, the runners were again going around the track. "Davis was cheered by the crowd, while jeers and catcalls were hurled at Glick, who sought refuge in his tent." He later apologized to Davis.

In 1888, former six-day world record holder, **Robert Vint** (1846-1917), an Irish-American and shoemaker from Brooklyn, New York, started complaining about an unknown runner Dempsey who was dogging his tracks during a six-day race in Madison Square Garden. "Before the trainers interfered, Vint received a blow in the mouth from Dempsey's fist, bringing blood. Vint called Demsey a name which he didn't take kindly to."

Robert Vint

Frank Hart and John Hughes Rivalry

Frank Hart

John Hughes

In 1881, several elite runners trained on a sawdust track at Wood's Gymnasium in Brooklyn, New York. **Frank Hart** (1856-1908), "Black Dan," of Chicago, Illinois, the former six-day world record holder, who was black, was training there one Sunday afternoon. One of his bitter rivals, **John Hughes** (1850-1921), "The Lepper," from New York City, was also on the track. Hughes would often yell hate-filled racist remarks to Hart.

That afternoon, Hart broke out into a strong run, and Hughes ran after him. "Within a few laps, Hughes showed his superiority as a runner and passed Hart easily. 'Never mind. I'll beat you in the match,' said Hart. Hughes, turned around and shouted, 'You lie, you black (n-word).' Saying this, he struck Hart with a powerful blow under the chin. Hart fell flat on his back but was up again in an instant and hit Hughes over the right eye."

Frank Hart	John Hughes
Age: 24	Age: 30
Height: 5'7"	Height: 5'7"
Weight: 140	Weight: 150
Chest: 36	Chest: 42
Thigh: 19	Thigh: 19
Calf: 14	Calf: 13 ½
Shoe: 8	Shoe: 9

They continued to deliver blows, but Hart was no match for the bigger Hughes. Trainer Happy Jack Smith jumped in and separated them. "As

Hart went away, Hughes shouted at him, 'I'll kill you the next time I meet you on the track." Hughes moved his training to the American Institute building. His wife said, "He does not wish to associate longer with such low brats as frequent the Williamsburg Gymnasium."

Hart and Hughes had many fights in races. In 1883, they raced against each other in Troy, New York. Hughes had a 21-mile lead but was drunk, taking in too much stimulating booze. He accused scorers of cheating, that they bumped up Hart's score while he was sleeping. Hart responded by punching him in the face and a "lively fight occurred for a few minutes until the crowd separated them." The police came and found Hughes bleeding from his nose. They cleared the hall and put an end to the match.

HUGHES HAS A ROW WITH HART.
Breaking Up a Walking Match with the Colored Man in Troy.

A month later, in Baltimore, Maryland, they went at it again during a six-day race. Hughes accused Hart of getting **George Noremac** (1852-1922) to run Hughes off the track. Hart denied it and called Hughes names. Hughes struck Hart, pounding him in the face and throwing him over the rail, and "a lively tussle" continued. "Mrs. Hughes, who has been a faithful attendant to her husband, interfered to separate the men. Hart tried to bite her, but only succeeded in biting the sleeve of her dress. The combatants were parted." The police stopped the fight.

Women Pedestrians

Many women took part in six-day races during the 1800s. Of the 900 total starters in 90 six-day races in 1879, more than 120 starters were women. Female pedestrians also exhibited some poor behavior during their races.

On March 15, 1879, a "Grand Ladies' International Six-Day Race" was held at Gilmore's Garden (soon to be renamed to Madison Square Garden) in New York City. For the first time in history, a women's ultrarunning race would include spectacular prizes for the winner. The first-place prize would be $1,000 ($28,750 value today), attracting eighteen very competitive women to take part.

During the race, the poor women had to endure laughing and insulting remarks from the crowds of men who would hang over the rail surrounding the track. Some women runners would blush and look down, but most would just face their tormentors with brazen looks and often answer back boldly.

Exilda La Chapelle (1859–1935), age 20, from Canada, was a very experienced and successful pedestrian who had recently walked 2,700 quarter miles in 2,700 consecutive quarter hours in Chicago on a track, 28 laps to the mile.

Bertha Von Berg was a boot and shoe seamstress from Rochester, New York. She burst into the pedestrian sport in 1878 when she walked 100 miles in 27 hours.

On the evening of day two of the six-day race, La Chapelle was leading with 140 miles, and Von Berg was just ten miles behind. La Chapelle was using a strategy to follow Von Berg closely during each lap to maintain her lead. This eventually bothered Von Berg. She stopped and said, "If you come within six feet of me again, I'll slap you in the face." La Chapelle backed off after that, but she said she would "wipe the floor" with Von Berg's face.

Bertha Von Berg

On day four, **Fannie Rich**, a book agent from Boston, would reverse her direction on the track and would not give the inside lane to the others. She looked like she was losing her balance and collided with the other runners. After being warned by the judges, she retired to her tent, making loud charges of fraud against the scorers. When her trainer tried to reason with her, she hit him over the head with a stick, got a whip and hit respected referee **Edward F. Plummer** across the face. She claimed he pulled out a pistol, but he denied that. She was removed from the race after 131 miles and complained about the unfair conditions she put up with compared to the other ladies.

Bella Kilbury (1862-1897) of Hoboken, New Jersey, was the youngest runner in the race. She began the race penniless and was described as "petite and fair, and altogether a lively girl dressed. "She is the only really graceful runner in the lot and called 'Dead-eye Dick' by friends because she had a glass eye." **Ada Wallace** was about 30 years old, and from Baltimore,

Maryland. She claimed to be the niece of **General Joseph Hooker** (1814-1879), a general for the Union in the Civil War.

On day six, Kilbury caught up and passed Wallace into second place. "After she passed Wallace, it was found necessary for one of the judges to escort her around the track for an hour to protect her from Wallace who lavished abuse upon the young Hoboken girl, calling her the vilest epithets and threatening her with bodily harm." Kilbury quickly extended her lead by several miles. The crowd gave her constant cheers and presented her with baskets of many flowers. She draped an American flag on her shoulders and walked around beating a kettledrum. Later, as things calmed down, all five women marched together to the music of "Yankee Doodle."

> The women pedestrians locked arms and walked together to the tune of "Yankee Doodle" at the close of their performance, and it is positively asserted that they pinched each other during the affectionate march only two or three times.

Criticism about the women's race flooded in many newspapers, much of it unfair against women, but some also pointing out the strange drama that took place nearly every day of the race.

> THE CRUEL TRAMP ENDED.
> VON BERG WINS THE BELT AND FIRST PRIZE. KILBURY SECOND, AND WALLACE THIRD.

It painted a picture of crude women parading around, flirting with men in an environment that encouraged the worst dregs of society to act vulgar in full display of the public.

Bias clearly affected the characterizations against letting women take part in such a sport. In Indiana, it was commented, "The five who persevered were not a lovely spectacle as they crawled around the ring. Their hair had not been fixed for half a week, their faces had not been washed and some of them had not changed their clothes for five days. To make a long and unpleasant story short, this show of disreputable women and shiftless loafers is over."

Whether or not fair, much of the public was left with an impression that the race was "public torture of women. One of the most brutal exhibitions afforded the public in some time." Negative feelings of women pedestrianism were expressed worldwide. England published this statement, "Woman is not physically organized for a six-day tramp and it is a shame to allow her to abuse herself."

Strange Running Tales: When Ultrarunning was a Reality Show

Runners Abuse Spectators

At times, the runners' anger would be directed at the paying spectators. **Patrick Cavanaugh** (1863-1908), an Irish-American living in Trenton, New Jersey, showed a particular temper during races. During the 1902 six-day relay, Cavanaugh's team was in the lead, but on day four, several of the runners were going "cranky" including Cavanaugh. "He was told by a newsboy that his picture was in one of the morning papers. This intelligence angered the Irishman for some reason or another, and he left the track and started after the boy on a run. Being unable to catch him, he threw a wet sponge at him, striking him on the back of the head, much to the discomfort of the boy and disgust of the spectators." Cavanaugh demanded that they find an Irish flag and give it to him, or he would quit the race. The race management provided him with one and he then rushed around the track, making the band play "The Wearing of the Green."

Early during a six-day race in 1882 in England, **George Cartwright** (1848-1928), of Walsall, England, who had a large amount of money riding on him to win, left the track to punch a spectator who was making fun of him because he had slowed down and walked. "The critic so riled the pedestrian that he lost his temper and endeavored to strike his annoyer who retaliated. Cartwright was struck upon the head with a bamboo stick. The blow was sufficiently violent to inflict a wound on Cartwright's forehead and draw blood, which flowed down the competitor's face. The police arrested the man for assault." The British were amazed, "There must be a pleasant variety about the sport of pedestrianism which embraces

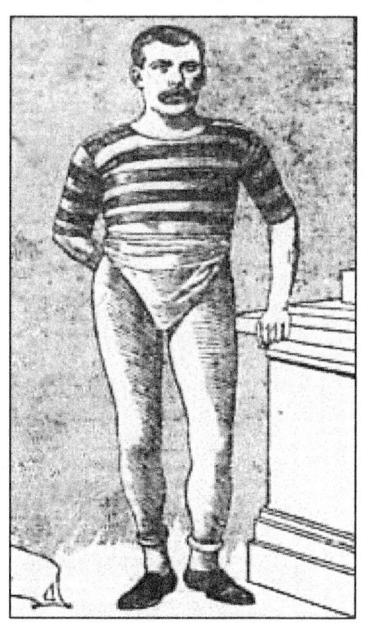

pedestrianism, boxing, and ruffianism, all within the space of a few minutes."

The most famous American pedestrian, **Edward Payson Weston** (1839-1929), also misbehaved at times. During a six-day race as he was reaching 360 miles, spectators were hurling offensive puns at him about his performance. "His fortitude and dashing manner however sustained him until some rash spectator remarked to a lady as he walked passed them by, 'Weston is a good walker, but he's got no Hart in him.'" (Referring to the latest champion, Frank Hart). "The effect  was almost fatal. The only effort Weston could make was to throw an orange at the band to quiet them. As soon as silence was insured on the part of the musicians, he walked into his room to recover from the shock."

At another race in 1879, a crowd of anti-Weston spectators were hissing him every time he passed. "It annoyed him very much, and he scowled and shook his cane at them. More of the crowd applauded vigorously to counteract the hisses."

CHAPTER SEVEN

Sickness and Death

Some professional walkers and runners from the pedestrian era, more than 120 years ago, became afflicted by mental and physical illness during and after six-day runs. This was likely caused by the powerful drugs and stimulants that were used at the time, and also because of mental stress breakdowns. Their financial backers put enormous pressure on them to be successful. Their "trainers" or crew would resort to measures that would have long-term effects on the health of their runners to get a short-term financial windfall. Not only would they load their runners full of stimulants, but would use cruel methods to keep them awake, including sticking needles in their skin, whipping them, and waking them up with very loud horns.

By 1884, critical reactions to the sport were common. In London, England, it was written, "We shudder at the Roman arena, we turn up our eyes at the Spanish bullfight. But for sheer brutality, it is doubtful whether a long-distance competition is not the most disgusting spectacle. One of these days a poor wretch will drop down dead on the track, and then one of America's worst gifts to England will be at an end."

Runners Accused of Becoming Insane

Sometimes, runners acted so irrationally that they were declared insane and committed to institutions.

In 1891, **John Gowan** (real name Robert Sherlock), called "the salvation army walker" took part in a six-day race in Madison Square Garden and had reached 278 miles. Just after midnight, Gowan showed signs of mental trouble.

Instead of sleeping during the night, he rested while singing gospel hymns.

In the morning, he started walking again, but his eyes grew wild and staring, and he let out a wild-west war whoop. "His trainer squeezed a sponge soaked in water and ammonia in his face. Gowan struck his trainer in the face and made a bolt for the Madison Avenue end of the Garden." He cleared the fence of the track in one leap. "Then the fellow rushed wildly down the paved lobby, cleared the brass railing at the ticket box, and ran out into Madison Square Garden arrayed in all the glory of dirty tights and a bright blue silk jumper. Two policemen gave chase and caught the escaped pedestrian. Bringing him back, the officers lifted him bodily over the rail, and his trainers led him back to his hut and put him to bed. A moment later one of them opened the door to take a peep at the fatigue-crazed pedestrian and Gowan plumped him a singing blow in the face."

They then locked him in his hut but later broke out, insisting on returning to the track, half naked. A policeman convinced him to change his mind. "The crazed fellow drank nearly a quart of kerosene oil that was in the hut which he had been locked into by the trainers."

His friends next took him to a room in Putnam House (a popular hotel) and locked him in. But he escaped through a window and down a fire escape. "Upon reaching the street, he sped down 4th Avenue in quicker time than was ever made on the tanbark. At this point he was spied by an officer. When the officer tried to arrest the man, he fought like a tiger and finally assistance had to be called. He was taken to the police precinct and thence in an ambulance to Bellevue hospital."

It was concluded that his illness was caused by a lack of nourishment. Authorities accused the trainers of giving Gowan so much whisky that it would have knocked out a man. It was believed that he had gone insane. A few days later, he had recovered. "A short rest was all that was needed to restore his mind." His sister commented he had not been fit for the severe mental or physical effort demanded by a six-day race. He retired from the sport.

Millie Rose, a very experienced pedestrian, suffered terribly during a race because of taking many "stimulating fluids, including beer and brandy." She collapsed on the track and during her next match, experienced an epileptic seizure while on the track. She was bedridden for the next several months and her abusive husband had her declared insane, left her, and took all her money. She eventually recovered, competed again, and had her husband arrested.

In 1877, people in Princeton, Illinois, believed that walking in a 24-hour match ruined **Carrie Parker's** life and drove her to insanity. She had become "a raving maniac," and was brought before a court. "Her father testified that ever since the walking match, his daughter had been suffering with great nervous prostration and recently, she suddenly conceived of the idea that her whole body was charged with electricity, and she would not touch her feet to the floor." She was sent to an asylum.

Ultrarunning Fans Committed

Not only were runners accused of going insane from six-day races, but there were also cases of spectators acting strangely. In 1888, **Julia Finley** of New York City had attended a six-day match with great enthusiasm. Afterwards, it was said that she was found constantly walking around her apartment, believing that she was beating the world record. "She was committed for examination as to her sanity."

In 1892, in Reading Pennsylvania, another walking woman was thought to be insane and taken to the state asylum. "She is crazy on walking. For years she read everything she could get about walking matches until she became convinced that she was dominated by the spirits of O'Leary, Rowell, Weston and other great walkers. Whenever she could escape from the house, she would go away on a long walk, sometimes not appearing again for days, during which time she would tramp hundreds of miles. Within a year, she extended one of her tramps as far as Chicago."

In 1879, in New York City, strange reports came into the police about a man running down Flatbush Avenue, creating intense fright among some. The man would move out of the way of carriages, but still continue fast. Police officer Hawxhurst took up the chase. A night watchman finally stopped the man and took him into custody. "He was fairly dripping with perspiration and looked like a man who had just been fished out of the water. His breathing came fast, and he evidently was in a much exhausted condition." When questioned, he pleaded to be allowed to "finish the race." He was taken to the police station but continued to plunge up and down in an approved pedestrian style. They figured out that "the poor fellow was a hopeless victim of the walking mania, and even when he was put into the cell, he continued to make lap after lap around the narrow circuit." A doctor suggested they take the prisoner from his cell and be allowed to walk in the yard in the fresh air. The man walked and ran for three hours until exhausted, then carried back to his cell to sleep for the night. In the morning, he awoke and asked to be put on the track. His friends were notified to come and get him.

Former Ultrarunners Never Fully Recover

There were several cases where former pedestrians later experienced some mental illness and their families believed that their ultrarunning had caused it. **James Noon** of Cliffwood, New Jersey, was one such athlete who competed in a six-day race. Several years later, in 1903, he was taken to the State Asylum at Trenton, New Jersey. They blamed his condition on the effects of that race.

In 1891, in Chicago, **John S. Dobler** of Chicago, a former very accomplished professional six-day pedestrian who had once held the world record for six days limited to 12 hours per day, had been delivering mail for the post office. "Recently, he began carrying away everything that attracted his attention in the stores where he left mail. He was declared insane by Judge Scales and was sent to an asylum." They found stolen bottles of cologne, brandy, cigars, and rolls of cloth in Dobler's room.

John Dobler

Health Scares

With the intense emphasis on very lucrative wagers, during this era of ultrarunning, the health of the runner was important, but seemed to be a secondary worry, even with doctors on the scene. Yes, a few deaths even resulted. Doping was not scrutinized. Some runners claimed to not use stimulants, but most did. Some even used powerful drugs to help them keep awake and moving. Doctors would even cut incisions in runner's thighs to help relieve muscle pressure. The long-term effects resulting in poor health became obvious.

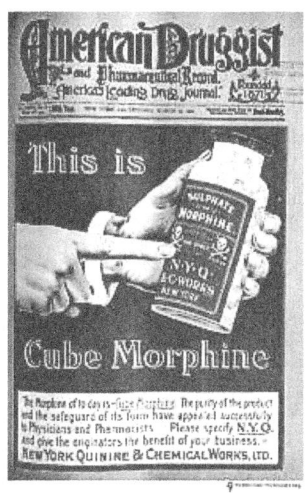

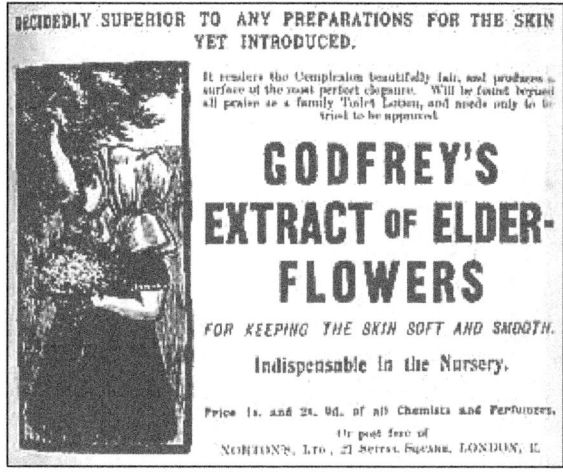

Fainting on the track during a race was common, and something that fascinated spectators. During an 1879 six-day race in San Francisco, **William Chenowith,** from San Francisco, California, started to act strangely on the track, staggering from side to side as though dizzy. He took a rest, came out again and then fell on the track senseless at about 412 miles. His handlers carried him to his tent and then he seized with a violent vomiting fit. Rumors circulated that he had been drugged to prevent him from reaching 450 miles. "Another story is that the trouble was caused by excessive use of a lotion on his feet, the skin being broken, the poisonous elements in the location getting into his blood, producing effects similar to strychnine. An antidote was administered, reviving him, but his chances were spoiled." He eventually recovered and competed in other six-day races the following year.

In another race, in 1902, during a six-day race in Philadelphia, **Patrick Cavanaugh** (1863-1908), of Trenton, New Jersey, also fell on his face on the track.

> **PAT CAVANAUGH FAINTED**
>
> Fell on Track, But Got Going Again in Few Minutes—Diehl Taken to Hospital With Dislocated Hip

"Without any warning, he suddenly reeled, and fell forward heavily on his face, throwing the spectators in the greatest excitement possible. He was picked up instantly and carried to his dressing room, where he revived in a few minutes." Doctors checked him out, and he was soon back on the track, winning the race with 532 miles.

Later in the year, while working on a building, Cavanaugh fell through an opening between two joists and seriously injured his hips. It was thought that he would be crippled for life, but a few months later, he was back to his winning ways. Six years later, while trying to make another comeback in 1908, Cavanaugh became critically ill with peritonitis (likely colon cancer) while training for a race in Erie, Pennsylvania. About a week later, he died at the age of 53 during an operation trying to fix his intestinal trouble.

In 1879, during the 5th Astley Belt Race in Madison Square Garden, **William H. Dutcher**, (1848-), a railroad fireman from Poughkeepsie, New York, fainted on the track after only 22 miles. He came back, but just one mile later staggered and dropped again. "It seemed that he was subject to convulsions. He was laid upon his cot and a physician attended to him. When he recovered consciousness, he begged in the most piteous manner to be allowed to go on the track again. But the doctor said, emphatically, 'If that man is put on the track again, I will not answer for his life.'" It was said that Dutcher "sobbed like a baby." He later explained, "I've got some trouble with my heart. I chewed a lot of tobacco while training and that brought on the trouble. My heart beats like a trip hammer. If I had gone on, they said it would have killed me." Dutcher was one of the early ultrarunning frauds, who had cheated during a solo six-day race by bribing timers and judges and skipped out of enormous debts. It was a wonder that they allowed him to continue competing. After this incident, Dutcher retired from the sport.

During an 1888 six-day race in Madison Square Garden, **Joseph Romeo Sullivan**, of Bangor, Maine,

> **Sullivan, the Bangor Ghost, Faints on the Track.**

"the Bangor Ghost" fainted on the track. He received little mercy from his friends. Less than two hours later, his trainers shoved him back on the track.

"There is not the ghost of a hope of his covering the 526 miles necessary to entitle him to a share of the boodle, but the poor fellow is pushed on by his friends." He finished with 383 miles. About ten years later, he died in a poorhouse.

There were plenty of other health scares experienced by the runners. **Gus Guerrero** experienced bleeding from his lungs, which scared him. After 400 miles, elite runner **Peter Panchot** (1841-1917), of Buffalo, New York, fell on his face from exhaustion and came out with a bruised and cut face.

In 1888, **John Dillon,** a railroad baggage master, of New York City, was running in a six-day race in Madison Square Garden and only needed 20 more miles to earn a lucrative share of the gate money. Several friends had brought the

Gus Guerrero

longshoreman a generous supply of "Jersey Lightning" which he drank too freely. Later on, he stopped on the track and refused to go on. Three of his competitors tried to help and took his arms, making him walk with them. But finally, he bolted off the track and refused to go on. He surprisingly withdrew and did not qualify for the huge payday.

Deaths

As professional pedestrianism became more popular, health experts of the era believed these ultrarunners were severely impacting their life expectancy. "Pedestrian contests have done much harm and any man who makes a practice of six-day walks cannot live to old age, because the strains wasted the nervous and muscular tissues." Also, "Physicians agree that these protracted strains upon walkers' system shorten their lives. It is the excess of the exercise that is dangerous." They, of course, had no data to back their guesses. In reality, the greats **Edward Payson Weston** and **Daniel O'Leary** lived into their 80s and 90s, far longer than the normal life expectancy of that era.

However, premature deaths occurred for assorted reasons. In 1879, **William Harris** was competing in a six-day event in Louisville,

WALKED TO DEATH.

A Man in Kentucky Kills Himself by Walking 220 Miles Less than O'Leary's Record in Six Days.

Kentucky, and was running in second place, when he died suddenly from "a congestive chill brought on by his striving to win the prize." He had reached 300 miles, left the track in exhaustion, and died the next day. Harris had no prior history as an ultrarunner, and it was his first attempt to run that distance.

During that same month in 1879, **Mr. Lavelle**, age 23, was competing in a walking match at Woonsocket, Rhode Island. He soon became ill and died in a few hours. He also was a rookie runner.

David L. Hoag (1846-1880), another rookie runner, died in 1880 two days after a match in Glens Falls, New York. According to the coroner's inquest, his death was because of the stimulants and morphine that were administered to him during a race. "One of the contestants says that the backers and trainers of the walker repeatedly gave him morphine without the doctor's knowledge and that one of the accused parties was seen personally kicking Hoag while in the ring in a collapsing condition to rouse him to action to win the race, which he did."

The trainer, **Richard H. Nichols,** was arrested for manslaughter, although the grand jury would be asked to indict him on first degree murder. "Hoag became so exhausted by over-exertion and improper care and ill treatment on the track and neglect after that race that he expired."

The *New York Tribune* thought the charges were ridiculous. "Nichols could have had no felonious desire to kill Hoag. On the contrary, his paramount desire must have been to keep him alive. His judgment may have been bad. He may have been criminally reckless and may have rendered himself liable to some penalty, but most certainly he did not commit murder in the first degree." No results of the case were found.

In 1879, **Benjamin Fowler** (1923-1899), a store clerk, age 56, and **George Leck** competed in a six-day match at Flushing, Long Island, New York. It was a very close race. They were only two miles apart during the last day, but Fowler started to show signs of failing. "He fell three times on the track but would not quit it in spite of the advice of his trainers. Fowler continued to lose time up to the finish, and Leck came in the winner. Fowler made 368 miles and was carried from the track in critical condition. It is feared he will die." Fowler retired from ultrarunning, continued in poor health, and in 1880 moved to Omaha, Nebraska, for a time, hoping to get better. He lived until 1899, died at the age of 76, and at the time was one of the oldest residents of Flushing, New York.

Two young men of Newburgh, New York, died and were said to have walked into their graves. **Elijah Van Keuren** was very active in walking early matches around New York City. "When he began, he enjoyed excellent health, but after walking awhile he began to fail, and then rapidly fell into hasty consumption (tuberculosis) and died."

James "Hoppy" Crawford, age 23, successfully walked 100 miles in 24 hours. "After completing the task, he was a perfect wreck. Crawford died of consumption after lingering for several months."

In 1879, **Clarence G. Howard** (1859-1879), a twenty-year-old young man, a laborer in a brickyard, who had taken part in various long-distance pedestrian matches on Long Island and Brooklyn, New York, died at his home on Long Island, "from prostration caused by excessive exercise."

In 1903, **Tom Cox** (1846-1903), age 47, a former six-day pedestrian who was coaching a track team for Christian Brother's College at St. Louis, Missouri, was murdered. One evening, he went to visit one of his students and, while returning home at midnight, he was stopped by a man who

TOM COX CANNOT LIVE THROUGH DAY

Trainer of Athletes Sinking Rapidly From Wound Inflicted by Highwayman.

stepped out from behind a billboard. "He commanded Cox to throw up his hands and, upon his refusal to do so, repeated the demand. Then Cox hit him over the head with an umbrella and in return was shot in the abdomen." He was taken to the hospital and had emergency surgery, but later died. "Cox was one of the best-known long-distance pedestrians in this country and had participated in matches in nearly every important city in it, besides making several trips abroad."

Suicides

A pattern of suicides afflicted many of these ultrarunners of the 1800s. There were likely many reasons, but it was common for successful runners to pile up a fortune of winnings, only to see it gone within a few years because of wild spending, gambling, or from being swindled. Health issues were also a factor.

In 1881, **Joseph Allen** (1846-1881), age 35, a very accomplished six-day pedestrian who once walked 525 miles in Madison Square Garden, but failed in his last race, was found dead on a road near North Adams, Massachusetts. "The physician's verdict was heart disease, although a man of his description jumped from a railroad train late Monday night at a point where his body was found. Allen participated in the last three six-day go-as-you-please pedestrian contests in New York City. He leaves a wife and several children in Adams, where he made his home since coming from Carlisle, England."

In 1883, **Charles M. Mitchell** (1852-1920) of Concord, New Hampshire, a well-known local pedestrian and boxer, attempted suicide by cutting his throat with a razor. He had been ill for some weeks and did not cut deep enough to do serious harm.

In 1888, **J. M. White**, a bookkeeper and pedestrian from Georgia, attempted suicide by swallowing a number of morphine pills.

In 1895, **Albert Wall**, of Australia, a professional pedestrian while suffering from "delirium tremens," (a psychotic condition typical of withdrawal from drugs, involving hallucinations), jumped from a tall building. "His head was smashed to pieces on the pavement."

The Sad Story of Mattie Potts

In 1879, **Mattie Potts** (1834-1882), a female pedestrian, and an actress from New York City, attempted a 2,600-mile walk from Philadelphia to New Orleans and back in five months. She claimed that she recently walked 225 miles in a six-day race, rested a week and then began her walk. She said she was a widow, had four children, but was now childless. She walked, carrying a cane covered with skulls and bones, which was a piece of an old umbrella, and a small satchel that included a revolver inside. She said her efforts were being made in order to win a $10,000 prize, or $5,000 (the number kept changing.)

Potts was described as blonde, tall and bony. "She wears a jaunty white straw hat, trimmed with blue ribbon, a short black walking dress and store shoes. She explains that she thirsts for glory." She kept notes as she journeyed and hoped to write a book. She generally walked on railroads and sent her luggage ahead down the line. Somehow, she found time and energy to put on paid walking exhibitions in evenings along the way. Curiously, she sometimes arrived in towns on a train. She complained about towns that would charge her for meals.

Potts said in Alabama she had trouble with a train. "A gravel train backed upon her while she was on a bridge, and she jumped on an iron bridge support and swung herself over the water and hung there." Along the way, she had eleven proposals for marriage.

Somehow, she completed her promised journey. She was a celebrity but did not receive the money. It was discovered that the $5,000 bet had never been finalized before she started her walk. Building on her perceived fame, she tried to put on walking exhibitions in New York City and Baltimore, in a garden and a saloon, but those were financial failures. Within a month, she attempted suicide "by placing her head on the railroad track. Poverty and failure to find employment led to the act." Someone noticed her in time and thwarted the attempt.

> **PROUD MRS. POTTS.**
>
> She Arrives in Baltimore and Tells How She Walked to New Orleans and Back.

She included a note in her pocket that said, "I am about to do a rash act, which I hope the world will forgive me for doing. It is nearly five weeks since I returned to Philadelphia. I was in debt for one week's board, and I was politely told by the proprietor that I could stay no longer." She tried to get employment, but rejected repeatedly. She concluded, "I want my body given to the medical students in Philadelphia. I am perfectly sane, but I have nothing to live on, nor nothing to live for. So goodbye to the world."

They locked her up for the night at the police station because attempting suicide at that time was a crime. "Whenever the long, shrill whistle of the trains speeding by near the police station were heard, the woman started up and begged to be let out that she might go and throw herself under the locomotive."

The next day, she was given a hearing in front of a magistrate. "She related that she was in an unfortunate marriage, her husband being a dissipated fellow, who died three years ago after the birth of three children. She had employment in a  suit store and was thrown into the pedestrian business afterwards as an alternative against starvation." She also explained that at the exhibitions in New York City and Baltimore, she had been swindled, became disgusted, and contemplated suicide. When asked who it was that swindled her, she declined to state. She said she felt well physically, but mentally had not improved, and if she did not get employment, she would try again to consummate her suicidal intentions.

The judge was smart and believed that she wasn't really a suicide threat, that she was just trying to generate sympathy and publicity. A well-known lady took an interest in her and collected donations for her.

Analyzing her walking pace, destinations, and her story along the way printed in many newspapers, her walk was a fraud, and she took railroad rides. She stayed for free at hotels and received many presents along the way. About a year later, she was seen "tramping across the continent" along with other frauds taking advantage of the sympathies of the public. "When last heard from, she was in Nevada. She carries a bundle in which she had clothing and provisions, and tramps along the road making an average from 25-30 miles a day." It is believed that she died three years later, in 1883.

CHAPTER EIGHT

Race Disruptions

Today's ultramarathons usually have very few disruptions from outsiders or spectators. The most serious disturbances are typically from people who take down course flagging which can cause runners to go off course, potentially putting them in serious danger. But during the era of pedestrianism more than 120 years ago, with thousands of spectators watching exhausted runners go in circles for six days, strange disruptions were commonplace. During high profile races, squads of policemen were required to keep the order.

In 1879, at Canarsie, Brooklyn, New York, an indoor six-day walking competition was held between five walkers in front of a nice crowd in Lehmann's Hotel. It was put on by **William Van Houten** (1857-1914). The event was going along fine until two well-known local men entered the room, **John Wilson**, and **Aleck Fisher**. At the time, most of the competitors were off track sleeping, and so were many of the spectators. "Wilson jumped on the track and commenced breaking it up, while Fisher went about the room, upsetting the benches on which were the sleeping Canarsieites."

"One of the walkers, **Clinton Drake**, requested Wilson to desist from breaking up the track, whereupon Wilson caught Drake by the shoulders, shook him and threatened to throw him out the window. Wilson broke the track up to such an extent that it became necessary to stop the walk." The two men were arrested by a constable but pleaded

not guilty. Drake pressed charges of assault and battery against Wilson, who pleaded not guilty to that charge, too.

In 1879 at the 3rd Astley Belt Race in Gilmore's Garden, New York City, as the leader **Charles Rowell** (1852–1909), was trotting on the track, a man rushed from the west side of the building and yelled "an offensive epithet" at Rowell. "At this instant the English pedestrian got afraid, and there was tremendous excitement. A policeman arrested the man and took him out, and a policeman accompanied Rowell round the track until order was restored."

A Gang Interferes

Apgar in later years

Also in 1879, a contest in the Industrial Art Building in Philadelphia experienced many disruptions. **Melville B. Apgar** (1950-1934), of New York City, who fought in the Civil War as an underage infantryman, was in the lead on day four of a six-day race when an incident ruined his race. "He was going around at a fair gait when a drunken man came on the track, and the acting referee, Jones, ordered him off. He refused to go, and a scuffle ensued, during which the drunken man fell against Apgar as he was passing and knocked him down." Apgar tried to continue for several miles, but he sprained his knee and he had to withdraw from the race. Apgar and his friends criticized the race management, and one of them, Clark, made a very inflammatory speech about the terrible treatment received. "He was instantly surrounded by a crowd, and cries of 'Put him out,' and 'Kill him' and the like were freely used, and a rush was made." The race manager asked the police to kick Clark out of the building and they did.

THE READING HOSE GANG

M'GLINCHEY AS LEADER OF THE INFAMOUS CROWD.

STORY OF THEIR CRIMES

Rumors circulated that there were further threats against Apgar and his friends from **John Comber's** notorious "Reading Hose Gang." The Reading Hose gang was an infamous group of ruffians that made their headquarters near the Reading Railroad depot. Over the years, several murders had been traced to the gang, along with many arrests for other crimes. "Night after night citizens were beaten, robbed, and left lying in the streets." It took many years for the authorities to break up the gang.

For the rest of the race, they brought in a large police force of officers to prevent any more disturbances. But still, **"Tricks" Muldoon**, a member of the gang, stole a cornet from a musician who was playing in the band during the event.

A Mob Ruins an Event

A similar disturbance occurred that same year during a walking exhibition at Oraton Hall in Newark, New Jersey. **Josie Wilson**, "The Jersey Peach Blossom," was seeking to walk 3,000 quarter miles in 3,000 quarter hours. She was described as, "twenty years old, comely, blue-eyed, brown-haired, plump in form and modest in deportment." After reaching 2,700 quarter miles, in front of several hundred people, it was announced that admission would be free the next day.

There was so much interest in the free tickets on a Sunday, the people were asked to take turns viewing in half-hour shifts. "A few gentlemen quitted the hall, but the majority refused to go. Meantime, the crowd outside struggled to get in. A rush was made, the street doors were burst open, and a howling mob surged up the stairway." The two policemen there were quickly overwhelmed and brushed aside. "A crowd of roughs entered the hall and refused to leave and make room for others. There was a row, which caused wild excitement. Oaths, curses and blows followed." A telegraph was sent asking for more police.

As Miss Wilson finished a lap, she became terribly frightened and nervous because of the unruly crowd. "Several ruffians began quarreling near the track. She trembled violently, and her face became white with fear. The next second she fell in a dead faint on the track. She was carried to her room and placed on a lounge. In another minute she was seized with an epileptic fit."

SCARED INTO A SWOON.
A Pedestrienne Faints on the Track and Abandons her Walk.

A squad of eight police soon appeared, but the trouble was over. The chief of police ordered that the exhibition be closed. "Practically, this was done already, for Miss Wilson, upon reaching her quarters, swooned away, and two physicians were called to attend her. It was said a matter of life and death, and her trainer therefore requested the audience to retire. In a few minutes, the hall was cleared." It took the doctors an hour before they could bring Miss Wilson back to consciousness. She would go on to compete in just one more event.

Gatecrashers

The pedestrian events were so popular in New York City that those who did not have the means to pay the admission fee would try all sorts of ways to get in for free. Tickets sometimes were counterfeited. Crashing the gate was the most common approach. In 1879, as midnight approached during the 3rd Astley Belt race, a gang of gate crashers used a beam of wood as a battering ram to break down a door to get in the building. Police eventually rounded them up, arrested them, took them out of the building, beat them, and then let them go.

Teenaged boys would gate-crash events by climbing up pipes through high windows and then later causing disruptions. During an 1882 race in New York, a group of boys started fighting among themselves right on the track. The police eventually caught them and evicted them from the building.

They sometimes enhanced the gate-crashing technique using a rope that they let down from one of the round windows up under the eaves of the south side of Madison Square Garden. "The rope was rather short for the purpose, and it was necessary to raise the candidate several feet from the sidewalk before he could catch hold of the end. When he had secured a firm hold and had given the word, he was slowly hauled up inch by inch till his heels disappeared through the window. Boy after boy was laboriously drawn up in this way. There were cheers loud and prolonged as each boy accomplished the ascent and the commotion drew a crowd."

BEATING THE TURN STILE.

At an 1884 race at Madison Square Garden, the crowds who wanted to enter were huge. People brought their lunches and stood in line for hours until the doors opened. "Outside the Garden, the sights were as remarkable as they were inside. Fully, 1,000 men and boy surrounded the building last evening, howling at every new scoresheet displayed and waiting for a chance to crawl in through the open windows. As policemen were distracted chasing a crowd of boys down Fourth Avenue, someone inside let a clothesline down from one of the portholes and 12 boys climbed up, hand over hand, to the roof and mingled with the multitude inside. Planks and barrels were taken from an adjoining car yard to aid in the assault on the admission fee."

Mob storms Madison Square Garden

The most violent known incident of gate-crashing occurred during the Third Astley Belt Race held in New York City in 1879. When the first mile took place, cheering inside Gilmore Garden (Madison Square Garden) was very loud. Those who were left outside the building heard the roar. They turned into an angry mob and rushed for the entrance, overwhelming the two policemen out there, broke down the door off its hinges and pushed into the building.

The dozen policemen inside rushed to meet the mob, led by police captain **Alexander "Clubber" Williams** (1839-1917) who was known for his brutality. "Then occurred one of the liveliest scrimmages seen in New York for a long time. The police used their clubs freely, and the blows fell thick and fast at random. This harsh usage was effectual, and the mob was driven clear of the building. The sound of the heavy blows rained upon the defenseless heads and bodies of the unfortunates who happened to be in the front ranks was sickening."

Clubber Williams

The riot that took place was not only because the crowd was denied entry, but also because of the police brutality that injured seventy people and sent them to the hospital. Rocks were thrown at the windows of the building, breaking at least one, and some climbed onto the roof. The police established patrol lines so that nobody could approach within a block of the Garden. Those inside the building didn't dare to venture out among the angry thousands. After two hours, the outside crowd finally dispersed.

A Brick Thrown at Runners

A bizarre incident took place during the Fifth Asley Belt Race in Madison Square Garden in 1879. As **George Hazael** (1845-1911) from London, England, and **Sam Merritt** (1850-) of Bridgeport, New Jersey, were walking around the track, a brick fell between the two, just four feet behind Hazael.

Police accused and arrested **Ephraim Holland** (1836-1887) of Cincinnati, Ohio, of throwing the missile to disrupt Hazael's race. Holland was a notorious figure, linked to election corruption (stuffing a ballot box with 300 fraudulent votes) and gambling fraud. He had served time in prison, but had been pardoned by **President Rutherford B. Hayes** for political reasons.

At a trial held the next day in the Jefferson Market Police Court, New York, as the race continued, Holland showed up, "a middle-aged man, well-dressed, and wore a brownish moustache." Unfortunately, **Frank Creamer**, of

HAZAEL'S ASSAILANT.

EPH HOLLAND, THE CINCINNATI GAMBLER, AT THE BAR.

The Witness Tell the Story of the Assault and the Attempt to Disable the English Walker.

Williamsburg, New York, the witness to the throwing of the stone, failed to appear. Another witness, **Otto Lecher,** signed an affidavit charging Holland with assault. Holland's lawyer asked for a dismissal because there was no evidence that the missile was aimed at Hazael. But the prosecution maintained that for 36 hours Holland had been trying to injure Hazael because he had heavily wagered on the order of finishers and Hazael was doing too well. Hazael's trainer testified, "He tried to get into Hazael's tent and at his food and was driven away." He had been warned that Holland would try to put drugs in Hazael's food. Holland yelled, "I never threw that stone."

Officer McCoy took the stand and testified that Holland was about fifteen feet from the track, and he had seen the brick pass over the heads of the crowd

> The Attempt to Assault Haznel—Arraignment of Eph Holland in the Jefferson Market Police Court—The Judge Directs a Complaint to be Drawn up Against the Prisoner.

and by several ladies and then rebound on the track. "Lechler, the complaining witness, testified that he saw Holland's arm raised as if to throw something and immediately afterward the stone fell." They needed the second witness to convict, but still did not show up. "Eph Holland left the court with a crowd of sporting men, who shook him by the hand and expressed their conviction that Eph could not have committed the act. Holland himself stoutly denied the throwing of the stone and claimed that he was the victim of a mistake."

Holland continued his corrupt activities. The following year, he was shot in the thigh on the streets of Cincinnati in a gambling dispute. He finally met his demise in 1887, at the age of 51, thought to be caused by

> THE DEAD GAMBLER.
>
> Eph Holland Laid to Rest in Spring Grove Cemetery.

the continued problems from the pistol ball wound in his thigh. He had been credited for establishing the largest gambling house ever run in the country up to that point.

Other Disruptions

Money Scramble

There were many other disruptions on the track. Sometimes wealthy spectators would cause a welcome distraction for the runners. They would throw money on the track in front of a group of runners and watch with amusement as the contestants sprinted to go secure the prize.

Race Officials Assaulted

Those who had wagers on the results were so intense that sometimes they assaulted scorers if they thought they were short-changing their runner of laps. This took place in 1882 in Madison Square Garden. An angry mob attacked a scorer named **Roberts** at 3 a.m. It was reported, "Many in this crowd were intoxicating and insulting. They accused him of putting up the wrong figures. Being unable to quietly rest under these aspirations upon his character, Roberts descended the ladder from the platform where he was on duty and undertook to reason with the excited men."

"They pitched upon him and beat him unmercifully. The police officers were at the other end of the Garden, and the ruffians only desisted in pounding Roberts when they were satisfied with their work." He left but returned to his scoring work the next day with "a bruised head and discolored eyes."

Scorers did make mistakes and had to be watched closely. In another race, an amateur athlete was keeping score on **Robert Vint's** score dial and gave him an extra mile. A young man in charge of the official score sheet discovered this. Because it was the second time for this mistake, they fired the dial-turner.

Angry mobs were a fear to those who officiated these races. In 1880 in England, during a 50-mile walking match held at Agricultural Hall in London, a mob brutally assaulted referee **George W. Atkinson** for disqualifying a walker named **Jack Hibberd** after repeated warnings. "The police were called upon to give Mr. Atkinson safe conduct from the building. He was attacked merely for daring to assert the rights of his office. For a time, the police kept them at bay, but finally the mob broke in, took possession of the track and surrounded the referee, who was threatened with annihilation. One ruffian struck the referee on the head, whereupon the police came to the rescue and no further violence was offered." One "rascal" tried to throw down another walker, and fights followed. Atkinson gave orders for the race to be stopped because it was impossible to clear the course and let the walkers compete safely.

Spectators Join the Race

At the 1st Oleary Six-day Race in Madison Square Garden in October 1879, the crowd was confused when a big man came on the track and seemed to be helping and pushing runner **Ben Curran** (1833-1907) along. "It was met with strong disfavor, and on the second lap which

Old Madison Square Garden

the big man made, someone who objected put out his foot. The big man stumbled over it and fell as a drunken man sometimes will fall. His hat rolled ren yards away, and he seemed to sprawl over the track. A great laugh went up, and the big man gathered himself up only to find that a policeman was escorting him kindly off the track."

During a six-day race at Madison Square Garden in 1891, a detained man broke out of a nearby building, rushed into the Garden and ran around the track. On his third lap, he was finally arrested, taken to the police station, and later sent to Bellevue Hospital.

In 1888, a one-legged boy of fourteen years came out on the Madison Square Garden track. "The cripple refused to leave the path of the men, and when the policeman attempted to take him out of the Garden, the boy fought him, using his crutch as a weapon. The rebellious lad was locked up."

Spectator Fights

During that same race, there were bigger disturbances. "A general fight among a lot of men who gathered on the track opposite **Peter Golden's** booth was created. There was a little clubbing by policemen and pummeling by combatants, but no

arrests were made although some men were 'fired' out of the building. Another 'come all ye' occurred in the big barroom during the morning hours, but there were no casualties." Even women caused disturbances. "Two loudly dressed women engaged in a fight in a box that distracted attention from the contestants until they were ejected."

Quest for Arrest

Oddly, during the morning of a race, a spectator came into the building and asked a man who had been there the whole week what disruption he could do to get arrested. "The boarder told him to kick in the glass of a showcase containing goods, placed on exhibition in the Garden. He did it. The hint proved a valuable one. The citizen was arrested with great promptness and could not find words to express his gratitude to the boarder."

Police Control

The police sometimes liked to show their muscle by causing their own disruptions. "Police Captain Reilly called on Race Manager **Frank W. Hall** and warned him that he was violating the law in furnishing music and selling liquor together, and Manager Hall concluded that there was more money in drinks than in music, and the band was dismissed." In another instance, the 12-year-old son of **Henry Vaughn**, of England, came on the track to run six miles in under an hour. The crowd cheered, but Captain **Clubber Williams**, always wanting to show he was in control "stalked over the sawdust with his club tucked under his arm and laid his hand on the boy's shoulder and said, 'that boy is underage, he must stop.'"

Unruly Spectators

Over the years, more events became unruly. The New York press noticed and wrote, "The walking mania has reached a queer stage. The halls have in many cases been turned into drinking places, and loafers spend their nights there in boisterous fun. Give us a rest."

At 1:30 a.m. of a race, a Mr. Waldron wanted free tickets from the race manager. When the manager replied gruffly, the man struck him with his fist, flooring him. Police took the man into custody. At 3 a.m. there was another small disturbance. "The only female in the audience emitted a sort of wail. She was carried out. Nobody seemed to know the cause of the wail nor the name of the 'wailer.'"

At times, the spectators would be amusing spectacles for the runners to watch. Frequently, people thought it was cheaper to sleep in the building rather than go home and pay another day's admission. One evening, a boy and his best girl settled into slumber in their box and soon were snoring. Runners thought it was funny to try to hit them with bits from the track as they ran by. Finally, the boy moved a little, causing the girl to slide off him. "She tumbled off the guard-rail of the box and down upon the floor of Madison Square Garden, going head over heels in the maneuver. Of course, this awakened her, and her escort realized the situation instantly. He reached over the railing and grasping her hand, pulled her back to the box, the crowd of spectators howling with laughter." The two quickly left Madison Square Garden "followed to the door by a crowd of hoodlums."

Pickpockets went to work as others slept. A fight between two spectators occurred. **John Clute** had been the most dedicated fan who had been there every day and night, never leaving. He ate at the in-house restaurant and slept for a while each night in the back chairs. On Wednesday night, someone stole his pocket watch while he was sleeping. On the next day, he recognized a man, **Charles H. Thompson**, who had been sitting close to him on the night of the theft. "He immediately accused him of having taken the watch. Hard words followed, resulting in blows. Clute proved too much for the man, and finally the stranger admitted he had taken the watch, but it was then beyond recovery. Clute had him arrested at the station house." The watch was eventually returned to Clute.

Sideshows

Sideshows sometimes were a distraction to the runners. During an 1881 six-day race in the Garden, a five-mile race involving 20 boys lined up on the track. "**John Hughes** (currently in second place) who had been in an ugly temper all day, became enraged and threatened to leave the building. The other regulars worked through the crowd of boys and jogged on uncomplainingly." As the sprint took place, half the competitors, including Hughes, went to their huts until it was over.

Fights Between Crews

Fights between runner crews were a risk for the events. In 1884, American **Patrick Fitzgerald's** trainer objected that a Mr. Mitchell was coaching Englishman **Charles Rowell**, even though he was not on his team as a regular handler or trainer. It was said that he had no business being on the track with Rowell. "Mitchell walked into the enemy's camp to explain matters, when a war of words occurred, and signs of a rattling sparring match grew promising. Partisans of both sides edged up. All were looking for a fight. It was reported that some of Fitzgerald's henchmen had procured brick bats to be used as ammunition. The referee requested Mitchell to return to the English camp. Policemen were placed on guard; the danger of any serious disturbance was averted."

George Cartwright Attacted by Spectator

CHAPTER NINE

Steve Brodie – New York Newsboy

The 19th century ultrarunner was a different breed of athlete compared to those today who take part in the sport. Many of those early runners were not necessarily the most outstanding citizens. For the vast majority, the motivation for participating was not just to see what they could accomplish running long distances. They were primarily motivated by greed and gaining fame. It should not be too surprising that many were involved in wild, free-spending lifestyles, scandals, illegal activities, and run-ins with the law.

A pattern emerged for many of the many successful ultrarunners of the 1800s. They would quickly gain fame and build up a massive fortune, only to come crashing down a few years later through their own mismanagement, dishonesty, and enormous egos. Even the most famous pedestrian of all, **Edward Payson Weston**, blew through his money, filed for bankruptcy, and was criticized for abandoning his family.

Steve Brodie

The story of seventeen-year-old **Steve Brodie** of New York City is a case study of one who gained fame and fortune ultrarunning but also treated many people terribly along the way, and eventually used fraud to revive his fame. The American vernacular term "do a Brodie," meaning to take a bad risk, or experience a complete failure/flop, came about because of Steve Brodie, the "New York Newsboy Pedestrian."

Stephen Brodie, (1861-1901) was the son of Richard and Mary Brodie of New York City. Richard was a member of the Bowery Boys street gang that menaced the city in the Bowery neighborhood in Lower Manhattan. The gang was an anti-Catholic, anti-Irish, and a somewhat criminal gang. The uniform of a Bowery Boy generally consisted of a stovepipe hat, a red shirt, and dark trousers tucked into boots.

A Bowery Boy

New York Draft Riot

His father, **Richard Brodie** was murdered shortly after Steve was born in 1861. The Bowery Boys reached the height of their power in 1863, taking part in looting much of New York City during the New York Draft Riots.

Strange Running Tales: When Ultrarunning was a Reality Show

Steve Brodie was the youngest of seven children. His older brothers were groomed for the Bowery Boys gang at a young age. Instead of attending school, Steve worked as a child selling newspapers, starting at the age of six. His older brothers constantly beat him and took his hard-earned money. At age nine, he moved out of his poverty-stricken home and moved into a boy's home and later went to live in a newsboy lodging house.

Newsboy

The career of a newsboy was explained, "You had to sell newspapers every day, or else your risked becoming homeless. You fought for street corners and fought to protect your property. Men robbed the boys and older boys robbed the younger boys." In his late teens, he led his own gang of newsboys. "He won the friendship of everyone he came in contact. He became acquainted with people of many classes, brokers, capitalists, lawyers, newspapermen, athletes, sporting men, actors, cranks, crooks, bums, and all the various kind of humanity that united to make New York an inexhaustible field for the student of mankind."

Brodie was a strong and daring swimmer who became a member of the Life Saving Corps organized on the East River front. As a youth, he was credited for making many rescues, including two women who fell off an excursion barge.

Brodie's First Ultra

In February 1879, at the age of 17, Brodie made his first attempt to break into the sport of pedestrianism. *The New York Daily Herald* took notice.

> ON THE TRAMP.
>
> STEPHEN BRODIE, THE NEWSBOY, TRYING TO WALK NINETY MILES IN TWENTY-FOUR HOURS—AN INTERESTING SCENE AT THE NEWSBOYS' GYMNASIUM.

"Pedestrianism has wrought its way into the favor of the upper circles of newsboydom, as was proven last evening by the commencement of the feat, proposed by Master Stephen Brodie, of walking 90 miles in 24 hours. The sawdust track of more than 20 laps to the mile was laid down in the gymnasium of the Newsboys' Lodging House, in New Chambers Street, and duly measured." Brodie was described as five feet seven inches and weighing 125 pounds. He felt ready but had only trained by occasionally walking from the newsboy's lodge to Macomb's Dam Bridge over the Harlem River, a distance of about nine miles.

Brodie's walk began at 7 p.m. on February 16, 1879. His first mile was completed in nine minutes, and he reached five miles in 52 minutes. His older brothers watched and were impressed. Two other newsboys did their best to keep track of the laps. Brodie fueled on beef tea, toast, and fried eggs. After five hours, because of a long rest of about an hour, he had only reached 22 miles. As he began again, as typical with rookie ultrarunners, he experienced his first trouble with nausea, requiring him to rest again. Eventually he settled down and started walking again.

Newsboys' Boardinghouse located on New Chambers Street

"He had been walking since the start in a pair of heavy, thick-soled brogans, and at 5:00 a.m. took them off and walked the rest of his journey in his stocking feet. He reached his 90-mile goal in 23:20 and then went off to bed. This feat has started the pedestrian fever among the newsboys, and a number commenced training, walking round the floor in the reading room."

Brodie Becomes a Star

Brodie quickly became a youthful pedestrian star in New York City. Next, in early March 1879, he attempted to walk 250 miles in 75 hours at the Fifth Regiment Armory, a site of many pedestrian events that year. He didn't succeed, but also didn't give up. A couple of weeks later, he walked 50 miles in 8:39:53 in front of 3,000 people at Eagle Hall, Hoboken, New Jersey.

Brodie's First Six-day Race

With this success, Brodie was accepted to compete in the American Championship Belt six-day race at Gilmore's Garden (Madison Square Garden), in New York City, April 14-19, 1879, with 40 runners. Because of his youth, he was a fan favorite and surprised the crowds of thousands with his bravery, and received many floral gifts. Early on he said with a grin, "I'm feelin' bully, an' will do my best."

Gilmore's Garden

He ran close to the frontrunners but started to look lame after the first day. "Brodie, the newsboy, was the picture of distress, and notwithstanding the opinion of his attendants that he was 'tough and all right,' it was evident that only their ignorance and his own pluck kept him moving around the track." He found his groove and continued strong. The common joke people yelled at the newsboy was, "Are they getting out new extras?" He was often seen chewing away at a large sandwich as he plodded along. His gait was described as, "a very slouchy manner, with his head hanging forward and his arms swinging violently."

By day three, the "youngster was astonishing everyone." He vowed to continue for the entire six days. He was a hero to all New York City newsboys. "Shivering newsboys, wet to the skin, stood in the half shelter of the building outside, inquiring eagerly of persons whom they supposed had just come from the inside. 'How is Steve Brodie getting along?'"

	1st.	2d.	3d.	4th.	5th.	6th.	Total Miles.
Panchot	104	86	70	77	70	73	480
Merritt	100	80	70	75	76	74	475
Krohne	94	69	78	80	71	63	455
O'Brien	90	80	70	73	63	55	431
Byrne	76	69	68	70	69	75	427
Noden	83	77	69	71	68	57	425
Brodie	86	57	49	63	51	69	375

By the final day, it was said that he was in the best condition of any of the eight runners who remained on the track. "Brodie, time and time again, ran around amid the cheers of the crowd." He smartly would run around the track carrying a bundle of newspapers, which he autographed and sold to the spectators at exorbitant prices. His friends solicited newspaper subscriptions for him in the crowds. For his six-day debut, he finished in a surprising 7th place with 375 miles and then immediately issued challenges to elite pedestrians.

Brodie Wins in Philadelphia

Brodie only had a brief rest and a week later competed in another six-day race in Philadelphia's Concert Hall against four others. He took the early lead. "The newsboy, a little black-headed fellow, reminding one, as he bobs around, with his head bent forward, of a small rat-terrier. He digs along on a rapid walk for a while, when he will fall back and plod along slowly till about the time when everybody is looking for him to retire, for rest, when he astonishes all by breaking out on a dogtrot, shooting past all his competitors and keeping up that run for several miles."

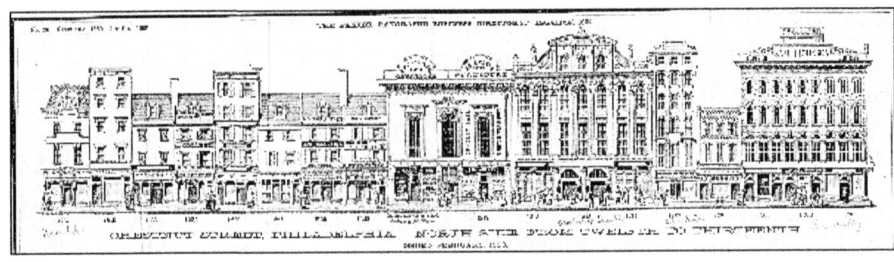

Philadelphia Concert Hall

On day three, he had the lead with 208 miles. With that lead, he started to use the strategy to dog the heels of his next competitor, **Henry Lyons** (known as "2 for 5"), a toothpick vendor, 13 miles behind, which made Lyons angry. "He grumbles and growls, and at one time stopped short to allow the newsboy to pass. Brodie, however, did not care to be in the lead and stopped also, compelling Lyons to go ahead. This created plenty of fun, and the crowd kept continually cheering one or the other of the pair." By day five, Brodie had extended his lead to a commanding 50 miles. Lyons dropped to third place "due to his own surly disposition and ill temper." He would stop on the track and jaw with the crowd, scolding them for applauding the newsboy. Brodie also showed a bad temper when he punched Lyons in the eye during an argument.

In the end, Brodie won with 390 miles, 82 miles ahead of the next runner.

Brodie	390	Murray	239
M'Lean	308	Ward	117
Lyons	301		

He won $500 valued at $14,800 today, an immense fortune for a young newsboy. "The lad was presented with a gold medal and watch and chain. He made a little speech. He was in excellent condition and is considered a promising pedestrian."

Brodie Competes in a Farse

Brodie, who obviously was managed by others wanting to have a piece of his fortune, continued to seek pedestrian opportunities for fast winnings. At the end of May 1879, he raced for 27 hours against two others at the Concert Hall in Philadelphia for $750. Brodie took the early lead. But when midnight arrived, it was obvious to the spectators that some collusion was taking place with Brodie and **John J. Dickinson,** agreeing to take long rests at the same time rather than really competing against each other.

Dickinson's trainer was so disgusted that he threatened to quit, but Dickinson refused to be on the track without Brodie. "In the sporting parlance, it was a put-up job between Brodie and Dickinson, that they should come out even at the finish, and divide the gate money. Dickinson, however, broke down at 64 miles. The time and number of miles at the finish amount to nothing and are not worth recording." Brodie did win with 95 miles. This event raised a sure red flag regarding Brodie's lack of integrity.

The event must have been a financial success, because only a few days later, Brodie was again the headliner for a 27-hour race at the same Philadelphia venue. Ten men started. "There were thin men and fat men, tall men and short men, young men and old men, and some of the men were boys, including a couple of newsboys." Brodie's fatigue finally caught up with his youthful body. He only managed 66 miles, finishing 5th.

Philadelphia in 1875

Brodie in Boston

Brodie next took his talents to Boston, Massachusetts, and competed in a 50-mile race against the famous pedestrian, **Peter Van Ness** (1853-1900) and **Charles Edward Holske** (1858-1940) a walker, for $50. Brodie lost, quitting after 40 miles when Holske had an insurmountable lead.

Brodie Goes to California

With his tail somewhat between his legs because of a string of losses, Brodie headed for California, hoping to compete against **Frank Edwards**, the recent winner of the Diamond Belt Six-day race with 371 miles.

Platt's Hall

Strange Running Tales: When Ultrarunning was a Reality Show

Edwards refused to accept Brodie's challenge, so the newsboy was left to find a venue and event for him to attract interest in watching him run. He chose to attempt to cover 250 miles in 75 hours at Platts' Hall in San Francisco. He failed to reach his promised goal again, reaching only 223 miles.

Race Against Horses

Brodie next entered a six-day race at San Francisco's Mechanic's Pavilion against horses and riders. Five runners competed against six horses on a 12-foot-wide track. Each horse had to be ridden by only one man the entire distance. Brodie boasted he would reach more than 400 miles.

THE NEW CONTEST.

Opening of the Match Between Men and Horses.

The unique contest attracted thousands of spectators on the opening night, October 15, 1879. *Pinafore*, a gray gelding of eight years, was the favorite, ridden by **John Levy**. Brodie and **Gus Guerrero** took the early lead. "The newsboy and the Spaniard are the only walkers who stand a chance of scoring more miles than the horses." But Brodie pushed hard. "Brodie challenged *Controller's* driver to a race, which was accepted, and man and horse ran around together twice, the horse passing Brodie on the straight stretch and Brodie gaining on the turns. Controller won the sprint." Brodie reached 100 miles in 23:13.

By the third day, betting turned against Brodie, predicting that he would not accomplish 400 miles and *Pinafore* had a 51-mile lead over the runners. It was speculated that the race was fixed, that Brodie went out fast on purpose to break Guerrero. After that, it was thought that Brodie would give up on purpose, leaving the victory to the horses. But that theory did not pan out.

Men.	Thursday 2 P.M.	11 P.M.	Friday 8 A.M.	12 M.
Brodie	70	100	104	114
Wilcox	45	70	85	97
Newhoff	56	70	90	100
McAlpine	54	77	86	96
Guerero	60	87	108	121
Horses.	2 P.M.	11 P.M.	8 A.M.	12 M.
Controller	63	89	99	119
Denver Jim	41	78	89	101
Dan McCarthy	56	90	113	130
Pinafore	67	103	131	150
Hoodlum	59	89	107	126
Nelly	63	95	111	133

Brodie's Vulgarity

But then it happened. "The ladies were out last night in nearly as large numbers, and we are particularly vexed that the boy Brodie, who seemed to be their favorite, should have taken it on himself to gratuitously insult them by his loud-mouthed obscenity and blasphemy. Mr. Brodie must bear in mind that he is not in the low Bowery Haunt, but in a place which the managers, by the exertion of care and judgment, have made, for the time being, a favorite resort for ladies. The repetition of any such conduct would have a disastrous effect on the success of any future exhibitions of pedestrianism."

> The Pacific Life says that Steve Brodie and Sallie Donley have degraded pedestrianism. It could not have been a very difficult job

Brodie had been much annoyed by a crowd of men who leaned over the rail trash-talking him as he ran by. But then he passed that annoyance onto Guerrero by passing him, stopping and purposely dodging in front of him as he came by to make him stumble. The crowd then really came down on Brodie and he replied with vulgarity. Many men yelled at him for his New York language. The hostilities toward Brodie and his vulgarity increased in "confusion and uproar." Finally, a policeman threatened to get a warrant for his arrest if Brodie didn't stop. He marched out of the building and came back and arrested Brodie for his vulgar language. He had to post $50 bail to continue racing.

> **Brodie's Bail Money.**
>
> Steve Brodie, the New York pedestrian, was arrested on Friday last for having made use of vulgar language, and Lawton & McNeill deposited $50 as bail to secure his appearance in Court. On the following day Brodie failed to appear, consequently the bail was forfeited.

By the fourth day, Brodie reached 217 miles but was far behind his goal and behind Guerrero, who reached 300 miles. *Pinafore* was running away with the contest with 405 miles. In the end, *Pinafore* won with 557 miles. Brodie was second among the runners, with a relative meager 262 miles to Guerrero's 375.

Brodie's Reputation Takes a Dive

Brodie failed to appear in court, forfeited his $50 in bail, and quickly left town. His very short, successful pedestrian career of eight months was crumbling around him like a house of cards. The immature 17-year-old clearly didn't have mature, experienced men around him to help keep his temper in check and work on his public relations.

On his return to New York City the next month, the hot-headed boy was arrested again. He and two companions became unruly at a restaurant. They were ordered to leave. "They refused, began a general assault on the waiters and threw a can of mustard over the proprietor." At their trial, they were each fined $10. Brodie didn't have money with him, so he asked his backer in California for help and was locked up in the meantime. His running abilities faded, but his ability to get into trouble continued.

Brodie's Pedestrian Career Ends

In February 1880, Brodie tried to revive his pedestrian career by competing in a big six-day race (12 hours per day) at the Music Hall in Boston, Massachusetts. His first 12 hours were pathetic, reaching only 23 miles because of cramping. The press referred to him as "a lame duck," and quickly withdrew in embarrassment. "This is not much, as his past record as a ped, with one exception, has not been of the most enviable. Beginning life as a newsboy, he still continues to base his calculations on paper."

Brodie's brief pedestrian career was over. He had accumulated $6,000 in winnings valued at $175,000 today. He married, **Bridget Breen**, the daughter of a bankrupt steamship captain, and started a family, but quickly lost his fortune gambling on horses. He got a job as a streetcar conductor.

Brodie was still a hero among his Bowery Boys. In 1882, a building caught fire and Brodie saved several lives by climbing a telegraph pole and throwing a rope to people in the upper stories of the building. He was awarded a gold medal. He loved the fame, reward, and attention.

The Bowery

In 1883, Brodie was back in court and fined $300 for assaulting his brother, **Dan Brodie**, "in a fight with some dull instrument." A few years later, in 1886, his two brothers got into a fight, were arrested and taken before the court. Brodie attended, and when his brother Dan saw him, he threatened to crush Steve's skull. The judge heard that and sent Dan to prison for six months. Yes, they were a loving family.

George Floyd, a printer, shot Brodie during a fight on the street a couple of months later. The wound was not serious. Brodie was in a down-spiral and needed to find a new way to get fame.

The Brooklyn Bridge

After fourteen years of construction, The Brooklyn Bridge was completed in 1883. Brodie had witnessed the construction for years. An idea came to him about how he could use the bridge to bring back his fame and fortune.

Robert Emmet Odlum (1851-1885) was a swimming instructor and daredevil. He announced he would make a leap off the Brooklyn Bridge. On the scheduled day, the police tried to stop Odlum's stunt, but he got across the bridge in secret, and made his leap into the East River, 135 feet below. He hit the water awkwardly and came up bleeding internally with critical injuries. He was hauled into a boat but quickly died.

A few months later, in 1886, Brodie got the idea that he could successfully make the jump. People made huge wagers, and he put together his plans. "For two weeks he had the big bridge in his head and planned to make the jump even if it would cost him his life." He first practiced jumping off High Bridge into the Harlem River. He even informed sports editors of his intentions.

On the big day, July 23, 1886, Brodie first met with reporters to let them take pictures and ask questions. He then went with friends in a wagon to the bridge. When the wagon had gone past the large granite bridge tower, it said that he slipped off his jacket, flung it in the face of his companions, and leaped into the roadway. "Climbing hand over hand down the outside iron railing like a monkey, he clambered down to the bottom of the iron structure. Then he reached down and took hold of one of the truss cables under the bridge. He swung by both hands free in the air. The boat containing his friends was in the middle of the river. A shriek went up from somebody on the dock below. Then Brodie let go."

STEVE BRODIE'S PLUNGE

From The East River Bridge.

The Young Man Who Jumped from the Big Bridge Into the East River.

He fell for three seconds feet first and disappeared into the water in a fountain of spray. The boat arrived as Brodie appeared on the surface. "He made a feeble signal for assistance and then began to swim toward the boat. He was taken ashore, drank two glasses of whisky, offered to dance a hornpipe, and threatened to thrash a policeman. He was locked up in the Oak Street station, arraigned in a police court while very drunk, and sent to a cell for the night." They charged him with attempted suicide and held him for a physical and psychiatric examination. Curiously, there were no significant bruises on his body, only a scrape from being brought into the boat. He boasted he could jump off anything on the earth.

Was the Leap a Hoax?

Was this reported story the truth? Brodie had a previous history of lies and deception. The newspapers mostly believed the story and made Brodie the most famous person in America that year. Some skeptics claimed Brodie had a friend toss a dummy off the bridge while he hid under a nearby pier, then swam out when the rescue boat approached. In **David McCullough's** book about the famed Brooklyn Bridge, he expressed the belief that the jump was a hoax.

It was said of Brodie, "Ever since he laid down his tights in Madison Square Garden and listened to the waves of applause washing against the four walls, Brodie has been famishing for notoriety. His principal occupation consisted of lounging about the street." He traveled around various cities for a time, doing stunts and telling his story in dime museums until those opportunities dried up.

In 1887, he opened a saloon in New York City's Bowery district, with a museum about his jump. He was no longer the newsboy. He was Steve Brodie Bridge Jumper. "Hanging above the bar was a massive oil painting showing Brodie making his famous jump from the Brooklyn Bridge into the waters of the East River. Next to it hung a paper signed by a boat captain swearing that he was the one who dragged Brodie from the river after he defied death."

Niagara Falls

In 1889, Brodie claimed he had gone over Niagara Falls in a rubber suit. He produced a 1,500-word version of his story that was printed by the *New York Sun*. But reporters finally became skeptical and realized that only three

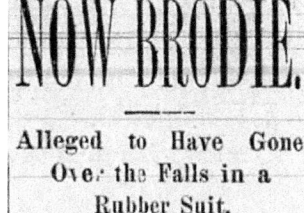

New York men were the ones who claimed to see him go over the Falls. They were Brodie's handpicked witnesses. It was written, "This faking business has ceased to be even amusing." People who were on the "Maid of Mist" gave a different story of seeing men hiding in the bushes, faking the entire thing, putting a man into a wagon in a blanket.

Finally, the *Buffalo Evening News* pointed out that the entire detailed story came from **Ernest Justin Jarrold** (1848-1912), who had a reputation of reporting outlandish stories to sell newspapers.

Ernest Jarrold

In the past, newspapers had printed stories that came directly from Brodie, and assumed the daring accomplishments were true. "His story has been corroborated again and again by his own hired men, who were with him in the dark and misty hours of the morning. He has never in any of his wonderful alleged performances timed his feats so that newspaper reporters could be present."

> **THEY SAY BRODIE DIDN'T DO IT.**
> Two Real Mean Men Who Give the Niagara Snap Away.
> NIAGARA FALLS, N. Y., Sept. 18.—

Dennis F. Butler (1856-1913), one of the best swimmers in America, called Brodie a faker. "I'll take his hand and we'll jump into the Niagara River and go over the Falls together. I know I couldn't come out alive, but I'd stand ten times as much show as he would." Later, in 1890, it was reported that Brodie admitted to throwing a large dummy over the Falls and subsequent news stories referred to the entire event as a fraud.

Brodie Performs on Stage

Brodie next went on stage as a star and played throughout the country for many years in a melodrama, "On the Bowery" purported to depict scenes from his life. He cleaned up his reputation by giving generously to charities and became "an instrument of philanthropy to the unfortunates in the slums of New York." But he continued to have legal troubles, and faced lawsuits related to outstanding debts from this theater tours.

Final Years

In 1900, he sold his famed saloon and museum in the Bowery and moved to Buffalo, New York, when he opened a saloon/concert hall there, building on his Niagara Falls fame.

> **COMING TO BUFFALO.**
> Steve Brodie Intends to Conduct a Saloon in This City.

He became a huge celebrity and was mentioned in the news nearly daily. His family life had been a mess. He divorced, remarried, and his son **Steve Brodie, Jr.** left home during his teens after fighting with his father.

In June 1900, Brodie's health began to fail seriously due to tuberculosis. He sold his Buffalo establishment, went back to the New York Bowery for a time, and then became hospitalized. In November, in desperation, he moved to better weather in San Antonio, Texas, hoping to recover. "He is greatly emaciated and speaks in a whisper, and though he realizes that death is not far off, he is cheerful." When asked if he had given up jumping off things, his reply, perhaps finally reflected on some of his fraud and the influence his fame caused others to lose their lives jumping off bridges. He said, "Never jump, young man; it don't pay in the long run. There are other ways of endangering your life without doing it foolishly. Better stick to the ground as long as you can, because when you die, it's for an awful long time, and then you are planted hard in old mother earth."

The Bridge Jumper Carried Away in San Antonio by Consumption.

STEVE BRODIE.

A New York man who knew him well wrote as Brodie was dying. "Despite all of Brodie's bluffs and his put-on slangy talk, he was a pretty smart individual, and had as many fine points about him as a porcupine."

Death

It was claimed that Brodie accumulated a fortune of $85,000 (valued at $2.9 million today) before his premature death on January 31, 1901, at the age of 39. "The body was taken to Calvary Cemetery for burial. A crowd of 500 or 600 men, women, and children, attracted by curiosity, remained in the streets during the services at the house, and many of them followed the funeral cortege to Ninety-Second Street Ferry on its way to the cemetery."

But Brodie's fame lived on for decades. In 1933, **George Raft** played Brodie in the film "The Bowery" and a Warner Bros. cartoon in 1949 showed Brodie being driven into jumping off the bridge by **Bugs Bunny**.

Was Brodie a fraud? He was for sure a brief accomplished ultrarunner, but his fame and fortune drove him to find easier ways to feed his ego and accumulate wealth. Most who have carefully examined his brief life full of accomplishments conclude that the only leap he truly made was during his "On the Bowery" performances, when he dived off a platform into a mattress. Today a marker stands at 199 Bowery, in New York City, identifying where Brodie's bar and museum used to be located.

CHAPTER TEN

Fraud, Theft, and Nuisance

By 1906, when the pedestrian era was over, most of the elite pedestrians turned to legitimate professions to support their families. **Daniel O'Leary** was traveling for a big publishing house. **John "Lepper" Hughes** was in the real estate business. **Jimmy Albert** was a Texas cattleman, **Robert Vint** was an oil agent in Russia. **Sammy Day** was a house painter in Pittsburgh, Pennsylvania.

But many others had a darker side, driven by motivations of greed and were not necessarily the most outstanding citizens. It should not be too surprising that many were involved in wild, free-spending lifestyles, scandals, illegal activities, and run-ins with the law. This chapter will concentrate on the strange darker side of the sport during the late 1800s.

Publicity Fraud and Redemption

The year 1879 saw an explosion of people trying to enter the ultrarunning/pedestrian sport with at least 90 six-day races held worldwide with 900 starters. That year, **Madame Waldron** and **Walter Moore** tried their hands at going after the fame and fortune of pedestrianism. Their story is interesting because they both degraded into serious fraud, but later, they turned around their lives, serving the downtrodden in their community.

Harriet "Hattie" L. (Waldron) Adams (1845-1911), of Brooklyn, New York (also known as **Madame Waldron**), became a female pedestrian in 1879. She married very young, in 1861, at the age of seventeen, to **Henry Adams** and they had a daughter, Emma. Henry likely died and in 1879, as the pedestrian craze took hold in America, Hattie turned to the sport to start a new life and attempt to earn a fortune.

Marriage Record

In January 1879, Adams (Madame Waldron) walked 150 miles in 50 hours at the Adelphi Theatre in New York City. Next, on March 3, 1879, she competed in an "International Pedestrian and Billiard Tournament," that was held at the Brooklyn Roller Skating Rink, near **Dr. Justin D. Fulton's** Temple. Pedestrians, male and female from nine countries, attempted various walks for huge money on seven sawdust tracks, each 20 laps to a mile, set up in the building. It was an amazing spectacle. "Its entire appearance had been changed from a mammoth, bleak and dreary barn to a bright and cheery place of amusement. Between the tracks were placed rows of evergreens, shrubs and flowing plants which gave the floor much of the appearance of a garden. Three full-sized billiard tables were placed in a space in the center of the rink. From the roof were pendant hundreds of bright flags. At the rear of the hall was a large music gallery."

ON THE TRACKS.

OPENING OF THE PEDESTRIAN TOURNAMENT AT THE BROOKLYN RINK.

Elaborate Preparations Made for the Event — Who Entered for the Various Contests — Feats Possible and Impossible Attempted — The Building Crowded by Spectators.

Adams/Madame Waldron and one of the most famous female pedestrians, **May (Mary) Marshall**, attempted to walk 4,000 quarter miles in 4,000 quarter hours. Adams was said to be "of large statue but attractive," 180 pounds, and claimed to be "the heavyweight champion of America." She did not succeed in the very difficult 1,000-mile walk, but had tasted the spotlight of fame and wanted more.

A couple months later, Adams competed against **Walter Moore** (1854-1915), a novice walker and construction worker from Brooklyn, attempting 2,700 miles in 2,700 quarter hours in Brooklyn at Bennett's Hotel on Atlantic Avenue. They did not make it, covered at least 111 miles, but they did evidently find love and got married. **Walter Moore** started going by the name of **Charles Livingston** and claimed that he successfully walked 4,000 quarter miles in 4,000 quarter hours, which was not true.

Fasting for 42 Days

After his short pedestrian career was over, to try to regain some fame, Livingston came up with a publicity stunt to fast for 42 days. He published a challenge for anyone to compete against him for $2,500. No one accepted, so he decided to do it solo. He shared his background with newspapers. "He began a business for himself when he was 19 years old, manufacturing calico wrappers, and built up a business which at one time employed 30 girls, but it failed, and he got into debt. He then went to work as a foreman of a construction gang." After his professional pedestrian career fizzled, he handled grain at stores along the East River.

Livingston's crazy fast began on September 7, 1880, at a beer saloon at 5 Willoughby St., Brooklyn, New York. He claimed that in the past he had fasted 23 days and he wanted to go after a 42-day record held by **Dr. Henry S. Tanner** (1831-1918), completed a month earlier. Livingston said, "I don't care for food. It has no temptation for me, and I can go without eating or sleeping without any inconvenience."

Henry Tanner

Beer Saloon

To verify the stunt, one "watcher" was always on duty. Livingston spent much of his days relaxing and chatting in an easy chair donated by a furniture store. He was allowed to drink water. He loved the attention that he was getting in the New York City newspapers, and his stunt was reported nationwide. Spectators coming to see him started to be charged admission after the second day. His manager, **T. J. Murphy**, said, "If he wants to starve, I will give him a good chance."

Many callers came each day to visit him, including **John Dwyer** (1847-1882), the ex-prize fighter and Congressman **Daniel O'Reilly** (1838-1911). "Livingston sat near the front window of the hall, and his wife sat most of the day by his side. He is her second husband, and they are an affectionate couple. She is many years his senior."

After just four days, Livingston, age 26, was getting thin and complaining that his clothes were too large on him. Oddly, his face still looked full, and he had not yet weighed himself. Dr. Tanner was very skeptical of the stunt, stating that "unless

John Dwyer

physicians watched him, the genuineness of his fast will be doubted."

On day five, Livingston felt well but "had a longing for food as he saw it in the restaurants which he passed in his walk." He wanted a notice posted in the saloon that people should refrain from mentioning food. Hattie livened things up by playing on the bar piano. She was increasingly becoming opposed to the stunt, mostly because it wasn't bringing in very much money. She accused one watcher of insulting her and threatened to fetch the police to make her husband go home.

On day six, Livingston said, "I am feeling worse today than I have any day of my fast. I am very weak and am losing flesh very fast. Just see how loose my coat and vest are." A popular daily postcard mentioned his effort.

Charles Livingston's Fast.

Six Days of Fast Beginning to Tell on the Young Man—His Coat Getting Too Large For Him.

On day seven, Hattie visited, still insisting that Livingston stop and told him falsely that his father died from a heart attack and that he must leave immediately to attend the funeral. Livingston didn't buy the story and didn't budge.

FASTER LIVINGSTON'S WIFE.

She Threatens to Call in the Police and Have the Fast Broken Up.

On day eight, Hattie, began insisting that he stop before he got deathly ill. She feared he was going to die and that his manager wasn't showing him the proper attention. Livingston refused to quit for his wife. "She wept at the decision and grew angry and threatened to call in the police and have the fast broken up." She vowed she would not come to visit him again during his continued fast. His father, who was not dead, came to visit and told him he was wicked for trying to fast longer than Jesus did. (See Matthew 4:1-11).

On the ninth day, Hattie sent word to her husband at the barroom that she was sick in bed with heart disease and wanted him to come see her. He and the two watchers went to his home at 358 Atlantic Avenue, but she looked as healthy as ever. She insisted he stop his fast or she would be the one who would die. Livingston refused to stop and returned to the bar.

Later that evening, Livingston's landlord rushed in, stating that Hattie had purposely taken bug poison and that he needed to return home right away. He darted out of the bar without his watchers. "The police were notified, and an ambulance was sent to the woman's house. The neighborhood was in a state of great excitement. Livingston reached his wife's apartment about the same time"

Hattie was moaning. A cup containing bedbug poison was on a table near her bedside. "He came out to his watchers and announced that after eight days and ten hours, he would stop his fast, as his wife was bound to get him home." The ambulance was going to take her to the hospital, but Livingston said that there was nothing wrong with her, that the poisoning was a ruse. The press wrote, "Starvation is the last resource of the lazy man. A lazy person would rather starve to death than work." It was believed that Livingston belonged to that class of people. Livingston immediately drank a glass of beer and ate three crackers. The next morning, he started to look for a job.

Fasting Fraud Revealed

About a week later, the truth came out. Livingston's landlady, Mrs. Fisher, revealed that the entire fasting event was a fraud. Hattie had secretly supplied him with food and stimulants and was in on the hoax. "Mrs. Fisher also let it be understood that the poisoning dodge was a job put up between Livingston and his wife as a dramatic close to the fasting imposture."

Livingston, the Faster, as a Runaway Husband.

A Gentleman Goes to See the Great Abstainer and Recognizes in him a Delinquent Son in Law—A Statement by his Landlady that he did not Fast and that the Poisoning Episode was a Job—Suit Against him for Absolute Divorce.

Desertion of Wife

During the event, **Hans Anderson** had been curious about the man fasting and went to visit him at the bar during his fast. It surprised him to find out that Livingston was the same man who was the lost husband of his daughter, Lillian. It turned out that Livingston's real name was **Walter B. Moorcroft**. He had married **Lillian Anderson** in 1878 when she was only 16 years old, and he had deserted her in 1879 when he started his pedestrianism. Since Mr. Anderson was Lillian's guardian, he went and filed charges and a divorce suit against Livingston. They attempted to serve papers to Livingston, but he had already fled.

Thomas Fields, a deputy sheriff, and Livingston's former manager, who was a watcher during the fast spotted Livingston on the streets of

FASTER LIVINGSTON SUED.

The Complaint of a Young Woman who Says she is his Real Wife.

Brooklyn. He convinced Livingston to meet him later at a certain place, and then had Anderson and his daughter secretly also be there to confirm, without a doubt, that he was actually Moorcroft. Fields then handed Livingston the summons divorce suit. Livingston was surprised, but admitted that he was Moorcroft and blamed Hattie for enticing him away from his true wife, Lillian. He had also gone by other aliases, **Walter Moore** and **Walter B. Morgan.** "If Moorcroft had brains to stick to one wife as tenaciously as he wanted to starve himself, he would have a partial outfit for a good citizen."

Lives Turned Around

Moorcroft and Adams became legally married three years later, in 1883. He became the superintendent of Emmanuel Mission which was "designed for the reclamation of fallen men." But at first, he was only using it as a charitable institution, probably for nefarious purposes. He was sued for nonpayment of goods for the mission and then it was revealed that he also owned the notorious Tenderloin Saloon on East 13th Street in New York City. It was known as "The Hole in the Wall" which had a "disreputable character," and likely contained a brothel.

Finally, in 1894, something happened. Moorcroft underwent a spiritual conversion one evening and immediately telegraphed his bar with instructions to close the business. His employees thought the police were after him. "But Moorcroft disabused everyone's mind by hurrying down to his saloon, taking out all the bottles of whiskey and emptying them into the sewer and then doing the same with every drop of alcoholic beverage he had in the place. Not a bottle of flask or keg was left unemptied by Moorcroft." He sold his business and donated the money toward fallen girls of New York City.

John Street Methodist Church

Moorcroft later explained, "I had a big business and made money, loads of it. I never was bothered by any pangs of self-reproach or remorse. I was a laughing sinner. One day, I was moved to enter the John Street Methodist church that I happened to be passing. A half hour later, I was a saved man, born again."

He then joined the Methodists and started work as a full-time missionary. He put his heart into the rescue mission and in 1895 was described as "a gentleman possessing an aggressive and intense personality, full of humane kindness, with the courage of his convictions, with one idea to administer succor to the outcast and abandoned." He and his wife lived at the mission.

Paterson, New Jersey

Later, they moved to New Jersey in 1901 and opened missions in Ridgewood, Lodi and Paterson and were involved with the Society for the Prevention of Cruelty to Children. "He took in free of charge hundreds of men and women rather than have them arrested for either drunkenness or disorderly conduct and sent to jail."

With his aggressive personality, Moorcroft would offend others. "At times he worked with and without the aid of the city's churches. His attitude was that the churches and pastors did not back up his efforts with the destitute, leaving him now and then without the support of the cloth. It can be truly said that he has never been known to turn anyone away, no matter what their condition, creed, or color, without giving them a fair chance to lead a good life."

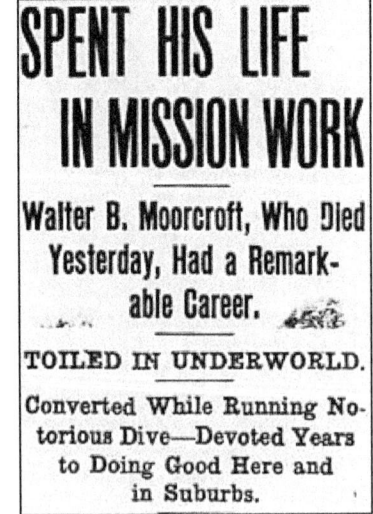

Hattie was also very involved and would sing solos during mission ceremonies. At times they were accused of using the

> **CONVERTED DIVE KEEPER DIES**
> Moorcroft Ran "Hole in the Wall" —Gave Last Years to Religion.

missions to gain money "under the cloak of charity," but evidence showed they were sincere in their efforts. Hattie went blind during her last two years of life, and her husband cared for her until she died in 1911 at the age of 66. He then was forced out of the "Red Light Mission" in Paterson, and opened a second-hand bookstore, taking boarders in, and just managed to make ends meet. He died in 1915 at the age of 61.

Runner becomes a Horse Thief

James Alfred "Alf" **Prater** (1857-1904), of Gainesville, Georgia, "the mountain wonder" was a champion pedestrian of the

> **A Walking Match.**
> ATLANTA, June 7.—A walking match is soon to occur between the mountain wonder, Alf. Prater, and F. H. Ricks alias Jim Alfred, a former clown of Castello's circus.

South. His nickname came from scaling several mountains in North Georgia. He started ultrarunning in 1885 at a three-day, 36-hour race held at Macon, Georgia where he placed second with 173 miles. He then gained fame in 1886 when he won a six-hour walking contest for the Georgia state championship. "One of the peculiarities of Mr. Prater was whipping himself while in the contest. While walking, he would carry a small riding whip which he would use in tickling his legs."

Prater was an engineer and gained national fame for constructing a model of the Brooklyn Bridge that weighed 750 pounds and had 350 figures (people, carriages, boats, etc.) But he was constantly in trouble with the law for beating people up and committing other crimes. He paid many fines and spent time in prison.

In 1898, a horse, buggy, harness, and bridle were stolen from different owners in Georgia. Through good detective work, Sherrif Durham believed that Prater was the thief and tracked him down in Albertville, Alabama, in possession of the horse and buggy. Prater had become very popular in the city with young people, attended picnics, and led a choir at Sunday School. But as the old adage says, "Things are seldom what they seem."

The sheriff arrested Prater and started to take him back to Georgia for trial. But on the way, several of Prater's friends blocked the road and forced the sheriff to take Prater before a justice of the peace. He testified he had bought the horse and buggy from a man in Alabama and promised to provide evidence in the morning. He was released on bail of $400, but didn't show up the next day and fled town. They returned the horse and buggy to their rightful owners. A $100 reward was issued for Prater's capture.

The police finally apprehended Prater a year and a half later. "A pair of handcuffs fastened to one end of a chain were snuggly clasped around Prater's wrists and the other end of the chain tightly held by the big sheriff, who said he was carefully guarding against the escape of his prisoner in case the old walking feeling should come over him again." At his trial, the jury found him guilty, but gave a recommendation of mercy. Before the judge rendered a sentence, Prater finally confessed that he was guilty. He was sentenced to two years in prison.

In 1904, out of prison, a train in Macon, Georgia, ran over and killed Prater. He met his death at a crossing that citizens called "a death trap." The train operated over the crossing with no regard for city laws. Prater left behind a wife and four children. His widow, Belle C. Prater, filed a $25,000 suit against Southern Railway.

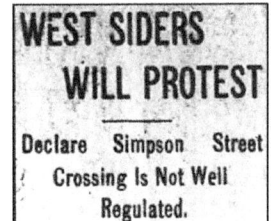

A Public Nuisance

In 1875 as Weston and O'Leary were gaining fame, in Pittsburgh, Pennsylvania, a man agreed to walk from the Opera House to Thirtieth Street, a little more than two miles, in 22 minutes for $25. "He started shortly after 7:00, dressed in an easy walking costume, and

Pittsburgh 1875

his rapid strides soon attracted an immense crowd, which kept increasing at every step he took. His followers were shouting 'there goes Weston,' 'look out for O'Leary,' etc. A detective considered the rabble somewhat disorderly and requested the walkist to desist, but as he signified his intention of walking on, the officer walked him off to the Central station." His friends paid for his bail.

Strange Running Tales: When Ultrarunning was a Reality Show

In 1885, **William Buckler**, age 36, "the great Newport pedestrian" who had just completed a walk of 306 miles between Aberdare and Pontypridd, Wales, in six days, was arrested and appeared in court. Buckler had been seen walking in Aberdare, in a light pedestrian costume, followed by a large crowd of

Aberdare, Wales

men, women, and children. The complaint was, "If anybody wished to drive a carriage along the street at that time, they would have had considerable difficulty in doing so." Apparently, that had happened several times before.

Buckler would advertise that he would do a walk, and many people would show up to watch or walk along. "Buckler said he could not help that people followed him, and he argued that there ought to be as much freedom allowed to him as to a show or a circus. Lots of people followed the circuses, but the police did not stop the procession. He had been in all parts of the world but had never been molested by the police before."

The judge was firm and said that they could not use the streets for walking matches or running races. Buckler promised to leave town as soon as possible. The judge said, "And remember that you have no right to run in the street and cause a crowd to follow you." Bucker countered, "I didn't run, I never run." The judge replied, "If you stand on your head and cause a crowd to collect, it would be the same thing." Buckler promised that he wouldn't attempt another walking feat in the town, and the case was dismissed.

For the next two decades, Buckler continued to attempt ultra-distances walking stunts in many towns, including his version of the Barkclay Match in 1907, walking 2,300 miles in 1,000 consecutive hours, 2 miles and 530 yards each hour for 41 days, in Halifax, England.

Apparently, such arrests were common in Great Britain. In 1876, four local pedestrians were convicted for foot racing on a public highway in Aberdeen, Scotland. "A crowd was collected, and the traffic obstructed. The defense claimed that the four had been allowed to race by two policemen, but then he waited until the first race was over and made the arrests."

CHAPTER ELEVEN

The Murder of Alice Robison

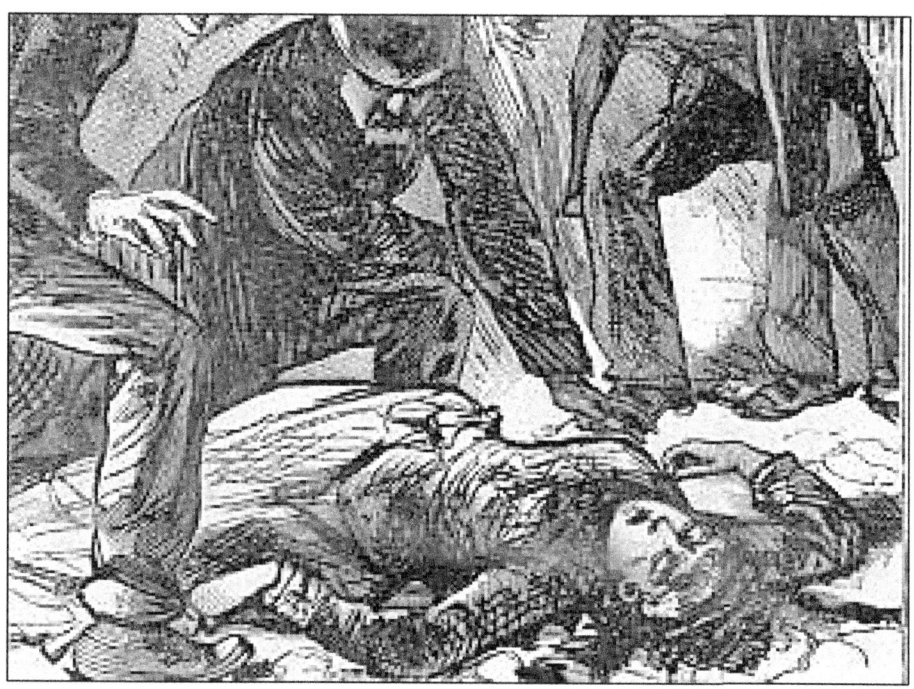

On April 24, 1897, ultrarunning/pedestrian champion **Alice Robison** was running in second place on the last day of a three-day race held at the Fifth Street Rink in East Liverpool, Ohio, with five runners. She was very intent on catching her long-time friend, who was a few laps ahead of her. Needing a rest, she retired to her room provided at the Hotel Grand next door.

That afternoon, a man came into town on a train from Pittsburgh, Pennsylvania. The mustached man wore a new suit with a price tag still attached, and a white hat with a black band. He went to the hotel and inquired where Alice was staying. He ascended the stairs and went to the third-story room. Shortly after, a gunshot was heard! The porter of the hotel rushed into the room and found the woman on the floor bleeding from a gunshot wound in her head and saw the man leaning over her, holding a revolver. How could this happen, an ultrarunner was murdered during a race!

Alice Robison (Jones)

Alice Robison's true name was **Agnes Jane Jones** (1860-1897). She was from Pittsburgh, Pennsylvania, the oldest of eleven children, a daughter of a coal miner.

Jones family in 1870 census

She married very young to James Waters, a coal miner, had three children, and later divorced. In 1882, at the age of 22, she next married again to **Zachariah S. Robison** (1851-1906).

Alice was Zachariah's second wife. His first wife, **Martha Alexandria** (1854-1881) from Kentucky, died in 1881 at the youthful age of 27, leaving behind four children who had gone to live with their Robison grandparents. Alice eventually took on the role of mother and stepmother to all these seven children ages 3-12, and then had two more of her own, **Robert Robison** (1883-) and **Georgia Robison** (1886-) for nine children in the home on a small farm.

Zachariah Robison

Alice's new husband, **Zachariah Robison**, was born in 1851. His Robison ancestors came from Ireland and settled in Beallsville, Pennsylvania, about 30 miles south of Pittsburgh, where his father was a cabinetmaker. Of Zachariah it was said, "from the time he was 5-6 years old, he was puny and sickly and frequently had epileptic fits." When his mother **Susan Robison** (1831-1906) would discipline him, he would fall to the floor in convulsions and remain unconscious.

Once married to Alice in 1883, the Robison family moved around to various places in the west suburbs of Pittsburgh across the Ohio River. Alice became the boss of the family and was in control of all the family finances, including property in Crofton, Pennsylvania, rumored to be worth $10,000. She worked hard as a washerwoman and house cleaner. Both Zachariah and Alice had drinking problems and would get drunk, causing difficulties in the family. The oldest son **David S. Robison** (1871-1931), when age 15 in 1886, did not like the manner of life led by his father and stepmother Alice, so he left home and learned the trade of a tailor.

Becoming a Professional Boxer

In 1887, Alice started to take boxing lessons. She was very strong and weighed about 165 pounds. A newspaper article revealed her motivation for learning how to fight. She was in serious conflict with **Hattie Stewart**, a boxing champion, who her first husband had become infatuated with years earlier. Alice wanted to fight her in some sort of dual. Zachariah was even trying to put up a $1,000 bet that she would win the fight. An editorial stated, "We have no concern whatever as to which woman comes off victorious, but if some fellow would just wallup Robison until she couldn't see straight for a month, we should experience a restful pleasure."

Zachariah also took lessons and the two would box each other. He even sold a small home to help pay for lessons. Alice was very serious, taking four lessons per week and started to make public challenges to fight other women and fought professionally.

A Female Glove Fight.

A match has been arranged between Annie Foster, of Seattle, Washington, and Alice Robison, of this city, to fight to a finish with gloves for $250 a side. Each contestant is to weigh not more than 135 pounds, and the contest is to take place within six weeks, at a point within 500 miles of Pittsburg. Ed. Smith matched Annie Foster and the husband of Alice Robson matched his wife. Mrs. Robson also offers to contest against any woman in the world in a 72-hour or a 142-hour go-as-you-please race for $1,000 a side.

Getting Into Pedestrianism

The Robisons became interested in following the sport of pedestrianism and by 1889, Alice jumped in to compete, probably at the encouragement of a female friend, **Frankie Flemming**, who had been competing and was also interested in boxing.

By 1889, at the age of 25, Alice joined the ranks of a dwindling female pedestrian sport. The female pedestrian heyday was back in 1879 when about 20 female six-day matches were held across America involving about 140 women starters. But after some particularly grueling races, criticism grew, and public interest waned. But several of the women pioneers continued to compete for more than a decade.

The "Robison" name was always confusing to the sports press. Thus, she was called by several names in competitions, "Alice Robison," "Alice Robinson," and "Alice Robson."

Alice's First Walking Match

Alice made her pedestrian debut near her Pittsburgh home, on February 21, 1889, at a three-day, 36-hour "Walking Match for the Championship of Allegheny County" against six other women, for prizes totally $250. It was held in the London Theater in Pittsburgh, Pennsylvania.

LONDON THEATER.
90 Fifth ave. and 63 Diamond st.
HARRY DAVIS......Proprietor and Manager
Commencing FEB. 21, closing FEB. 23.
12 M. to 12 P. M. DAILY.
Grand 36-Hour Female Walking Match for Championship Allegheny County. $250 in Cash Prizes. List of Entries: Aggie Harvey, Lulla Zellette, Alice Robinson, Lizzie Anderson, Clara Bella, Jennie Ranson, Lulla Hart, Mamie Wood. General admission, 10c
fe17-57

3,000 people witnessed the first day of the event "and everything passed off as smoothly and quietly as a church service."

Alice did surprisingly well, although she was "broken up in a terrific struggle for second place,"

	Miles.	Laps.
1. Miss Jennie Ranson	70	28
2. Miss Aggie Harvey	95	17
3. Miss Lulu Zeletta	121	0
4. Miss Alice Robson	111	3
5. Miss Clara Bell	131	7
6. Miss Mamie Wood	130	2

reached 56 miles in 12 hours, and 83 miles after 24 hours. "She is a somewhat heavy but courageous lady. Mrs. Robson's heroic efforts are worthy of the attention of men and women of superior pedestrian abilities." Alice finished in third place with 111 miles, with her feet in "a sad condition." Despite the painful experience, after several months of recovery, Alice competed again in shorter races.

Alice's Greatest Race

Alice's greatest race came in December 1890, at a six-day, 12-hours per day race in Wilkes-Barre, Pennsylvania, in the Nineth Regiment Armory Building. The race began on December 1, 1890, and her husband, Zachariah crewed Alice. Among her competition were veteran champions,

Armory Building in Wilkes-Barre

Sarah Tobias "an old walker, with many medals, and the champion 142-hour woman walker of the world," and **Bella Kilbury,** the six-day world record holder.

The track in the Armory building was a tiny seventeen laps to a mile. "The armory is admirably adapted for the exhibition and is well-arranged for the comfort of the walkers and the spectators. Outside and inside of the oval track are numerous seats and the walkers are seen to good advantage either by daylight or under the glare of the electric lights."

Alice was described as "a tall, black-eyed girl in red and black striped garment with short skirts, is the noisy one of the lot and a good stepper."

> **Seventy-Two Hour Female Pedestrian Tournament**
>
> —AT—
>
> **NINTH REGT. ARMORY,**
>
> —COMMENCING—
>
> **MONDAY, December 1st.**
>
> From 12 o'clock, noon, till 12 o'clock, midnight, each day for the six days.
>
> **LOOK AT THE LIST OF ENTRIES.**
>
> Madam Tobias, New York, champion 142 hour runner of the world.
> Bella Kilbury, New York, the champion heel and toe walker who holds twenty-three medals won in contests.
> Happy Jarbo, Pittsburg, the little wonder, only 15 years old.
> May Allen, Pittsburg, pedestrian and bicycle rider.
> Bessie Macbeth, Philadelphia, who holds the championship record as a long distance runner.
> Kittie Lawrence, Philadelphia.
> Alice Robson, Pittsburg.
> Goldie St. Marr, Philadelphia.
>
> **Admission, 25 Cents,**
> SEASON TICKETS, (Six Admissions), $1.00.

The big surprise in the running field was the debut of Alice's 13-year-old daughter, **Mary Jane Waters** (1877-1951), who had the stage name of "**Happy Jarbeau.**" It was reported, "Early in the day she showed signs of unwillingness but was urged on and was pluckily gaining on her competitors by running at the top of her speed for several laps, cheered on by both walkers and spectators."

Alice quickly built a big lead, reaching 51 miles during the first 12-hour day. "When occasionally the orchestra strikes up an

NAMES.	MILES.	LAPS.
Madame Tobias	40	2
Lizzie Harvey	39	10
Bella Kilbury	38	4
Alice Robinson	51	0
Happy Jarbeau	39	7
Goldie St. Marr	41	10
Mary Allen	41	12

unusually spirited air, the walkers all become imbued with new life, and fly around the track with swishing skirts and twinkling heels, a sight worth beholding."

On the second day, Alice withdrew her daughter, **Happy Jarbeau**, worried that she could not handle the continued strain of the race. The crowd was relatively small, about 500 people. The women had a goal of reaching at least 225 miles, in order to get a share of the gate profits. By day four, Alice was leading with 171 miles.

On the last day, Alice became drunk. It was reported, "Alice Robison held her big lead easily. She got quite hilarious towards the close of the contest, her trainer (husband) having resource to liberal stimulants to keep up her strength. Although she might with safety have gone off the track early in the evening, she did not do it but kept steadily at work all night." Alice was the surprising winner with 252 miles, twenty-seven miles ahead of Sarah Tobias. She won $150.

		Miles	Laps
1.	Madame Tobias	225	5
2.	Aggy Harvey	128	7
3.	Bella Kilbury	122	3
4.	Alice Robinson	252	14
6.	Goldie St. Marr	190	10
7.	Mary Allen	226	11

Champion Pedestrian

In 1891, Alice became bold, publishing challenges in newspapers. "All the female pedestrians seem to be afraid of me. I claim the championship, and I am prepared to defend it against any female in the world for any amount of money." She also competed in boxing that year, fighting **Annie Foster** of Seattle, Washington, for $250.

> Mrs. Alice Robson of Pittsburg stands ready to accept the challenge of Belle Fuller of Woodlawn, Ala., to race with any woman in the country from a 72 to a 142-hour race.

She continued to race and bring her daughter to run 5-10 miles as a side-show, probably bringing in some nice additional money. But at a 72-hour (six days, 12-hours per day) race in Baltimore, Maryland, the police showed up and ordered that the young girl be taken off the track because of her youth. Alice again did well, finishing second, reaching an impressive 238 miles.

> **A Pittsburger's Record.**
> CHICAGO, May 21.—Mrs. Alice Robson, of the Thirty-fifth ward, Pittsburg, made a record yesterday in the eight-hour per day female pedestrian contest now going on here. In the afternoon she completed 100 miles in 23 hours, which is quite a performance for a woman.

Alice was feisty in her races. In April 1892, she wanted to enter a race in Minneapolis, Minnesota, but was refused entry. Race manager and experienced pedestrian, **Henry O. Messier**, (1862-1945) explained, "Alice Robson was barred from the race because she has been guilty on several occasions of improper conduct on the track. I have seen her put off tracks twice for improper conduct."

But Alice continued to compete in many races elsewhere in 1892-1893, including Washington D.C., Chicago, Illinois, Detroit, Michigan, and Baltimore, Maryland, where she went over 264 miles. As a popular champion, she was away from home on long road trips. But then she took the next three years off, as competitions further dwindled.

The Robisons continued to move around and lived for a time in the East Liberty section of Pittsburgh. Family life became a struggle. Zachariah's health declined with his drinking and smoking. Alice brought in most of the family income but was also helped by stepson, **Thomas**

East Liberty, Pennsylvania

Robison (1873-) who took up painting jobs with his father. Zachariah's mood became melancholy. Thomas said, "I noticed it in his walk. He stooped over and never looked around." He would complain of sleeplessness, act erratically at times, and fall down on the floor, experiencing a fit like he had as a child. Alice said that it seemed like he was losing his mind.

Chuck Stewart Arrives

In 1895, a young man, **Charles "Chuck" Stewart** (1872-1924), age 23, came into the lives of the Robisons. He was known by police in the area of being a "troublemaker." He

Pittsburgh Workhouse

had been convicted of burglary in 1891 and was in and out of the workhouse/prison eight times for being convicted of assault, battery, and disorderly conduct. He was generally lazy and did not hold down jobs. When he did work, he was a slate roofer and was said to be a big, good-looking man.

Stewart started to visit the Robisons regularly and drink with them. He claimed to have no place to live, being thrown out of his house by his father because of his drinking. Alice took pity on him and wanted him to move in with the family, but Zachariah would not consent. Since Alice was the family boss, she let him move in any way. He was pretty much a freeloader, rarely taking on work, would come in drunk, and sleep in late.

Every few months, the three of them would go on a big drinking binge when Alice would bring home as much as a gallon of liquor. As Zachariah became drunk, Alice and Stewart would even pour booze down his throat and then go out together, sometimes all night. Son, Thomas, became suspicious and warned his father that something was going on between Alice and Stewart. But Zachariah couldn't believe it. He loved her so much. When he confronted Alice, she scoffed at the idea, claiming that nothing could ever come between them, and that Stewart had a transmittable disease, anyway.

Three-Day Race in East Liverpool, Ohio

Alice decided she wanted to make a pedestrian comeback and run a race in East Liverpool, Ohio, about 60 miles away. Her longtime friend, **Agnes "Maggie" (McShane) Weigand** (1870-), who had entered the race, invited her to go. Maggie's stage name was **Aggie Harvey**, and she was a very

East Liverpool, Ohio

experienced pedestrian who held the world record for a six-day, 8-hours per day race distance of 200 miles. Alice asked Zachariah if she could go, and he consented. She left their East End, Pittsburgh, Pennsylvania home on April 19, 1897.

5th Street Rink

The race, held at the Fifth Street Rink, was rather disorganized. They held a men's race for the first three days and then started a women's race that ran for 3 ½ hours on the third day. By the next day, Robison was in second place, chasing her friend Agnes, who was only five laps ahead. She was confident that she would overtake her. It was reported, "The scenes at the race during the week were disgraceful in the extreme."

A Love Letter Found

While Alice was away, Zachariah found a love letter to Stewart from Alice, inside Stewart's coat pocket, and read it. It had just arrived from East Liverpool and started, "My Darling: How I miss you. I hope you made it all right at the house. Let me know, dear old darling. It is so hard to be without you. I love you better than my life, darling."

Zachariah showed the letter to his son Thomas, who confirmed his suspicions that Alice had been unfaithful. Robison became distraught, could not concentrate on work, and left to go confront Alice in Ohio. He first stopped to see her close pedestrian friend, **Frankie Fleming**, and showed her the letter. Frankie had been increasing disgusted with Alice's lifestyle and mentioned that once on the road for a race in Manchester, New Hampshire, she had discovered Alice drunk in bed with multiple men. This further disturbed Zachariah and he left.

Confrontation

Zachariah arrived at East Liverpool by train and immediately went to the Hotel Grand, next door to the rink where the race was being held. He first got a shave from the barber and then took a half hour to figure out which room Alice was in. He finally knocked on the right door. Her friends, **George and Agnes Weigand,** were there, along with the race manager, **Edward G. Wilson.** They were preparing for the final six-hours spurt of the race and Alice was packing up her things to leave for home the next day. Zachariah went right up into her room, and Alice spoke to him and telling him she was glad to see him. She had been expecting him to come and help for the last day of the race. She asked how the folks were doing at home. His calm reply was, "Whom do you mean, your lover?"

Hotel Grand in East Liverpool, Ohio

Her friends left the room so they could be alone. Zachariah then confronted her about the letter. About ten minutes later, he went to the room of her friend, Agnes. He asked her if Alice had been receiving letters from **Chuck Stewart.** Agnes later said, "He said she had been unfaithful and called her the vilest of names. While he was talking, Alice came to the door of the room and asked him to come to her room, as she wanted to see him."

Rink Band

They talked, came out, and Agnes warned Alice that she should stay away from him until he cooled down, because she saw he carried a revolver in his right hip pocket. Zachariah and **George Weigand** went out of the hotel to view the track in the rink and get some drinks at **Joseph Geon's Saloon.** Zachariah stated that he planned to help Alice with her race during that night. While he was away, Alice, probably fearing that her husband would see more of her mail, went to tell a porter that if any mail came for her, that they should deliver it to Agnes.

Fatal Shot Fired

When Zachariah came back, he again went alone into Alice's room. A rattle was heard against the door, as if someone was thrown against it, then a shot rang out.

George Weigand had heard the shot, tried to get in the door, but it was locked. He went down and got **George Perry** and the hotel porter, **Robert Donaldson,** from the hotel bar to go with him to investigate. He said, "I went into the room. Mrs. Robison was lying on the floor and he was kneeling beside her, sponging her eyes. Robison said it was only a flesh wound, and I told him he had better give the gun to Perry." Alice was moaning with blood streaming from a hole in the corner of her right eye.

The porter said, "The woman lay on the floor. I walked up and saw the bullet hole in her head. Robison raised up and wiped the blood from her face." He asked Robison if she would live. He replied, "Why certainly. The only thing I am sorry about is that I came so wide of the mark." He then showed the porter and the others the letter that began, "My Darling," explaining that it caused the tragedy.

A doctor was telephoned for, but there was no hope. Zachariah showed no emotion. He went back over to where Alice lay, then leaned down and kissed her. He kept saying, "It is only a flesh wound. She'll be all right in a little bit." When the doctor came, Zachariah mentioned he did not want to pay for the bill. He was heard mumbling, "This is what women get for trifling with their husbands."

Robison Arrested

The police and firemen took Robison to city hall, where an officer claimed Robison tried to stab him with a putty knife. "Then he was overpowered, the knife was wrenched from his grasp, and he was locked up." Within a half hour of the shooting, Alice was declared dead. Later, not knowing that Alice had died, Robison told reporters, "I never was so surprised in my life when the thing went off. I didn't know whether I had hurt her or not. She fell on the floor."

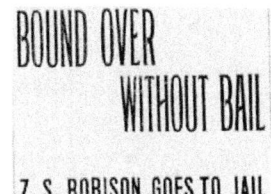

Strangely, the race continued. "Often the opinion was expressed that the place should be closed by the authorities. There was a crowd at the race Saturday night, and when a well-known resident asked a young man connected with the race why the place was not shut up in view of the tragedy, he brutally replied, 'Oh a little thing like that wouldn't affect us.'" Soon the match was stopped by the police, and they detained all of the participants as witnesses. The race manager, Wilson, quickly skipped out of town without paying the bills.

The next day, Major Gilbert of the police visited Robison and informed him that his wife was dead. A hearing was held, and Robison plead not guilty to first degree murder.

Robison's Trial

Robison's ten-day trial started about two months later, on Jun 15, 1897, in Lisbon, Ohio, and certainly was the trial of the year for that area. They carried multiple pages of details daily in the local newspaper. Dozens of witnesses were called. The defense strategy initially was to prove that Robison was insane or that he was defending himself from an attack by Alice while they were alone in the hotel room.

On the second day of the trial, they read the love letter from Alice to Chuck Stewart, and it was the first time Robison showed any emotion. "On hearing the terms of endearment in the letter addressed to Stewart, Robison's form was shaken with sobs, and for five minutes he wept piteously."

A doctor testified that he was not insane, although there was much discussion about the effects of lead poisoning from his painting jobs. The doctors concluded he was in the early stages of paresis, which they said was a paralysis of the gray matter of the brain which sometimes causes delusions.

Columbiana County Courthouse
Lisbon Ohio

HE IS NOT INSANE

That Was the Unvarnished Statement of Dr. T. B. Marquis.

His elderly father, **Thomas Robison** (1827-1907) age 60, came to the trial but his mother was suffering from paralysis and could not attend. "After his father arrived, Robison merely glanced at him, and then burying his face in his hands, remained in that position for some time. His father testified that there had never been a stain on his family name and that he deeply felt the disgrace brought on by the action of his son." Zachariah's sons **Thomas** and **David** also testified. "The prisoner chews tobacco, and constantly keeps his jaws moving. When his sons desire to talk with him, they shake his arm."

STILL DRAGS ALONG

Many Pittsburg Witnesses Remember Zach. Robison.

Chuck Stewart's Strange Testimony

Chuck Stewart was called to testify and asked about the infamous letter that Alice had sent him during the race from the Hotel Grand, on hotel stationery. Stewart said, "I never got no letter like that." His testimony seemed to conflict with earlier statements. "He looked half ashamed of himself as he took the stand." He stated a belief that Zachariah wrote the

CHUCK STEWART TOLD HIS STORY

And Emphatically Denied That Mrs. Robison Had Sent Him the Letter

letter. Robison's face was bathed in tears as he returned to jail, and he did not want to see anyone. His son, David, sent him a huge bouquet of flowers before returning to his home in Punxsutawney, Pennsylvania.

The Prosecution's Case

As the second week of the trial opened, Robison took his seat with the same mechanical stare. "He had nothing to say, and after carefully putting his hat under the chair, looked straight to the front." The prosecution's case was short, claiming that the evidence showed that he was guilty of murder in the first degree, and that he was not insane. He was called, "a wicked, jealous-hearted murderer."

A VERDICT TOMORROW.
Judge Smith Will Probably Send Out the Jury Tonight.

Later in jail, Robison complained about the pain in his heart from the death of his wife. He said, "I don't care. They can send me in the chair and electrocute me if they want to." He seemed to be detached from the reality that he caused her death.

Closing Arguments

The defense claimed that Robison stood in that hotel room with the letter in one hand and the gun in the other, about to shoot himself, when Alice grabbed the gun, which accidentally went off, causing her death. The judge would not allow the jury to consider second degree murder, or manslaughter, only premeditated first degree murder. It was first-degree murder or acquittal.

FIGHTING FOR ONE MAN'S LIFE

Robison's Attorneys Plead With the Jury.

THE IDEA OF PREMEDITATION

The Verdict

After six hours of deliberations, the jury reached its verdict. They were at first split, five for manslaughter, five for second-degree murder, and only two for first-degree murder, but after eight ballots they came to their unanimous decision. The foreman handed a sealed paper to the judge, and the

clerk read that the prisoner was guilty of murder in the first degree. "Robison did not move a muscle. He looked out of the window and no man could tell that he was the person most interested in the words that had just been spoken. No one approached him. He sat alone."

Later, back in his jail cell, Robison said, putting down a Bible, "The past four months are like a dream. My mind, at times has seemed blank. I have been dazed and I think it took something like the shock of the verdict to make me normal. I am innocent of killing my wife. But it was through me she died, whether intentional or not, and I feel that I loved her well enough to suffer death now for the harm I have done her."

The news went out across the country, "the story of the tragedy is the old one of woman's frailty and man's maddening jealousy."

The Death Sentence

The defense immediately appealed for a new trial claiming misconduct by the prosecution springing surprise witnesses, including **Chuck Stewart** who clearly committed perjury, and because additional evidence had been found. The judge refused to grant the defense a new trial. He then gave Robison his sentence. 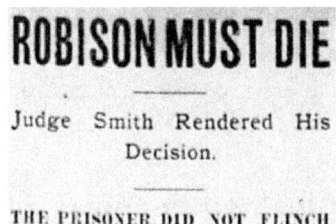 "On the morning of November 26, before sunrise, a sufficient amount of electricity shall be passed through your body to cause your death." Robison did not flinch. He took his chew of tobacco from his mouth, threw it in the spittoon and sat down. He later said he was willing to die because he has nothing to live for now that his family has broken up. He continued to maintain that the killing was an accident.

A letter written by Robison during an appeal trial was later found in his jail cell. He wrote strangely, "I can look upon this a mysterious blessing to my wife. If this had not occurred, my poor wife would have met a fate a thousand times worse than her death. I now truly believe she was taken by the mercy of God. I never intentionally harmed her. If God had not interfered when he did, I am fully satisfied it would have been the eternal damnation of both of our souls, for she would have gone to the lowest depths of sin, while I, in my wild, made passionate love for her, could never have stopped, nor could I have controlled myself until

I had drunk myself into my grave. As to my dearly beloved wife, if she wronged me, it was forgiven. When I reach that other shore, I believe hers will be the first hand to greet me."

The Appeal

A couple of months later, the judge claimed that a technical error was found in the proceedings of the case, and he referred the matter to the Circuit Court. He sent a book of 891 pages, five inches thick, to the court.

Columbus Penitentiary

In the meantime, Robison was the model prisoner in the Columbus Penitentiary. He mostly kept to himself, reading, and he received a few letters from family and friends. His youngest children went to live with their Robison grandparents.

On October 5, 1897, the Circuit Court decided Robison should be granted a new trial. "The court found error on the part of Judge Smith in refusing Robison a new trial when his conviction was accomplished in part on evidence of **Chuck Stewart**, whose perjury on the witness stand was so apparent." Since the trial, Stewart's comments made it apparent that the letter was real. It also found problems with **Agnes Weigand's** testimony. They set the new trial for November 8, 1897.

Zach Robison Will Be Given Another Chance.

CHUCK STEWART SETTLED IT

The Plea Deal

But then, something unexpected happened. A plea deal was made, and Robison plead guilty of murder in the second degree on October 20, 1897. He was sentenced to life in prison. The prosecutor still believed that he was guilty of first-degree murder but knew that the witnesses were scattered across the country, and it would be impossible to gather them in

SENT UP FOR LIFE

Zach Robison Was Sentenced This Afternoon.

MURDER IN SECOND DEGREE

time for the new trial. At the sentencing, Robison again declared that he had no intention of injuring his wife when he walked into her hotel room. He broke down with emotion when he made his statement.

Prison Life

Columbus Penitentiary with water tower

A STORY ABOUT ZACH ROBINSON

Now Engaged In the Hazardous Task of Painting the Immense Standpipe

At the Columbus, Ohio Penitentiary, they assigned Robison to work in the painting department and he quickly became its superintendent. In 1900, at the age of 49, when the 150-foot-high water tower (standpipe) needed painting, he insisted on being the only one to do the dangerous job, suspended on ropes and pulleys, not wanting the young men with families who would be released soon to put themselves in danger. He believed that if he fell and died, no one would mourn him. The other prisoners cheered him. "Every day for the past week, Robison could be seen on the top of the standpipe working away, apparently as self-possessed as if he were painting a garden fence." The water tank was painted with a red roof and a black body.

Later in 1900, he became too sick to work, affected by his lead poisoning disease. He was such a model prisoner that public opinion expressed the idea that he should be pardoned. "His behavior has been equal to that of any citizen in Ohio, as the officials themselves will cheerfully admit." In 1902, Ohio politicians endorsed an application for a pardon and his son, **Thomas Robison,** hired a lawyer for him. The warden even took him out of prison occasionally to paint his home. Alice's family supported the pardon application. It was said that because of his illness, he would only live for a few more years. The application was turned down

ZACH ROBINSON.

The Columbiana County Life Prisoner is Suffering With Ill-Health at the Penitentiary.

because one person on the pardons board objected and stated that Robison had not yet been sufficiently punished.

Robison Released from Prison

By the end of 1903, another push was made for a re-hearing. Letters from Robison's original jury and judge were obtained supporting a parole. On July 14, 1904, after being in prison for seven years, the pardon board recommended clemency. **Governor Myron Timothy Herrick** (1854 – 1929) had Warden **E. A. Hershey** bring Robison to the statehouse, where he gave him a pardon and reduced his sentence to eleven years. He was given some good advice by the governor and immediately released.

Governor Herrick

Robison went to live quietly with his son Edward, who worked for the railroad in Donora, Pennsylvania, 25 miles south of Pittsburgh.

Zachariah S. Robison died Sept 9, 1906, in Mercy Hospital at Pittsburgh, at the age of 54 from alcoholism and lead poisoning. They buried him in Beallsville Cemetery, where his first wife and other family members were buried. His mother

Beallsville Cemetery

died a week earlier, at the age of 75, and his father died the following year.

Alice Robison has been forgotten for more than a century. She has hundreds of descendants living today who never knew the tragic story of their famous ultrarunning great-great-great grandmother Alice Robison.

Davy Crockett

CHAPTER TWELVE

Love Scandals

Ultrarunners/pedestrians, both male and female, spent a prolonged time away from their homes and families as they traveled to compete in races across America and in England. As with other professional athletes and celebrities, even in our day, love scandals would at times emerge that made for popular gossipy news stories. Many of these ultrarunners became instantly wealthy and had many adoring fans and friends who wished to be part of this new wild, free-spending lifestyle. Some of these love scandals were covered in newspapers all over the country.

Fannie Edwards' Love Triangle

In 1879, **Fannie Edwards** (1856-) of New York City, born in Portland Maine, burst onto the stage of pedestrianism when she succeeded in walking 3,000 quarter miles in 3,000 quarter hours at Brewster Hall in New York City on March 20, 1879.

But along with her fame came scandal. She became quickly involved in a love triangle. She had been seen in public with **Frank Leonardson** for several months in the New York City area. Frank, also a pedestrian, was described as very good looking. He served as her trainer during her successful month-long walk. Fannie was described as "quite young, below the medium height and of slight 100 pounds, almost fragile physique. She has large lustrous brown eyes, an abundance of dark hair, and well-rounded features, suffused with the glow of health."

Fannie Edwards

LENARDSEN, THE TRAINER.

DESERTING HIS WIFE AND CHILDREN FOR A FEMALE PEDESTRIAN—A SCENE IN A POLICE COURT.

In March 1879, Frank's wife of seven years, **Delia Leonardson**, filed for abandonment and wanted some of his estimated $800 of pedestrian winnings for the support of their two children. Frank was arrested, and a trial was held. "Lenardsen admitted the marriage and desertion, but said he could hardly support himself, but was willing to do whatever he could for his wife." He claimed he had only earned $31 as Fannie's trainer but omitted mentioning his previous success as a pedestrian. He had started to compete in May 1878, in a 36-hour race, as a member of the Scottish American Athletic Club in New York City. He could balance a quart bottle filled with beef tea on his head as he walked. They had been likely involved for a year. "It was learned during the hearing that Miss Edwards induced him to forsake his wife for her company, sharing her earnings with him." She had even hired his lawyer for the trial.

The judge ruled Frank must pay his wife $200 and pay $3 per week for alimony. "Fannie screamed, 'Is that all?' with delight and surprise. She then bounded, brushed past Mrs. Lenardsen, and offered her gold watch and chain, her necklace, bracelets, and earrings to the court as security to have Frank released." The judge said, "The court is not a pawnshop for lovers." She then wrote out a check for the $200 and $156 for a year of support, and said, "That's cheap enough. I'd pay a thousand dollars to be rid of her." Delia was left in a corner of the courtroom "crying as if her heart would break." Frank and **Fannie Edwards** went off together. To get away from the scandal, they went to California to compete.

At some point during their relationship, Frank took on the stage name of "Frank L. Edwards," and they told people in California that he was

> Frank Edwards, the pedestrian, returned to the city yesterday, having in his possession the California diamond belt won by him at San Francisco on the 15th of July last. The belt is a beautiful specimen of its kind. It contains fourteen ounces of solid gold and twenty-two ounces of solid silver and is adorned with thirteen diamonds. It displays the

Fannie's brother. They weren't discrete enough. The press noticed that Fannie soon had a diamond ring that they figured out came from Frank. But evidently their relationship only lasted a few more months.

Fannie Edwards Ruins Another Marriage

Fannie Edwards was not through ruining marriages. **William A. Cousins** (1858-1880), of Greenpoint, Brooklyn, New York, who was called "a well-known pedestrian" was arrested on November 18, 1880, in Brooklyn for having two wives. He was described as "a well-built young man, of 22 or 23 years, and of rough exterior." (It is interesting to point out that even though Cousins called himself "a champion pedestrian," no successful pedestrian accomplishments have been found for him.) He was the son of a machinist and had a younger brother, **Hiram Cousins**, who had recently died in a tragic fire at a box factory.

Cousins married **Isabella M. Remer** on October 11, 1880. She was called "a handsome blonde of eighteen." Isabella had known Cousins for a year and on her wedding day, he brought **Fannie Edwards** to her mother's house, announcing that he had selected her to be a bridesmaid. "He explained that

Name:	A William Cousins
Gender:	Male
Marriage Date:	11 Oct 1880
Marriage Place:	Kings, New York, USA
Spouse:	Isabella M Renner
Certificate Number:	2672

Index for marriage certificate

Miss Edwards being a pedestrienne, he made her acquaintance in a professional way." But after only four days of marriage, because of serious arguments between the two, Cousins deserted Isabella and sought to marry Edwards.

Isabella said, "The next week, he came to see me and asked to see the certificate of marriage, which as soon as I gave it into his hand, he tore up and burned. He then said that that ended our marriage and that I need not trouble myself any further about him, as he was going to marry Miss Edwards. He then went away. I was astonished, but I could do nothing."

On his next visit to Isabella, he brought Edwards and let her know they were engaged to be married. Isabella said she was his lawful wife and that she would fix him if he married again. She said, "He threatened to knock me down and kill me if I interfered with him in any way. Miss Edwards heard all and simply said that our marriage was of no account now that the certificate was torn up, and that she would marry Cousins anyway, as she was more suitable for him. He again threatened my life if I troubled him and went away with Miss Edwards."

The two pedestrians married about three weeks after Cousins' first marriage, on November 2, 1880. He then visited Isabella again, laughed and threatened Isabella some more. But she was determined to see him arrested. With some detective work, she found the reverend that had married the two and got a warrant for Cousins' arrest. The police arrested Cousins. He couldn't pay the $1,000 bail, and they kept him in jail until the trial.

At the trial, **Reverend Francis Joseph Schneider** (1832-1903) a pastor without a church, known as "the marrying parson," testified that he remembered marrying Cousins and Edwards. Edwards testified that her real name was **Frances Alvina Wurms**. She denied that she had been married to Cousins and had never seen the Reverend before. She had lived as a boarder at Cousins' house for two months. She was then caught in several lies, even denying that she had been known as **Fannie Edwards**. She denied ever meeting Isabella, and that she

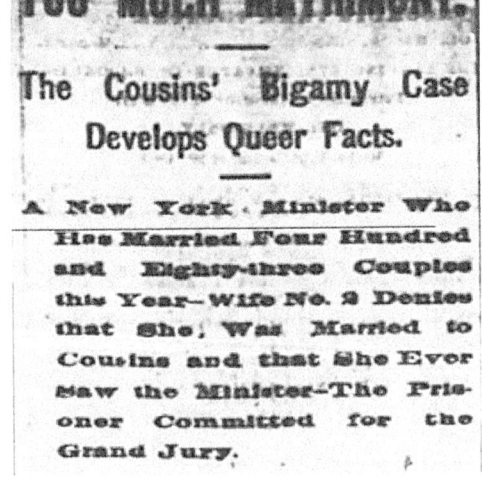

wasn't the bridesmaid at their wedding. Witnesses and a marriage certificate showed that Edwards' testimony was full of lies.

The defense claimed that the Reverend ran an unreliable "matrimonial bucket shop performing 400 marriages per year" and that Isabella's arrest warrant was just motivated by her own jealousy. The Reverend corrected the number, he had performed 483 marriages so far during the year for 2-3 dollars each. (Reverend Schneider was indeed a shady character, who was a wife beater, and the following year was sent away to prison for 18 months because of larceny.)

HE'S A SPECIALIST

Pastor Schneider Has United in Marriage 15,756 Couples.

The Judge decided to refer the case to the Grand Jury. Two months later, in January 1881, Cousins was acquitted of bigamy because of a lack of proof. "Cousin's first wife made a scene by denouncing him and predicting that evil would befall him." Isabella was evidently correct. Only two months later, Cousins was killed on March 18, 1881, when he fell from a scaffold while painting at Bayonne, New Jersey. Fannie Edwards disappeared from the sport. Isabella would remarry, have children, grandchildren, great-grandchildren, and die at the age of 81.

William Cousins, a pedestrian, was recently tried and acquitted at Brooklyn of bigamy. His first wife predicted evil would befall him. Friday he fell from a scaffold and was killed.

Mary Marshall's Love Triangle

Getting romantically involved with trainers seemed to happen often. **Mary/May Marshall** (1841-1911) was one of the most famous and successful female pedestrians of the 19th century. Marshall's true name was **Tryphena (Curtis) Lipsey**. She was married to **Thomas Lipsey**. After they moved to Chicago, they experienced financial trouble, which motivated her to try pedestrianism in 1875, taking on the stage name of Mary Marshall.

Mary Marshall

After experiencing great pedestrian success and being away from her family during long road trips, in 1877, Marshall, still married and age 36, got romantically involved with the 23-year-old pedestrian **George F. Avery** (1854-1885) of Maine and Massachusetts, who called himself, "**P.T. Barnam's** Great Pedestrian." He had been Marshall's trainer. But to Marshall's dismay, Avery soon left her for the much younger pedestrian **Bertha "Bertie" LeFranc** (1859-) originally from Paris, France, who was only 18 years old. Her true name was **Matilda Colom**. The scandal went public because Avery walked out with LeFranc while Marshall was competing in Massachusetts. She was left without her trainer and failed in her walking efforts. The scandal resulted in the breakup of Marshall's marriage to Thomas Lipsey. Her husband and son moved to Iowa. Avery and LeFranc married and about a year later, she gave birth to a girl. Avery worked as LeFranc's trainer.

Bertha LeFranc

Marshall changed her public name to "May Marshall," but then stopped competing for a time because she was with child and gave birth to **Stonewall Lipsey** (1878-1963) (He later was known as **Allen Stonewall Curtis**, raised by Marshall's family). She returned to competition in 1878, giving the excuse that she had been away because of yellow fever, evidently trying to keep the birth a secret. In 1882, she married pedestrian, **Harry Hager**. She continued to perform for several years in various publicity stunts, including races against skaters and people pushing wheelbarrows, and died in 1911.

May Marshall

A common question in the family had always been whether her son **Stonewall Lipsey** was a product of Marshall's marriage, or of her affair with Avery. Marshall's great-great-grandson solved the mystery with a DNA test, confirming that he was also a descendant of the pedestrian **George F. Avery** who died in 1884 of heart disease.

James W. Ford had Two Wives

On June 25, 1884, a six-hour race was held in Atlanta, Georgia, which was won by Atlanta's champion, **Alf Prater** with 37 miles. **James Willliam "J. W." Ford** (1853-1943) a furniture salesman, and Macon Georgia's pedestrian champion, was the favorite, but he quit unexpectedly mid-race. Some suspected that he threw the race on purpose, but a much more bizarre reason soon surfaced.

Atlanta, Georgia

During the race, "it was said that as he passed a certain point on the track, a lady with a pleasant face, but plainly attired, was observed to lean forward and whisper words to the champion." She noticeably startled Ford, but he kept up his pace. When he came by again, the lady said, "you shall be arrested before 9:00." Ford went to his tent, followed by the lady and he soon quit the race, claiming that he had taken ill.

The lady made her story public to reporters, and it was printed nationwide in newspapers. She was **Mollie Kerr** (1862-) a 22-year-old worker at a paper bag factory in Atlanta. She claimed she was Ford's wife, who he abandoned and had not seen for five months. She said that she had eloped with Ford six months earlier. But after only a few days, she returned to her parents' home in Atlanta, where she discovered Ford had another wife, **Fannie White**, and two children who lived only two blocks away.

Ford came for her and at first denied that he was married to Fannie. Mollie said, "I loved him, but he has blighted my life." After five months, she had him arrested. She said, "I hate to send him to the penitentiary on account of his two little children." Ford already had a police record. A few months earlier, he was convicted and imprisoned for cheating and swindling.

> **FORD TO BE PROSECUTED.**
> The Macon Walker to Get in the Clutches of the Cobb County Court Next Month.

The entire scandal was played out in public in the newspapers. It was a "she-said, he-said" story worthy of tabloids. Ford soon confessed that he had two wives, but claimed that Mollie had gotten him drunk and then married him. He then painted a sinister picture of her. He said after she had gotten his attention during the race, that she followed him to his tent. "When I laid down in my tent, she rubbed my head and said, 'You have got to pay me, and well, too. You have ruined me, and I am going to have you arrested at once.'" He begged her to wait until he finished the race. She refused and said, "You know you can't beat Prater. He is my fellow, and I never intended you should beat him in this race. I am going to marry him. He brought me to the match and paid my way in." She had indeed sat next to Prater's sister at the race.

> **WHOSE HUSBAND IS HE?**
> FORD, THE MACON CHAMPION, BESET BY A LADY.
> Who Insists That She was Duped Into a Marriage and Deserted—What the Father of the First Wife Says and What Ford Himself Has to Say—He Denies He is a Bigamist.

According to Ford, he and Mollie left the race together and returned home. Mollie expressed her love for him, but knew he didn't really love her, so still demanded that he pay her so she could get a divorce. He accused her of being married to another person, too. Finally, he agreed to give her the money for their divorce and then left, hoping to never see her again.

Mollie did not let it rest there. The public was hungry for more details about this strange scandal. The county grand jury summoned Mollie to appear to indict Ford for bigamy. It was rumored that she knew Ford had another wife when they got married. Ford's defense lawyers were going to claim that he was drugged when they married.

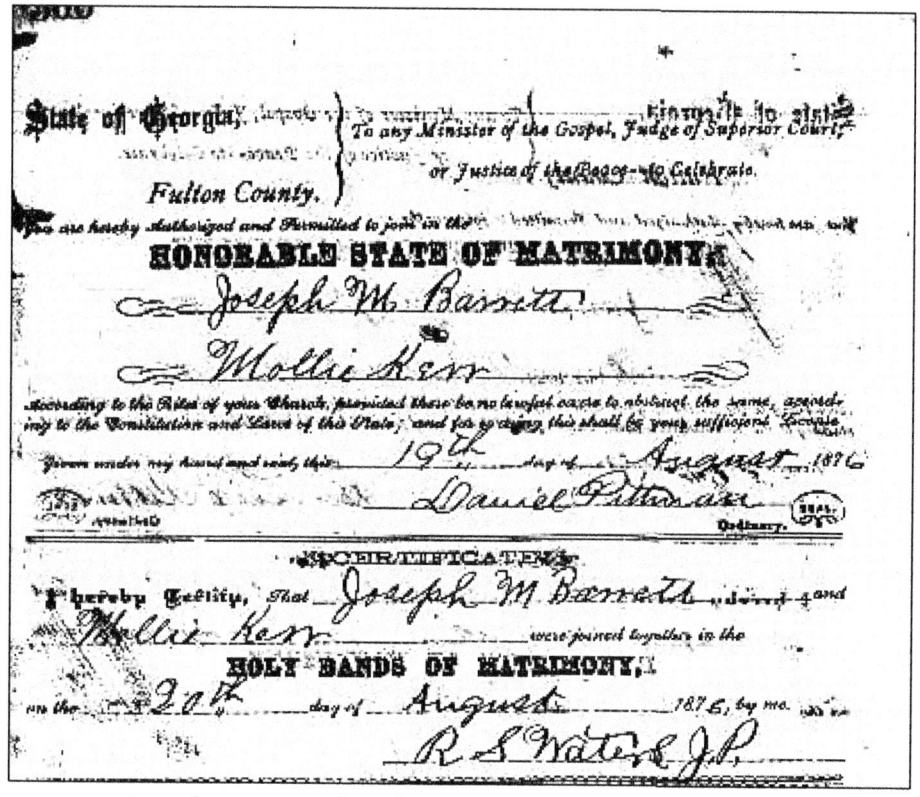

Joseph Barrett and Mollie Kerr's Marriage License

An Atlanta reporter dug deeper, interviewing many involved. Mollie was described as "a dark-eyed, brown-haired, moderately good-looking lady." She claimed that before marrying Ford that she had been divorced from a **Joseph M Barrett** (1747-1887) (They had been married in 1876). Ford and Mollie had dated for a couple months, he proposed, and then they were quickly married. After four days, she found out he had another wife, but he promised to never see that wife again. They had "a lively quarrel" and separated.

Next, the reporter interviewed **Jabez M. White** (1839-1908), the father of Ford's first wife. He claimed that Ford and his daughter, Francis **"Fannie" Augustus White** (1861-1931) had been married for six years. He had suspected that Ford was being unfaithful with Mollie, went to see her, and found out that she was also married to Ford. He told the shocking news to his daughter. She wrote to Ford and essentially told him to get lost. **Jabez White** said, "The next train brought him to Atlanta and when he entered the house about sunrise, I got up and hunted for my pistol to kill him, but my wife had hidden it. I then had Ford arrested. My daughter went almost crazy, and her physician said if I did not release Ford, she would lose her mind." White dropped the charges, but his daughter remained ill.

Finally, the reporter interviewed Ford. He claimed he had never formally married Fannie White, so actually did not have two wives. That was a lie. His valid marriage license on file was proof. He even tried to deny the race incident, hoping the public scandal would go away. He claimed that the lady at the race was just trying to get him to go out with her. He said, "It would take more than one woman to get me off the track." He claimed falsely that it was the first time he had met Mollie Kerr and that he had quit the race because he drank some champagne by mistake, that made his stomach revolt.

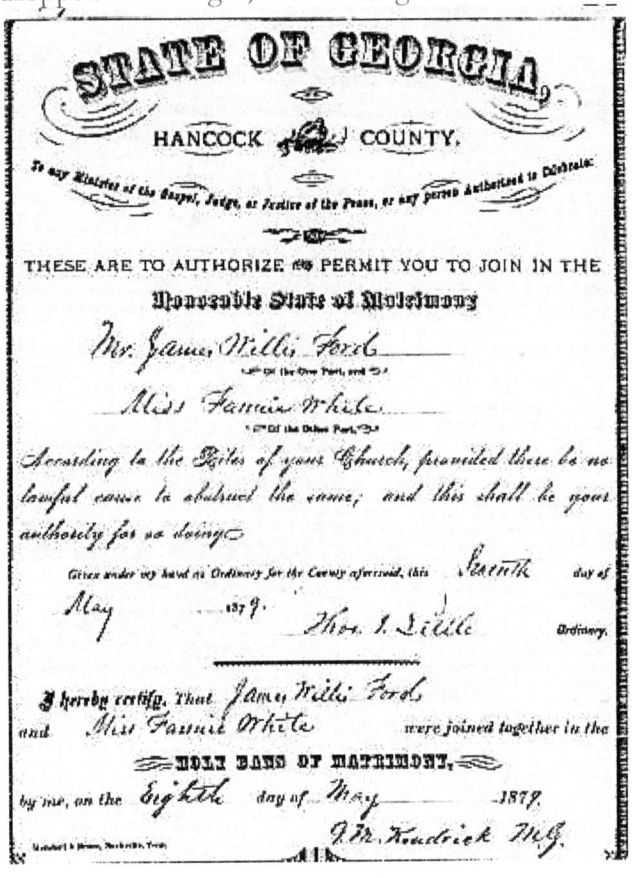

James Ford and Finnie White's Marriage License

No report was found to show that the bigamy trial was ever held. Ford returned to his first wife, Fannie, and they moved to Macon, Georgia. About three years later in 1887, he returned to Atlanta for a quick visit and again was arrested, because of a warrant issued by a furniture dealer, **J. W. Hinman** waited for a chance to force Ford to pay him $75 that he said was owed to him. He got an arrest warrant to be issued for bigamy and theft.

Ford turned himself in, determined to fight the bigamy charge. Mollie Kerr refused to testify in court. She had completely back peddled on the claim that they were ever married. In a letter, she stated, "If Ford and herself were ever married that they were drinking at the time, and she knew nothing of it."

Macon, Georgia

She wrote that the complainant, Hinman, had previously approached her about a plan to blackmail Ford. Interesting enough, a Miss **A. P. Prater**, likely Prater's sister, witnessed the letter, strengthening the idea that their Mollie and the Prater may have conspired to get Ford to quit that race. Ford settled the case by paying $70 to Hinman and court costs. Hinman withdrew the warrant.

So, what really happened? We are left to guess. **Mollie Kerr** continued to live in Atlanta for many years. **Fannie White** was indeed Ford's wife, and they stayed together for many years until she died in 1931. Together, they raised five children. Ford died at the age of 89 in 1943, as a well-respected citizen in Macon, Georgia, and owner of a furniture company.

Charles Harriman Runs Off with a Man's Wife

In 1879, **Charles A. Harriman** (1853-1919), age 25, a shoemaker, was originally from Maine but living in Haverhill, Massachusetts. At the age of fifteen, he ran away from home and enlisted in the Navy, where he served for several years. He returned home and went to work in a shoe shop. When he was about 20 years old, the shop owner challenged him to a foot race in Auburn, Maine. Harriman won, and that started his love to run.

Charles A. Harriman

By 1879, his ultradistance experience was recent, but impressive, breaking the existing walking 100-mile world record with a time of 18:48:40. He applied to the Third Astley Belt six-day race in New York City with no six-day experience and was accepted.

Stackhouse Marriage Record

A week before the race, Harriman trained in Central Park and stayed at the St. James Hotel where he flirted with **Katie (Lapp) Stackhouse** (1856-), the beautiful wife of the St James hotel steward, **George W. Stackhouse** (1852-). She was described as "a handsome brunette of about 22 years of age."

During the March 1879 race, the very tall Harriman was a fan favorite among the women and received many bouquets of flowers from them. Katie was among his most enthusiastic admirers and would go each day to watch him run, "casting bewitching glances," and she gave him a large basket of flowers. For his final day, she made him a red, white, and blue sash which he wore around his waist.

Charles Harriman

He ended up placing third with 450 miles, winning $3,679, valued at $105,000 today.

After finishing his race, Harriman had to be carried to a carriage back to the St. James Hotel. A day after, his eyes were still bloodshot, but he looked well and was being cared for by Katie. "She carried dainties to the weary pedestrian and relieved the heavy hours by reading to him. It is said that by these means a tender feeling sprang up in the bosoms of both."

After he recovered, he was seen around New York City on the streets with Katie. People noticed them

HARRIMAN, HOW COULD YOU?

The Long-Legged Pedestrian Walks Into the Affections of Another Man's Wife.

riding together in Central Park and visiting places of amusement. Stackhouse suspected something was going on and found them together at a masquerade ball. Katie said of her husband, "He was like a crazy man. He raved and swore and picked me up bodily and threw me into a carriage and home we went." As Harriman went on a southern pedestrian tour, the two wrote letters to each other.

A GO-AS-YOU-PLEASE MATCH.

Harriman, the Pedestrian, Elopes with Another Man's Wife—The Outraged Husband in Pursuit—The Guilty Couple in Medford at the End of the Last Lap.

In July 1879, Katie went to visit her parents in Philadelphia, but went missing after a few days. She ran off to join Harriman in Richmond, Virginia, where Harriman was competing. Her husband hired a private detective to track her down. She was finally found with

Harriman in Medford, Massachusetts. They had been staying together at the Eagle House Hotel and she registered as **Katie Wilson**. They were seen several times together in public, including on a ride on the steamer *General Bartlett*. "The lady was dressed in the height of fashion. Her dress had a long trail, her gloves had fourteen buttons, her bracelets were large, and she wore a ring with seven diamonds. She dined with her gloves on."

Stackhouse went to Medford and found the two together at the Mystic Hotel. He also discovered love letters between the two.

HARRIMAN AS AN ELOPER.

The Pedestrian Accomplishes a Feat Not in the Sporting Line.

Stackhouse filed for divorce and also sued Harriman for $10,000. Stackhouse was successful in freezing Harriman's bank account. Once Katie learned that the scandal went public, and that Harriman couldn't spend his money, she returned home and begged to be forgiven and taken back by her husband. She also wanted Harriman's money freed up. Stackhouse refused to accept her back. "Mrs. Stackhouse on her knees again implored forgiveness and again was denied. Finding her husband obdurate, she left." He sold all her belongings, including her piano. "Stackhouse started out armed with a six-shooter and determined to perforate the amorous pedestrian as soon as he could discover his whereabouts."

The police arrested Harriman, and he posted a bail of $5,000. Katie told the press that she had been an abused woman by Stackhouse. She threatened to prosecute her husband for confiscating her belongings unless he would abandon his suit against Harriman. Eventually, three months later, a settlement was reached "through mutual friends", and Stackhouse withdrew the suit and was likely much richer. Harriman and Katie quickly got married. She became a fiery staunch defender of her new husband. A year later, she horsewhipped a Mr. Ladd for making offensive remarks to Harriman. She was arrested for assault and fined $5.

Harriman

Harriman continued to compete into the late 1880s, traveling to several countries. At some point, he joined the Texas Rangers and was seriously wounded in a battle with outlaws. He claimed that he was also shot at the Battle of Wounded Knee, where Sitting Bull was killed. In 1884, Katie sued for divorce, charging Harriman for deserting her and failing to provide support.

He returned to Maine in 1897 and a few years later organized a labor union for lime kiln workers in Rockland, Maine. Into his late 50s, he put on walking exhibitions. Late in life, he became an evangelist pastor. He died on March 14, 1919, at the age of 66, of Bright's Disease and was survived by a second wife and five children.

Harriman

Elsa Von Blumen

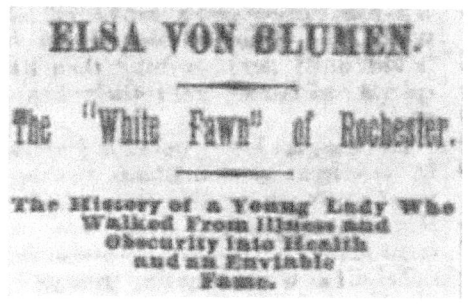

Elsa Von Blumen

Elsa Von Blumen (1863-1935) "Queen of Lady Pedestriennes" became a famous pedestrian. She was the daughter of a German widow, living in Oswego, New York. She was said to be "a young girl so delicate in health that physicians told her that unless she left and sought a drying atmosphere, she could not live long." The family moved to Rochester, New York, where a doctor told Elsa that she needed to walk daily. Her health improved, and she was discovered by **Burt Miller**, who trained her to compete as a pedestrian. She began her career in April 1879, when only sixteen years old, attempting to walk 100 miles. She was described as "a young lady of some five feet four inches in height, and weighing not far from 125 pounds, some eighteen years, with ringlets that are quite pretty. Her appearance is singularly attractive, and modest in the extreme."

A few months later, Von Blumen walked at Hillsboro, Ohio, attempting to walk 100 miles in 27 hours at the Music Hall. "Miss Von Blumen made a good impression upon her audience. She is good-looking, and lady-like, full of pluck, and possesses great powers of endurance. She was neatly and appropriately costumed and walks quite gracefully."

PEDESTRIANISM.

Miss Elsa Von Blumen to Walk in Hillsboro

During this exhibition, trouble brewed. The wife of her manager/trainer, **Burt Miller**, became very jealous of the attention that her husband was giving to Von Blumen. Mrs. Miller's mother seemed to be at the root of the problem. "She made Miller's wife jealous, and basely slandered Miss Von Blumen and circulated false stories about her."

The result was a very public "grand old row," among them that created great excitement among the citizens of the city. It was reported, "The manager's wife and Miss Von Blumen became reconciled the next morning. The Miss Von Blumen seems to

Elsa Von Blumen

have the sympathy of our citizens, and no imputation against her character are intimated. It is an unfortunate affair all around, as the entertainment was drawing full houses and giving good satisfaction." Von Blumen finished her 100-miles as promised.

Miller continued as her manager. There actually was something between the two, because he later left his wife and the two were married. People discovered he had been cheating measurements for Von Blumen, using a mile that was 660 feet short, and **Burt Miller** became infamous for the "Miller Mile". "The plan was, hire a reputable city surveyor; have him mark out on the floor of the hall a path, and get his official certificate thereto, then, as soon as he goes home, rub out his marks, lay down a different path, 660 feet shorter each mile."

> —Burt Miller managed the 100-mile bicycle race for Miss Von Blumen. Miller is the genius who invented the elastic distance known as the "Miller Mile."—Gazette.

Von Blumen later became an incredibly famous endurance cyclist and rode 1,000 miles in six days in 1881 on a high-wheel bicycle and continued to ride into her 70s.

QUEEN OF WHEEL DIES
Elsa Von Blumen In Eighties Gave First Exhibition Here on Fair Grounds

She later became known as Mrs. **Caroline Roosevelt** and claimed that she was the widow of two civil war veterans, cousins of Theodore Roosevelt. She died on Jun 3, 1935, at the age of 72 in Rochester, New York.

John W. Jackson

John W. Jackson had multiple loves. He competed in an 88-hour walking match in Dayton, Ohio, in 1889. As

> A PEDESTRIAN'S TRIALS.
> He is Jailed for Perjury and His Sweetheart Takes Morphine.

soon as it was over, he and a woman in his company, **Grace Gillespie**, were arrested on a charge of perjury, accused by **Samuel Vinson** about some falsehood they made under oath. Jackson had sold some property but swore that the two had no property.

The two were taken to jail and while there, news came that a girl named **Emma Martin** had attempted suicide by taking strychnine. "She was found in an unconscious state, but the doctors say she will recover. A note was found by her bedside addressed to Jackson, saying she could not live without him and wanting to die. A trial was held and the case against Jackson and Gillespie was dismissed.

Katie Stackhouse cheering for Charles Harriman

CHAPTER THIRTEEN

Corruption and Bribes

With the outstanding success of ultrarunning in the 1880s, and the millions of dollars of legal wagering involved, corruption raised its ugly head in the sport. "Match Fixing" was the most common form of corruption used. This practice made it possible for bookmakers to maximize their profits. Sports history scholar **Mike Huggins** wrote, "The fixing of sports events has a history that is probably as old as organized sport. Persons off the field directed match fixing to make often illegal financial gains using a mixture of legal and illegal sports betting platforms, sharing some of that profit with those connected to the sport who executed the fix on the field."

In this chapter, some strange stories are shared about attempts to fix pedestrian matches. They are only the "tip of the iceberg" for what actually took place.

Bill Daly Runs for Six Days Without Fatigue

In 1894, a strange story was published in *The Washington Post* about a six-day race that occurred in 1880 in Denver, Colorado. The publication of the story widely affected public opinion about the sport and the corruption involved. **Mark Montgomery Thall** (1858-1901) and **James Henry Love** (1852-1902) organized the

Denver in 1880

race. They were celebrated agents and promoters with a firm in Denver. Previously, together they established Forester's Theater, one of the first in Denver.

Mark Thall

Thall was born in Montgomery, Alabama and went to California with his family in 1865. After living in Placerville for four years, he ran away from home and joined the circus at the age of eleven. He rose to become one of the best-known theatrical men in the country.

Thall and Love were referred to as "hustlers" and had been involved in organizing six-day races as early as 1879 in San Francisco, where he was arrested for running off with $85 of the proceeds. The following year, Thall went to Denver and established a theatrical business with **J. H. Love** called "Love, Thall & Co."

Strange Running Tales: When Ultrarunning was a Reality Show

The race in Denver was held in a big tent on a track going around the edge with raised seats in the middle. About sixteen runners started, including **Peter Napoleon "Old Sport" Campana** (1836-1906) and others. A rookie started that no one really knew–**Bill Daly**, who did not look very strong. Another local runner participated, **"Rocky Mountain Sam,** who traveled around the track with an impressive long stride. The race was popular and kept the tent full of spectators.

By day four, young Daly caught up with the leader, Rocky Mountain Sam. "The pace had been so swift that day that Sam was all used up. His feet were swollen, and he was sick, but he kept up after Daly." Most of the other runners had dropped out. It was a two-man race, or so they thought.

Old Sport Campana

After a rest, it amazed everyone how Daly would come out so fresh, skipping around and whistling "Yankee Doodle." Sam's backers tried to encourage their man on, and even had a brass band march along with him. On the last day, a large crowd came to watch the finish. "It got down to the last hour. Bill Daly was running easy and gaining one lap in five on poor old Sam." In the end, Daly won by over 40 miles and received a check for $3,000.

The Hoax is Discovered

However, something seemed wrong, and Sam made an investigation. "It didn't take him long to find out that it was a fixed race. You see that damned Bill Daly was twins. His twin brother Jim looked just like him to a dot. Bill would walk until he got tired and then he would go into the tent, and in an hour or so, Jim would come out. Neither one of them could walk much, or they would have beat the world record."

It appeared that the race organizer, Thall was in on the hoax. He put on another race in Oregon with the Dalys doing the same thing. With the fixed win, the Dalys split the winnings with Thall. But Thall got the last laugh when his check to the Dalys bounced.

They are lucky they didn't pull this scam in England. In 1902, a trainer there sent a Leeds athlete into a race, impersonating another runner. They were discovered, arrested, and sent to prison for six months, doing hard labor.

Mark Thall died in 1901 at the young age of 41 from pneumonia. He was an owner of the Alcazar Theater in San Francisco. He left behind about $9,500, valued at about $317,000 today along with a contested $20,000 ($670,000) ownership in the Alcazar.

In February 1888, after **James Albert** of Philadelphia, Pennsylvania broke the six-day world record with 621 miles, an unsubstantiated charge surfaced that Albert had a twin brother and that they alternated times on the track. Albert denied he had a twin, or even a brother, and his record was eventually accepted. **Charles Bibbins** of Omaha, Nebraska, who floated the rumor, later admitted that he was wrong.

Bribery

Bribery was a prevalent method to fix matches. Like the Black Sox scandal in baseball, runners would be bribed to throw races. It became very tempting for a runner experiencing great pain to take the easy way out to reduce that pain by accepting money and going slower or quitting altogether.

Ephraim Clow Gets Bribed

Ephraim Clow (1854-1927) was born on Prince Edward Island, Canada and emigrated to the United States in 1872 at the age of 17. He was a shoemaker and settled in Arlington, Massachusetts. He started six-day ultrarunning in 1879 and quickly rose to become one of the elites in the sport, finishing with 460 miles in the Rose Belt. In May 1881, he competed for the Second O'Leary International Belt in Madison Square Garden. There were heavy bets on **John Hughes**, the defending champion, to place second in the race. As the race progressed

Ephraim Clow

on day five, Clow was in second place, doing well. Some bookmakers had been seen visiting Clow's room and afterwards his pace slowed down, allowing John Hughes to overtake his second-place position.

"When Clow **Ephraim** had scored his 502 miles, he entered his cabin, and shortly afterwards emerged dressed in his everyday clothes and announced that he would walk no longer." This was a shock

Clow and Littlewoood Leave the O'Leary Race.

The Former Said to Have Been Bought by Book-Makers.

because he had looked like the freshest runner on the track. "He gave various excuses, all of a flimsy character, and finally bluntly said that he would not stay in the race until $500 was placed in his hand."

Someone had clearly bribed Clow to quit. **Daniel O'Leary** didn't want to see him quit and promised him a check of $500 to stay in the race, but Clow declined, saying that checks were "no good." He went to leave the Garden. **"Old Sport" Campana** was sitting at the Garden door when Clow left. "Campana, in language more forcible than polite, upbraided Clow for leaving the track, and asked for the price of the dozen bottles of imported ginger ale, which he had purchased. Clow **Ephraim** told him to collect the debt in Hades and Campana walked away in disgust."

"The impression prevails that Clow has been captured by the bookmakers. Certainly, his conduct afforded good ground for such a suspicion. O'Leary was very much disturbed by Clow's withdrawal and damned up hill and down dale." Later, word came out that Clow's backers

were offered $12,000 to take their man off the track.

Clow **Ephraim** left the sport, moved to Minnesota with his brothers, turned to farming and died in 1927 at the age of 72.

Old Ben Curran

Bookmakers even tried to bribe some of the most respected runners. **Benjamin Curran** (1833-1907) was from New York City. He served for two years in the Civil War with the 21st Calvary and then became a longshoreman on the New York City docks. Like so many others, he tried his hand at pedestrianism in 1879 and became an instant hero of his fellow longshoremen as he achieved 428 miles in the 1st O'Leary Belt race held in October 1879 in Madison Square Garden.

Curran must not have aged well. Even though he was in his mid-40s, he was referred to as "Old Ben Curran." In fairness, the average age of the professional pedestrian in 1879 was about 30 years old or younger compared to a modern era ultrarunning age average of about 40. But Curran must have been an aged sight. One reported said, "the ancient longshoreman looks like a member of the first Napoleon's Old Guard." He was described as having "a battered face, weather-beaten, that becomes more worn, day after day."

During his first six-day competition in 1879, at the age of 46, betting odds were largely against Curran, because he looked so old. Spectators were stunned that such an old man could do so well pushing toward second place. "He proved himself throughout, a most persistent veteran. To all appearances he bore about his person as he walked a good many perplexing aches and pains, but he strangled these as well as he could and pushed closely for second place. His valiant march was applauded on every hand." Curran milked the attention by overstating his age by about five years.

"Entering the cubby house that is his quarters, he would throw himself upon the bed and giving order for a change of tights, a shampoo and a shave, and sink instantly into a placid sleep. Five skilled trainers attended to his wants. Two stripped him of his boots and anointed his feet. One deftly searched out the grizzled stubble in the deep furrows of his old parchment-colored face with a razor. Another flitted about like a phantom towel-rack with numberless compartments for sponges and bottles. The renewal of the veteran completed, up he got again then, and betook himself and his pains and aches once more valorously to the track."

Bookmakers try to Bribe Curran

Original Madison Square Garden

In March 1881, at age 47, Curran again competed for the O'Leary Belt in Madison Square Garden. He was a fan favorite because people thought he was so elderly. "The old man's legs are gnarled and twisted like the limb of an oak, but they have done him better service than anybody ever expected they would." The press was critical of having such an old man in the race. "There is nothing to be hoped for by the friends of Ben Curran, as his aged frame and inelastic limbs can scarcely stand the present strain put upon them. A man of his years would be better employed working at his legitimate daily labor than competing with younger men in a contest that demands youth and elasticity."

Large wagers had been made that the runner **Dick Lacouse**, of Boston, Massachusetts, would finish in second or third place. However, Curran was performing so well, twelve miles ahead, that he was disrupting these wagers. Lacouse's backers boldly approached Curran to give up third place for $1,500 worth of wager tickets. "Unfortunately for the longshoreman's reputation, he accepted the $1,500 bribe."

When the race manager, **James E. Kelly** (1832-1903), heard of it, he immediately wanted to stamp out the corruption going on. He saw the tickets in Curran's hut and Curran said he was used up and quitting. Kelly threatened to bring in the reporters to witness a doctor declaring that Curran could perfectly continue running. "If Curran cared to be exposed, he could accept the bribe. Curran decided that he wouldn't leave the track and Mr. Kelly then gave him a new $500 bill." He then stuck the bill on the end of his walking stick as a signal to those who knew that he had declined to be bribed, that the $500 was a "reward for Roman virtue."

The spectators were confused, so went to the reporter's stand and said, "I do not wish this to be misconstrued. I have paid this $500 out of my own pocket as I do not wish injustice done." It is interesting to note that Kelly's business, "Kelly & Bliss" was a bookmaking firm that also operated pool rooms and horse racetrack betting. He had been a pioneer in American legal bookmaking that was brought from England in about 1873. But he was indicted at times for illegal activities. Yes, bookmakers were even putting on pedestrian events. Curan indeed finished in third place with an impressive 504 miles. Lacouse finished with 489 miles in fourth.

Curran continued to race six-day events until his last in 1888 at the age of 55. That race did not go well, and he quit on day three "exhausted and broken-hearted at his failure. **Sammy Day** passed around his hat and $50 was raised for the old man, who will never be able to run again."

In 1892, Curran applied for a military pension as a Civil War invalid veteran at the age of 59. Ten years later, he was in a home for disabled veterans. He died in 1907 at the age of 74.

Daniel Burns Bribed

Daniel D. Burns (1860-), from Elmira, New York, came into the sport in 1879 as a 19-year-old newsboy. He gained great fame for allegedly walking a horse to death during a race in Chicago in 1880, where he reached 578 miles in 6.5 days. He raced in many other six-day races and placed well against some of the best in the world.

Atlanta, Georgia

In Atlanta, Georgia, in May 1885, a three-day walking match was held. Burns, age 25, was doing well and expected to win. But he started to fade which worried his chief backer, **John Thompson**, who had wagered $1,000 on Burns to win. To help incentivize Burns, he paid him $150 to push harder.

But later, Burns also took a $350 bribe to lose the race. He was seen lagging behind even though he looked fresh. After he lost, Thompson investigated, and the truth of the bribe came out. "Burns and his trainer Brooks were both arrested and taken to the calaboose, still in their skin-tight suits. Friends of the arrested men protested that the men would die if kept in such a place after three days walking and a guard was detailed to watch them at their rooms at a boarding house, but later they were taken to prison."

Thompson wanted his $150 back. Burns was defiant and said that he would never give the money back, "that he had rather go to the chain gang a dozen times than give up. He asserts that

Mr. Thompson offered him the $150 for a tip." Brooks agreed that there were no conditions put on the tip. The outcome of the trial is unknown.

You would think that Burns would be run out of the sport, but no. A few months later, he was competing again. He ran many races in his hometown of Elmira, New York. He became a well-respected proprietor of the Columbia Hotel in Elmira.

For his last seven years, he worked as a bartender at a hotel in Binghamton, New York. He and his wife had seven children. He died in 1914 at the age of 53. His obituary remembered his pedestrian feats. "Mr. Burns' favorite racing was the go-as-you-please race. He was often matched against the most famous racers of their day."

James Albert Offered Bribe

Not all the runners accepted the huge bribes that were offered. One particular pedestrian showed huge integrity. **James "Jimmy" Albert** (1856-1912), was from Philadelphia, Pennsylvania. His true name was **James Albert Cathcart**. He started his pedestrian career at the age of 22, in May 1879, when he achieved 450 miles at Philadelphia, Pennsylvania. He then started competing against the best ultrarunners in the world but became significantly injured and left the sport for a few years. In 1888, he was back and thought he could win a big international six-day race held in Madison Square Garden from February 6-11, 1888.

After Albert had reached an amazing 545 miles on day five, he knew that breaking **Patrick Fitzgerald's** 610-mile world record was within reach. The bookmakers had offered such high odds at the beginning of the race on bets to those who thought the world record would be broken, which distressed them. They were in danger of losing a fortune.

Stories circulated gamblers were going to try to poison Albert's food or cripple him in some way. "But Albert's good-looking wife watched closely over her husband and the only chance they had left to prevent

record-breaking was to buy off the record breakers."

Sure enough, Albert was approached with bribes to stop short of the world record. He said, "I was told that there was $10,000 waiting for me if I kept under 610 miles. They argued that this would be nearly double what I would receive from the race, but as I was not in the market, I declined the proposition." He passed over a dollar amount that today is valued at $312,000. Mrs. Albert added, "They were bothering me too. I was asked to persuade him to take the biggest money and let the little go. But we want to leave this race with a good reputation and Jim won't take anything."

Mrs. Albert

Policemen were placed on guard, but the bribers used unknown men to get into quarters used by the trainers and the runners. Efforts were made to forcibly remove Albert from the track, but those didn't work. "Fourteen policemen were watching him, prepared to arrest the first individual who should make the slightest hostile demonstration."

Albert Breaks the World Record

As word spread that Albert would likely break the record, the crowd packed Madison Square Garden, and the excitement intensified. He broke the world record at 7:23 p.m. and kept going. "A surging crowd followed Albert along the rails cheering him on. The roof of Madison Square Garden shook with the shout that went up as Albert passed the scorer's stand." In the end, he quit with two hours to spare, reaching 621 miles and immediately received congratulatory telegrams from some of the greatest ultrarunners in the world.

Albert, who believed his reputation and the world record were greater than an easy fortune, gave a humble speech at the finish announcing his retirement from the sport because he was "getting old now," at age 38. He said, "I wanted to make my final effort a good one. I knew I had to leave the track, and I wanted to leave my name upon it." His wife was pleased. "Mrs. Albert stood alongside her husband. She looked at him with pride. Her eyes danced with delight, and she could not conceal her emotion. Tears of joy filled her eyes. Three rousing cheers were given for Albert, his trainer, and his wife." It was

estimated that he received $5,800 for his win, far less than if he would have taken the bribe.

Albert's retirement did not last long. After **George Littlewood** (1859-1912) broke the world record with 623 miles, later in the year, he wanted it back. In 1889, he entered a six-day race in San Francisco, California and explained, "My sole purpose in entering this race is to eclipse that and place the record so high that it will not be touched for years to come. When I made the record in New York, I still had five hours to spare (actually two hours) and could have made 650 miles without trouble." Albert won the California race with 533 miles but was far off the world record. It would not be until 1984 that the world record was broken again. Yiannis Kouros shattered the record with 635 miles in New York City.

Albert returned to New York stating that something about California caused "weakness attacks to the legs" and that new world records could not be broken there. "It is an unprofitable country for pedestrians, but the promised land for boxers." After a couple more years, Albert finally retired from running. During his career, he invested his winnings wisely in real estate in Atlantic City, and by 1889 it was valued at $50,000 (or $1.5 million today).

Atlantic City, New Jersey

He became very wealthy and developed the famed boardwalk area, funding the construction of a 1,200-foot iron pier out into the ocean that included a dancing hall.

James Albert Cathcart died on Dec 24, 1912, at the age of 56. It is believed he died of a heart attack while alone in a small boat during a storm. He failed to return from his duck hunting trip in the evening. A search went out for him on Christmas Day. They found him lying face down in the boat anchored two miles from where he started out. He left behind an estate of $50,000 and left a generous amount to a hospital.

RICH REAL ESTATE MAN FOUND DEAD IN BOAT

Overcome by Exhaustion in Storm That Hit Atlantic City Tuesday.

Trainers Bribed

Trainers were bribed too. In the 1881 O'Leary's six-day race in Madison Square Garden, **Dick Lacouse**, of Boston, Massachusetts claimed that one of his trainers was bribed $2,000 to drug him, to make him fail. This was the same race where **Old Ben Curran** was bribed by bookmakers on the other side, to let Lacouse finish in third place.

Lacouse explained about the drugging. "The first dose was administered a few hours before the race started on the pretense that it would settle his stomach. He alleged that his trainer used chloroform or physic mixed with ginger ale purposely to make him unfit for the track throughout the race." Lacouse said, "I covered 489 miles, yet was compelled to be off the track in all 54 hours, almost twice as much as any other man, so I feel confident that I was good for second, if not first place." On day four, the trainer took him off the track and gave him something that "seemed to set his frame on fire" causing him to become feverish. Was it true, or just an excuse? He finished in fourth place.

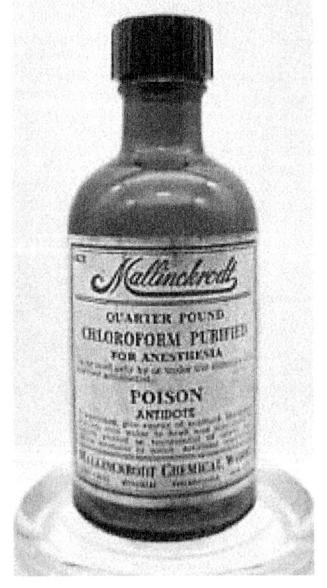

Strange Running Tales: When Ultrarunning was a Reality Show

Rumors of Trainer Bribed

Pedestrian Fitzgerald an Alderman.
Patrick Fitzgerald, the pedestrian, was appointed a member of the Board of Aldermen of Long Island City, at a meeting of that body last evening to fill a vacancy caused by the death of Alderman Johnson of the Third Ward.

PATK. FITZGERALD,
610 MILES IN 6 DAYS.

At times, runners were so "out of it," that they accused their hard-working trainers (handlers) of being bribed to drug them. **Patrick "Paddy" J. Fitzgerald** (1846-1900) was born in Ireland and, while an infant, his family moved to Canada. When he was twelve years old, he won a two-mile race against nine competitors. He emigrated to New York in 1864, and that summer ran a mile in 4:32. He first became a cattle driver but later became involved in city government on Long Island and was eventually appointed the alderman of Long Island City. He became one of the fastest runners in the world from five to fifty miles. Starting in 1879, he became a very experienced six-day runner, one of the early pioneers. In 1881 he broke the world record with 582 miles, but then lost it to **George Hazael** (1845-1911) of England, the next year with 600 miles.

HAZAEL'S RECORD BEATEN

FITZGERALD THE WINNER OF THE SIX-DAY RACE.

ROWELL ONLY EIGHT MILES BEHIND HIM AT THE FINISH—INCIDENTS OF THE LAST DAY'S STRUGGLE.

In 1884, Fitzgerald was determined to get the six-day world record back. During the late stages, he believed his highly experienced and respected trainer, "**Happy Jack**" **Smith**, of being bribed to drug him. It had been rumored that **Charles Rowell's** backer, **Peter Duryes**, had paid Smith off with $2,000 to do the dirty work. Fitzgerald's backer even got into an argument with Smith and threatened to fire him. Fitzgerald, in poor shape, heard the rumor, was distressed, and confronted Smith. The wise Smith knew his runner needed sleep and put him to bed. After an hour, he woke him up, told him falsely that he had been sleeping four hours. That worked. Fitzgerald's mind was cleared, and he apologized for doubting Smith. Fitzgerald went on to break the world record with 610 miles, beating Rowell by only eight miles.

Fitzgerald had legitimate reasons for being paranoid during races. Once during a race, a mysterious man in a cream-colored slouch hat shadowed him. "He was clad in a respectable suit of black, and often carried a long cape over his shoulders. He had restless and piercing black eyes. He had never been known to speak to any person during a race, but always kept his eyes on the weakest-looking man." When Fitzgerald started to fail, the man intercepted him in his laps. He turned out to be a wealthy eccentric man from Harlem who would wager $10,000 that a pedestrian would die on the track.

Champion Walker Dead.

New York, Nov. 12.—Patrick J. Fitzgerald, once champion six-day walker of the world and still holder of the 100-hour go-as-you-please record, is dead at his home in Long Island City. He died from dropsy, after a brief illness. Fitzgerald was born in Ireland in 1847 and came to America in 1864.

Fitzgerald used his riches to establish a training park, athletic hall, hotel, and a saloon in the Ravenswood neighborhood of Long Island (Queens). He died in 1900 of dropsy at the age of 55.

CHAPTER FOURTEEN

Richard Lacouse - Scoundrel

Richard Lacouse was once a famous, elite, ultrarunner from Boston, Massachusetts, during the late 19th century, one of the most prolific six-day pedestrians during the early years of the sport.

As with other runners of his time who amassed a fortune in winnings, he chose to use that money for nefarious purposes, rather than for good. His life turned from a race around a track for six days to a race to stay ahead of the law and to dodge one of the most skilled detectives in the country. In his wake, he left behind abuse and corruption until deciding to make an honest living in Montana in the mine industry to conclude his life.

Early Circus Life

Richard "Dick" Amos **Lacouse** (1848-1923), a French Canadian, was born in Sainte-Marcell, Quebec, Canada, the oldest of eight children. He was the son of **Joseph Octave Lacourse** (1825-1876), a carpenter, and **Emelie Guilbert** (1826-1892). His Lacourse ancestors had lived in Quebec, Canada, for many generations. By 1870, the family moved to Fall River, Massachusetts. Once he reached adulthood, Richard left home seeking adventure and athletic performances, and for unknown reasons dropped the "r" in his last name for half of his life.

Parents: Joseph and Emelie Lacourse

He claimed he became acquainted with **Charles Blodin** (1824-1897), a man who had shocked the world by walking over Niagara Falls on a tightrope in 1859. Blodin taught Lacouse how to rope walk, but the young man gave it up after a serious fall during an exhibition. He next became a trapeze performer for several years, claiming to be a star in **P.T. Barnum's** circus. In 1873, he gave up the circus, settled in Boston, Massachusetts, married **Catherine Buckley** (1844-), and started a fish market. The business venture failed, and he became a bricklayer.

Lacouse first appeared in newsprint in 1875, not for a significant accomplishment. He was arrested and accused of stealing $150 worth of property from various people outside of Boston. He was living in the slums of Boston, where he worked as a bouncer and bartender in various houses of ill-repute.

Beantown Pedestrian

In May 1879, at the age of 31, Lacouse made his debut in pedestrianism when he took part in the first big ultrarunning event in Boston, Massachusetts. It was an interstate pedestrian tournament relay race between teams from Massachusetts, Maine, and Rhode Island. It was also called "The Bean Pot Tramp" held in a mammoth tent at the Riding Academy in Back Bay, Boston.

Back Bay from the State House 1857

With the popularity of pedestrianism taking fire, Lacouse tried out for the big event. It was reported, "He said he was undersized at that time, but his legs were hard as iron and sinews of steel wire. The tryout was a revelation to the management of the tournament, which immediately bargained with Lacouse to join the Massachusetts team." He was described as weighing 135 pounds, standing at 5'7", a "stocky Frenchman," who lived on Barton Street in Boston.

Each state's team was comprised 12 runners. Each day, for six days, two runners on each team would run for six hours each. Maine came out on top, but Lacouse, often referred to as "the Frenchman," ran more than 35 miles during his turn, which was the second furthest of all the runners in the competition, earning him $75.

For the final week of the tournament, he competed in a six-day walking match with 20 others. He put on an impressive performance. "Lacouse is still in the lead. He is a wonderful specimen of humanity. His feet are badly blistered, yet he walks with apparent ease, and for pluck he has no equal. During the morning he frequently spurted around the track for two and three laps at a time."

On the final day, he was in close competition with **Frank Hart** (1857-1908) for the win, but then ran into serious trouble. "Some outsiders gave Lacouse some stuff to drink, which in a few moments acted on him in a strange manner. He looked insane and began striking himself with a stick and showing other signs of insanity, which caused him to be removed from the track for some two hours." He lost his lead, and when he came back out, he fell senseless on the track. His friends plead with him to quit, thinking that he would die. "At this time, he looked wild and ran out of the tent as he said, to get ice water. He was immediately taken back to the tent, where he begged for rest. But his trainers insisted on him staying on the track."

```
1st Prize—Lacouse, 427 miles................$300
2d Prize—Hichborn, 424 miles, 5 laps........ 150
3d Prize—Coughlin, 400 miles................ 100
4th Prize—Wheeler, 356 miles................  75
5th Prize—Durgin, 338 miles.................  50
6th Prize—O'Connor, 320 miles, 3 laps.......  25
7th Prize—Hurley, 319 miles.................  15
```

The referee made a doctor check him over and diagnosed that he was delirious and suffering from congestion on the brain. They put him to bed, rubbed for an hour, and he fell four miles behind Hart. Lacouse insisted on returning to the track and after being given some stimulants he "started out and ran like a deer." Hart also collapsed and it was thought for a while that he was dead, but after an hour he was revived and taken home. Lacouse won the race with 427 miles, three more than Hart, winning $300 (valued at nearly $9,000 today), and made a big splash for himself in the sport in Boston.

Prolific Six-Day Runner

In July 1879, given his growing ultrarunning reputation and that he included all the principal winners of long-distance races in New England, O'Leary accepted him to run in his six-day 12.5 hours per day race in a field of twenty at the Music Hall in Boston. Instead of running for 24 hours for six days, it was discovered that audiences enjoyed watching more competitive, fresher runners, who would all sleep through the night. Lacouse was obviously still a rookie. "Lacouse stopped frequently before the scorers' stand looking at the score, evidently forgetting that he was in the race, and it required all the energies of his trainers to force him along." Later on, his mind seemed to go to mush. "Lacouse showed signs of mental suffering. He talked at random, and once or twice became so forgetful of the real work he had in hand as to stop to talk with various parties on the track." He finished in a respectable fourth place with 256 miles, winning $50.

Lacouse and his family still lived in a rough neighborhood of Boston. They couldn't stay out of trouble. Just a week later, his landlady, **Bridget Costello** confronted Lacouse's wife, **Catharine Lacouse**, for their rent money. Catharine picked up a stone and threw it at Costello causing a wound on her forehead. Costello's sister, Kate, then hit Catharine with a clothing pole, which also hit their fifteen-month-old son, **Joseph Lacouse**. The confrontation blew up, hit the newspapers, and Catherine Lacouse was convicted of assault.

Lacouse was away from home much of the time, trying to compete and win money in all the nearby races. In August 1879, he ran in a six-day, 75-hour race in Providence, Rhode Island. "Lacouse is looking in good condition for a man that has during the past few months been in so many pedestrian contests. The little Canadian deserves much credit for his pluck." But Lacouse experienced the fatigue that eventually catches up with an ultrarunner. After 107 hours, he dropped out because of sickness.

Did he learn? Perhaps not. The next week he competed in another 75-hour race in the Music Hall in Boston.

	M.	L.
Lacouse	281	02
Hanson	272	01
Colston	255	14
O'Connor	252	13
Colbert	251	07
Crowley	212	04
Harriman	196	04
Collyer	157	

He showed amazing determination in a close race and won the race with 281 miles, earning him the Ennis medal, and $200. His winnings were piling up, and he was becoming a very rich man. He quickly went to Dover, New Hampshire the next week and entered yet another 75-hour race with 16 others. He placed a surprising second place with 250 miles.

The following month, October 1879, he competed in Captain **T. E. Halleck's**

Names.	M.	L.	Names.	M.	L.
Chow	399	01	Madden	407	05
Faherty	243	01	Lacouse	406	06
Hughes	226	04	Ingram	367	07
Barry	202	01	Allen	140	02
O'Connor	213	05	Coughlin	322	01
Geldert	304	06	Durgin	304	02
King	187	02	O'Toole	195	00

Worcester, Massachusetts, six-day 75-hour race at the skating rink there. He finished in second place with an impressive 406 miles, winning $150. In

November, he ran in yet another six-day, 75-hour race in Worcester, Massachusetts. He won again with 332 miles.

Lacouse was ready for the big time, the Rose six-day race in Madison Square Garden in December 1879, against 65 of the country's best ultrarunners, including talents such as **John Hughes**, **Steve Brodie** the newsboy, **Frank Hart**, and "**Old Sport**" **Campana**. But Lacouse's recent massive miles finally caught up with him and he quit after reaching 188 miles. During his short 1879 pedestrian career, he had already run 2,280 miles in eleven races and won about $1,500.

1880 Competitions

In 1880, Boston still had a great interest in pedestrian races, and Lacouse was among their favorite sons. A 70-hour six-day race was held in the Music Hall in Boston. For the first two days, he was on the "sick list" but recovered and continued going over 200 miles. After he failed in another race the following month, he then wisely backed off and competed in lower distance ultras. He still tried several six-day races but did poorly.

Finally, he was again victorious at a six-day race held at the Boston Athletic Club's covered training grounds, 520 Albany Street, winning with 475 miles. At the end of 1880, he raced for 130 hours at Boston's Music Hall, "Lacouse never looked so well on a track before. He runs like a deer and is feeling confident of taking first place. He shows no sign of fatigue whatever, and his trainer, Mr. **James Robinson**, says that he will carry off the laurels." He won with 425 miles in 127 hours. "On his leaving the track, he was loudly cheered by those present, and the wily little Frenchman kicked up his heels and remarked, 'I never felt better in my life.'" He won $700.

Strange Running Tales: When Ultrarunning was a Reality Show

1881 O'Leary Championship Belt Race

The most prestigious race of his career came in February 1881, the O'Leary

	7 p. m.	8 p. m.	9 p. m.	10 p. m.
Panchot	535	537	539	541
Krohne	515	520	521	523
Curran	500	504	504	504
Lacouse	487	489	489	489
Campana	450	450	450	450

Championship belt in Madison Square Garden in front of thousands. "Lacouse looks remarkably fresh, but he is believed to lack the grip necessary to carry him through the week." He surprised many and climbed the leader board into fourth place by the final days. Large wagers of $5,600 had been made that he would finish in second or third place. However, **Old Ben Curran** was performing so well, twelve miles ahead, that he was disrupting this wager.

Lacouse surrounded himself with shady characters. His backers boldly approached Curran to give up third place for $1,500 worth of wager tickets. He accepted the bribe, but the race manager later discovered it and made this public to keep the race legit. Lacouse finished in fourth place with 489 miles for a personal record. Curran reached 504 miles.

Lacouse didn't even trust his own men. He felt that they cheated him and had taken bribes to drug him. On day four, the trainer took him off the track and gave him something that "seemed to set his frame on fire" causing him to become feverish. Was it true, or just an excuse? He fired his trainers and disappeared from the sport for nine months. It was said that he was training himself, hidden in the woods of Massachusetts.

Comeback Attempt

In December 1881, Lacouse attempted a comeback and competed in the Ennis Six-Day race at the

Fitzgerald	582	miles.	55	yards.
Noremac	565	"	495	"
Herty	556	"	275	"
Krohne	509	"	1590	"
Lacouse	501	"	275	"

American Institute Hall in New York City, this time without a trainer. He started weighing only 116 pounds. At this race, **Patrick Fitzgerald** broke the world record with 582 miles. Lacouse stayed with the front-runners and broke 500 miles for the first time, finishing in fifth place with 501 miles, winning $100. In a weak condition, he was carried to his dressing room, and he allowed his attendants to pull off his shoes and socks that had not been removed for six days. He said, "By Jingo, my toenails, all of them came off with the stockings and the out skin halfway to my knees." Lacouse again disappeared from the sport. During his three-year storied career, he competed in at least 23 races, winning six of them, reached more than 6,000 miles, and earned about five times the typical annual salary of the time.

Locouse's Den of Ill-Repute in Gloucester

Instead of using his fortune for good, Lacouse turned to illegal activities to earn easy money. He established a boarding house in "Five Points" in Gloucester, Massachusetts. This was the red-light district of the city, a "den noted for harboring females of poor character. It was famous for assaults, shooting affairs, and attempted suicides." Lacouse's place was called a "resort" but was actually a brothel, saloon, and gambling hall. It was reported, "Lacouse made money fast and eluded justice on several occasions."

By 1882, Lacouse had divorced or left his wife **Catherine**. She would marry again in 1887 to **Patrick Mahoney**, a fisherman. Lacouse married (or lived with) his housekeeper in 1882, **Maud (Lindsay) Edson**, who had recently given birth to his son, **Richard Lacouse**. On June 19, 1884, Lacouse's six-year-old son **Joseph Richard Lacouse** (1878-1945), (by his

Gloucester

first wife Catherine) was playing in the upper story of the building on Porter Street and fell out of a window, causing a gash on his head and internal injuries. They feared he would not live and took him to the hospital. He did recover.

Attempted Suicide?

Two months later, in August 1884, after Lacouse returned home from a trip to Portland, Maine, he had a terrible argument with Maud. "She stated that he attempted to shoot her, and that she took away the revolver twice. He then shot at himself, the bullet entering the back of the head. The shooting, she said, took place in the bedroom, but appearances indicated that he was on the sofa in the front room and fell forward on the floor." The authorities were called. Lacouse was conscious and a doctor "probed for the ball. The bullet went through the outside of the skull and was not found." It was said the cause for the shooting was because of jealousy, but "the true version of the affair could not be ascertained." Lacouse recovered and stayed with his wife. He later claimed that either Maud had fired the shot, or the gun went off accidently, that he did not try to commit suicide.

> **I HEREBY GIVE NOTICE**—That I will not pay any bills contracted by my wife, known as Maud Edson. RICHARD LACOUSE, Gloucester.
> 2t s6

A couple of weeks later, he published a strange notice in the newspaper stating that he would not pay any bills contracted by his wife.

Lacouse became an American citizen in October 1884.

A detective caught the notorious crook, **John Houlett**, at Lacouses's house of ill-repute at the end of the year. "The thief made considerable resistance and offered to pound him, but clubs were used and Houlett was dragged and locked up at Short Street. The police record shows that Houlett is one of the worst crooks in the city."

The Mayor Attempts to Close Down the Business

In April 1885, it was said that Lacouse was operating a "den of infamy" in Gloucester. The new **Mayor John S. Parsons** (1836-1911) was determined to shut it down. Once taking office, Parsons began a campaign of moral reform, and launched several raids on Gloucester's brothels, including Lacouses' Porter Street operation. Lacouse was arrested for "maintaining a nuisance." He was freed on bail.

John Parsons

Arrested for Beating Maud

Four months later, Lacouse was arrested again for assaulting his now former wife, **Maud Edson**. She had sold her furniture and intended to leave for Boston. Lacouse was accused of beating her. "On the night of July 28, 1884, while the revels were at their height in Lacouse's den, a piercing cry of murder was heard by the patrolman on the beat, and upon forcing an entrance into the place, he found Maud Edson lying bleeding on the floor, her features so battered, that recognition was well-nigh impossible. The girl was insensible at the time and was removed to the hospital."

At the trial, it was reported that he had thrown Maud down the stairs, which caused her to be terribly disfigured. When the case was called, Maud could not be found, and it was alleged that Lacouse had arranged for her to be hidden away. "The testimony in the case by officers showed that his voice was heard cursing his wife during the disturbance. When arrested, he said it was lucky that he was not arrested for murder. The judge said it was one of the most aggravating assaults that had come under his jurisdiction for a long time, and that the remark about murder was a confession." His case was referred to the grand jury, and another bail was instituted of $600. Lacouse came up with the bail again and was released.

Porter Street Dive Again Raided

Lacouse's "Porter Street Dive" was again raided, and illegal hard liquors were found.

LACOUSE FOUND GUILTY.
He Gets Eight Months and a Fine of $100, but Appeals.

"Officers saw five for six girls upstairs. The girls said they boarded and lodged there. The reputation of the house has not been a good one." One girl said that Lacouse had knocked her down once and dragged her downstairs. The entire place was said to be noisy and disorderly. They held a lengthy trial with witnesses, including Lacouse, and he boasted that he did not have to pay police hush money to keep his place going, that instead he would make sure the annoying Mayor Parsons was voted out at the next election. (He was reelected). Lacouse was found guilty of operating a place for prostitution and gaming, was fined $100, and sentenced to eight months in prison.

Lacouse Flees to Texas

A month later, on October 5, 1885, Lacouse's assault case came before the grand jury, but despite the $2,100 bail, he had fled to Galveston, Texas, where he went to work in a saloon. Maud, who was apparently his wife again, followed him there. Lacouse got into an argument with his employer over money and right after he quit, the building was discovered to be on fire. They suspected him of causing it, but they couldn't find any firm evidence. He next opened a small restaurant and a cheap boarding house with Maud.

Apprehension and Escape

In 1886, the district attorney in Gloucester hired the Pinkerton firm's best detective, **M. J. Healy,** to locate and apprehend Lacouse. The detective was successful, arrested Lacouse in Texas, and they started for Massachusetts by the steamship *San Marcos* to New York. Before leaving, Lacouse tried unsuccessfully to bribe the detective to let him go ashore. They put Lacouse on suicide watch when he went on a

hunger strike on the way. "He was handcuffed for some time, but after a while, Lacouse was freed from the iron bonds and mingled with the passengers in the cabin." The steamer stopped at Newport News, Virginia, for coal, anchored about eleven miles from shore in Chesapeake Bay.

One evening, Lacouse was playing cards in the cabin. The detective went on deck to light a cigar, and five minutes later, a passenger reported Lacouse had left the cabin. They searched the area but couldn't find Lacouse. "Several people were on deck at the time, and it was clear moonlight, but no one had seen a man go overboard." An intense search was made of the entire ship, including the cargo areas that were storing cotton.

WHERE NOW IS LACOUSE?

Said to Have Jumped Off an Ocean Steamer.

Gloucester's Very Bad Man, Who Left His Bondsmen in the Lurch.

One of Pinkerton's Men Found Him in Galveston.

DICK LACOUSE'S ESCAPE

The Sensational Story of His "Leap in the Dark"

Denied by the Captain of the Steamer San Marcos.

How a Detective is Said to Have Guarded the Prisoner.

When the ship arrived in New York, the detectives closely watched until all the cargo was removed, but they did not find Lacouse. "It was believed that Dick jumped overboard, as he would take any chance to escape, but as the sea was running high, there seemed no possible chance for his escape from drowning. The detective felt the loss keenly, that Lacouse was only the second man lost by the Pinkertons in 35 years." The authorities presumed that Lacouse was dead. Some who knew that he was an extraordinary swimmer believed he had escaped and would eventually turn up.

Lacouse Found and Brought to Justice

To the great surprise of everyone, Lacouse lived and indeed had escaped. On June 3, 1885, he was arrested at Middlegge's Place, "a pleasure resort" about five miles from Galveston, Texas. He had indeed swum ashore and made his way back to Texas and linked back up with his "pseudo wife," Maud. "Last night, to the astonishment of the police, she appeared and swore out a warrant, charging that Lacouse had again attempted to kill her. She divulged his hiding place."

The Chief of Police, Jordan, engaged four mounted officers to ride down the island to apprehend Lacouse. "Lacouse saw the cavalcade in the distance, guessed they were after him, and down the island he flew. The officers followed; their horses taxed to the utmost to overtake the runner. The chase continued five miles along the seashore and Lacouse was finally captured under a farmhouse."

Lacouse claimed that on the ship, a man from Boston aided his escape and some of the crew who sympathized with him. "He was provided with a life-preserver, and while the detective was doing the honors for some of the lady passengers, he quietly slipped overboard and swam

San Marcos Steamship

toward the shore." He said he saw Detective Healy and the officers of the San Marcos flashing their lights over the side of the ship looking for him. "He was laughing at them from the dark water in the distance." It took him five hours to swim to the shore. He then went into a town where he found clothes, took a train to Baltimore, and returned by steamer to Galveston, arriving two weeks later. Old sailors said his story was improbable.

On returning to Galveston, Lacouse had discovered that Maud had already taken up with another man and had sold his restaurant. He had demanded money from Maud, wanting to flee for Canada, but she refused, and they got into a fight during which he tried to kill her again, leading to his arrest.

The Pinkerton Detective Agency just couldn't accept the wild escape story and believed that he had stowed away, escaped the search of the ship and returned to Galveston by the same steamer. The Boston Globe was also skeptical of the amazing story. "The story of swimming ashore, sounds a little fishy. If the story be true, he ought to be fitted out as a cruiser to protect our fisheries."

C. Burrows, the captain of the *San Marcos* gave a different story. He believed that when the ship went into dock at Newport News to obtain the coal, that Lacouse, who was not being watched well by the detective, had simply lowered himself

Pinkerton Agents

over the rail and swam 150 yards to the dock. Once they were out in the sea again, a search of the ship was made. The captain said, "The story of Lacouse's jumping from the steamer 11 miles at sea is a good yarn to help a man (the detective) out of a difficulty, but I don't like to see the public gulled."

At a Galveston trial for threatening bodily harm on Maud, she promptly withdrew her charge, but the trial went forward. Bail was set at $750, and he remained in jail. The Pinkertons were again engaged to take Lacouse back to Gloucester, Massachusetts, to face trial there. Legal wrestling occurred to extradite him. Lacouse wanted to remain in Texas, where he said he had the best jail that he had ever stayed in. After a couple weeks of wrangling, Pinkerton Detective Healy got his man and took charge of Lacouse with the help of Texas **Governor John Ireland** (1827-1866). This time he took the prisoner to Boston by railroad. Lacouse soon found his new home in Salem Jail, in Boston.

Montana

No details were found about his trial, but about 1890, Lacouse, age 42, resurfaced in Butte, Montana, involved in mining with the Anaconda Copper Mining Company, working as a bricklayer, building smelters. He changed his last name to "Lacourse" and soon became a respected member of his community of Anaconda.

When legendary **Daniel O'Leary** came to town on a barnstorming trip with other runners in 1891, Lacourse quickly organized a six-day race championship at Evan's Opera House, that he also took part in. He was confident that he could win, so he held back during the early stages to let the betting odds against him increase. Then he poured it on.

"Presents were showered upon him, which were of nominal value. One-dollar bills which he had no time to examine did the work of tens or twenties urging him to further efforts. He ran his feet off and went into the lead on the fourth day." He won with 501 miles, received a gold trophy with the figure of a man walking, and declared himself the champion of Montana. O'Leary reached 401 miles.

Lacourse made a false claim that he ran in 17 six-day races in Boston and won 16 of them. "He says he can stay as long and run as fast as he ever did." Lacourse finally retired for good and concentrated on making money in the mining industry, but a few other Montana races were held.

Final Years

In 1893, He married for a third time to **Annie Lawson Lacourse** (1866-1955). A daughter **Helen Lacourse (Doran)** (1896-1990) and a son **Octave "Otto" Lacourse** (1899-1987), would soon be born. Even though Lacourse seemed to have cleaned up

Anaconda Smelter Stack

his life over the years, it wasn't surprising that he got involved in fights and lawsuits. In 1916, at the age of 68, he fell off a scaffold at a smelter and suffered some serious injuries. In 1921, at the age of 73, he and his wife, in retirement started to travel, taking vacations in California and Mexico, where he became ill. "He said he began to feel like his natural self as soon as the train carrying him came within sight of the big smelter stack."

RICHARD LA COURSE DIES UNEXPECTEDLY AT 81 YEARS OF AGE

At One Time Partner of Blondin; Natural Athlete; Famous Record.

MANY PRESENT FOR PIONEER'S FUNERAL

Friends From Surrounding Country Pay Last Tribute to Richard LeCourse.

On November 4, 1923, Richard Lacourse died at the age of 75. He had not been feeling well since returning from an annual vacation in California. "He was in a jovial mood when he sat down to the supper table with his wife Sunday evening, and after eating, remarked that he would lie down a while and rest. Shortly after, he laid down, his wife stepped to his side to inquire how he was feeling and found him dead. Death had come peacefully and without pain." A long obituary was printed in the Montana newspaper that outlined his pedestrian accomplishments but left out his wild escape in Texas. They held a large funeral for him attended by the bricklayers' and masons' union. He was buried in Mount Carmel Cemetery, in Anaconda, Montana.

Legacy Left Behind

What legacy did **Richard Lacouse** leave behind? We can see it in his son who did not come with him to Montana. Back in Massachusetts, **Joseph Lacouse** appeared in the news regularly. He became a notorious criminal in the Boston area, involved in burglary and escaping from prison. He followed in his father's terrible activities and in 1903, he and his wife, **Winfred Lacouse**, were arrested, accused of operating a brothel in Gloucester, enticing young girls from

COUPLE ARRESTED.

Joseph Lacouse and Wife of Gloucester.

Accused of Enticing Girls There From Boston.

Also Said to Conduct Place in This City.

Boston to be part of their business that was frequented by sailors and longshoremen. They were sentenced to prison and fined.

His son **William Lacouse** was arrested for breaking and entering a house in 1906. They found him hiding under a bed. "He swore that he hadn't stolen anything and wanted it to be believed that he had crawled under the bed to go to sleep."

Son, **Otto Lacourse** became a stonemason in Montana, moved to Sacramento, California, working as a bricklayer. In the 1950s, he was a patient at the Napa Mental Hospital. He died in 1987 at the age of 92. Daughter **Helen Lacourse** married **Joseph Doran**, an iron moulder, and raised three children in Anaconda, Montana, and then moved to California. She died in Oakland, California, in 1990 at the age of 95.

Davy Crockett

CHAPTER FIFTEEN

Arrests

Ultrarunners/pedestrians of the late 1800s were a unique breed of determined and aggressive individuals who were in the sport primarily trying to cash in on the huge prize money potential and to get their names in the newspapers as "world champions." They would gladly endure the torture of running hundreds of miles in a week for a perceived easy way to earn life-changing money. Such opportunities obviously attracted individuals that weren't necessarily the most outstanding citizens and had run-ins with the law. But the law and others at times wanted to bring down the sport and the athletes, and thus confrontations occurred.

Race Accused of Disorderly Conduct in a Saloon

In 1885, two female pedestrians, **Emma Frazier** (1861-1914) and **Elizabeth Carr,** were arrested in Philadelphia at a saloon on Walnut Street, along with 25

THE WALNUT STREET RAID.

The Proprietor of No. 823 Held for Trial—
The Other Prisoners Released.

spectators and the race manager, **James B. Jamison** (1830-1900) for disorderly conduct.

A policeman visited the event and went to get an arrest warrant. They conducted a raid, stopped the race, and made arrests. It was discovered that Carr was a minor, age 19. "The excitement over the match was at its height, some thirty persons being assembled in the bar and showroom. The raid had been carefully kept secret and was completely successful. Everybody in the house was taken out of it and marched in a melancholy procession to the Central Station, where they were locked up to await a hearing the next morning. One of the young pedestrians had the good fortune to be wearing a calico skirt over her bloomer costume, but the other, in the regulation fancy dress tights and short jacket of red, was marched through the streets, to the amusement of the 'groundlings.'"

RAIDED BY THE POLICE.

An Unexpected and Unpleasant Interruption to a Female Walking Match.

Jamison, who also had a retail store, had previous run-ins with the law and believed the raid "was a piece of spite work on the part of a neighbor with whom he was competing in business." At the hearing, they testified that the place was noisy and disorderly. "Mr. **J. L. Grotenthaler**, the owner of the competing business, said the place was interfering with his business, and he was losing his lady customers. Officer Watson said that he visited the place because of complaints that young girls were enticed into it. He saw a man guarding the entrance to the showroom, allowing nobody to enter without one of the checks presented by the barkeeper with each glass of beer or liquor sold. He saw both men and women drinking. Jamison was held for $1,000 to answer the charge of keeping a disorderly house and the other prisoners were released."

Walnut Street Theatre near saloon

Strange Running Tales: When Ultrarunning was a Reality Show

Mark All, the 60,000-mile Pedestrian Arrested

Mark All

Mark All (1828-1925), of England, was an interesting pedestrian character. He claimed to be one of the mega-mile "around the world" walkers of the time and claimed to be the "champion walker of the world." Most of these professional walkers were taking advantage of the naïve Americans, but Mark All was a rare elderly walker who was entertaining the British.

All was born in Greenwich, England, in 1828, where he went into an electrical engineering career. For years, he was employed by a firm of engineers. But during a great strike of 1897-98, he lost his employment. Since he was 72 years old, he decided to start a walking tour and find employment wherever he could, to prove that a man isn't "used up" in old age.

All claimed that he started a long walk on August 6, 1900, and walked 30,000 miles before the sports newspapers of that era noticed his efforts in

AGED PEDESTRIAN.
WALKING 60,000 MILES.

Mark All, the aged engineer who is endeavouring to walk 60,000 miles in seven years, passed through Leeds yesterday, on his way to London,

1904. He said that three of the papers raised a £500 prize for him if he could continue and reach 60,000 miles in a total of seven years. He was described as "a ruddy-faced, white-haired man, carrying a black bag containing small engineering tools, a walking stick and having a picture of his dead British bulldog suspended from a button of his waistcoat."

By 1906, he claimed he had traveled through the British Isles and many European countries. Like most of the "around the world," walkers of the time (the majority who were frauds), he alleged that the conditions for his long walk required that he could not solicit donations but could receive them if offered. "When the opportunity presents itself, he does a day's work. He was stabbed when in Spain, and on two other occasions, he had been stoned and robbed. But the proudest moment of his life was undoubtedly when King Edward spoke to him on the road near Newmarket, gave him a couple of sovereigns, and called him a brave old veteran."

He claimed that his usual pace covered 50 miles in 10 hours, 250 miles per week, and that he never walked on Sundays. Another time, he said he walked 27 miles per day. A good pair of Army boots lasted him two months. He said at age 77, "My life on the road has been one of many vicissitudes, with few to recognize me or give a helping hand. Still, I am alive. I am without a rival or companion on the road, having beaten all previous records at my age. I will never despair, but struggle on to the end."

During 1905-1907, All became famous across England. He would always visit newspaper offices and try to get his story in the local papers. He said that he allowed himself a little beer when "off duty" and enjoyed a pipe before his daily exercise.

In 1907, at the age of 80, he was arrested for drunkenness in Ashbourne, England. The judge was shocked to see such a famous man in his court. The night before, he had fallen, cut his chin, and was arrested for being drunk. The judge did not want to "deal severely" with the famous old man, so he let him off with a fine.

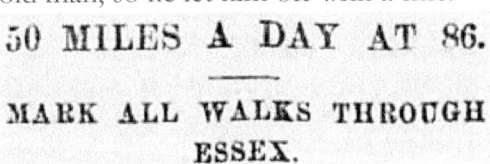

Just a year later, All claimed that he was walking 100,000 miles in 8.5 years, which would have required him to walk 40,000 miles in just a year and a half in his 80s. His prize amount curiously jumped to £2,000 and then to an outrageous £3,000. He then boosted his mileage amount to 200,000 miles. Obviously, it all was a farse, but no one seemed to want to confront the old man.

His tales to reporters became more and more outlandish. "Mr. All has suffered as many persecutions as St. Paul, been flung into prison, attacked with knives, shot at, stoned, baited with dogs, and had many adventures and extraordinary escapes."

1911 Census in a Workhouse

Starting in 1909, authorities finally recognized that he was a homeless traveling tramp, and he was committed or admitted voluntarily over and over again to workhouses. These public assistance institutions were intended to provide temporary accommodation for homeless people. They would do work such as digging for potatoes.

All stated in the past to reporters that there were important conditions for his walk, "that he shall not enter a workhouse or fall into the hands of police." Well, records show, he was committed to workhouses continually. He would get out and visit local newspaper offices, claiming that his walk was continuing, with a trip even to America. Reports never saw him walking, he was only seen in newspaper offices.

Mark All died on March 31, 1925, a pauper in at Shirley Warren Poor Law Infirmary, Southampton, at the age of 96. Actually, there is no true evidence of his age. People said he looked 20 years younger than he claimed. No one at the infirmary knew who he was until they went through his papers left behind. He claimed impossibly that in 25 years he had walked 356,000 miles. "One was never quite able to come to the conclusion of whether he was a hoaxer." As it turns out, Mark All was one of many "around the world" walking frauds, who would turn up in towns telling stories about meeting the kings and sharing unbelievable survival stories. These tales were great for entertaining news stories. He and others like him just looked for attention and free room and board.

Death of Mark All.

350,000 MILES WALK.

Mark All, the pedestrian, who, it is stated, during the last 25 years had been engaged on a walk of 350,000 miles for a reward of £3,000, has died at Shirley Warren Infirmary, aged 95. An entry in the diary written on his 95th birthday reads:—
"Since 6th Aug., 1900, I have walked 356,000 miles. Finished in Exeter. Now got to walk to London to get my reward."
Mark All had called at "The Citizen" Office on several occasions in the course of his long tramp.

As All was nearing death, he stated he hoped that in the afterlife he "may travel on a beautiful highway where there will be no bloomin' motor cars to choke an old fellow with dust."

The Tax Man Cometh

Samuel F. Mishler (1860-1931), a steelworker, was an accomplished pedestrian from Reading, Pennsylvania, who walked 100 miles in 23:27 and he won a 24-hour race with 107 miles. In 1879, he was arrested in Reading, Pennsylvania for non-payment of taxes. "Many persons expressed indignation, as they allege it was a put-up job to prevent a walking match in which Mishler is engaged."

Assault with a Pewter Pot

In 1881, **George Pegge** (1830-1884), age 51, a shoemaker from Derby, England, "a well-known pedestrian" who had recently walked 102 miles in 25 hours and accomplished 382 miles in a six-day match, was charged with a violent assault on a butcher, **Henry Thorpe**. "On Monday, Pegge entered the Old Neptune Inn and offered to walk against anybody to the town of Burton for £20. He then offered some money to Thorpe, telling him to cover the bet, but when he declined, pushed it away and the money fell on the floor. Pegge gave him a blow on the head with a pewter pot, injuring him severely, and saying he would knock his brains out. The tankard hit Thorpe's head, cut the scalp, and caused a wound which had to be dressed at the Infirmary." Pegge was sentenced to three months in prison with hard labor. He had been convicted of other crimes before, including stealing a hare from a neighbor. He had been called a "foolish, drunken freak."

Neptune Inn

Cruelty to Children

In 1881, in New York City, **Thomas Smith Sr.** was arrested for cruelty to children. At the American Institute Building, he forced his 15-year-old son, **Thomas Smith Jr.**, to take part in a walking match, "in which, after having walked 98 miles under the use of stimulants and influences, the boy fell insensible on the track, completely broken down." The father made him continue, supporting him as he tottered around the track. But when that didn't work, he carried his

AMERICAN INSTITUTE HALL, 1079 THIRD AVENUE, BETWEEN 63D AND 64TH STREETS.

son to his tent, and then he sent him home in a carriage "in a dangerous condition." At the trial, the boy denied that he had been forced to compete, but Smith pleaded guilty. He was sentenced to ten days in prison and given a $100 fine.

In 1893, **May Robison**, age 16, "**Happy Jarbeau**," (real name, **Mary Jane Waters**) was determined to follow her mother, **Alice Robison**, into a career of being a professional pedestrian. Her stepfather, **Zachariah Robison**, forbade her from participating and placed her in a Columbus, Ohio convent. She escaped and walked to Cincinnati, where she appeared in a race of female pedestrians. By then her mother was dead and stepfather was in prison. (see chapter 11). From there, she went to Chicago and New York, where she was chased out of walking matches three times by Humane Society officers because her childlike appearance was obvious. Finally, she was arrested in Pittsburgh, Pennsylvania, by the "Anti-Cruelty Society" and placed in a foster home. When arrested, she boasted, "I took second prize money in a race at Chicago last winter."

Wife Beater

In 1881, **Michael S. Tynan**, a shoemaker from Staten Island, New York, competed in the 3rd O'Leary Belt six-day race in Madison Square Garden. He left the track after reaching 85 miles in the first 24 hours. His friends had pressured him into entering the race and he went home with a feeling of disgust about failing. He took it out on his wife, **Alice Tynan**, and beat her, giving her black eyes and tearing out much of her hair. "It was shown that Mr. Tynan was of irritable temper, especially at times when he was in training, and that it was customary for him to throw dishes around the house, break glass and raise the wind generally. He promised to reform before leaving the court and marched down Butler Street, followed by two of his misguided backers in the recent contest." He was fined $20 which was paid by his employer.

Runner Charged with Sexual Assault

In 1904, **Tony Todd** (real name **Hugh Sloane**), age 22, of Bolton England, was attempting to walk 2,000 miles in 1,000 hours at the Coach and Horses Ground, Dronfield, England. An eighteen-year-old girl, **Emily Bennett**, visited his tent during his attempt. Sloane's wife had been lodging with the girl's parents and went off to wash his dirty clothes. "Sloane, it was alleged, after three other men had left the tent, fastened the door by placing a bar of iron across it, and then committed the offense. Afterward, he gave her a shilling, which she at first refused." Emily cried long and often the following day and let Sloane's wife know what happened. He denied the allegation, became violent, and struck and knocked down his wife. The police went to the venue and arrested him. At his trial, Sloane testified that he had never been left alone with the girl and claimed the payment given was for washing his clothes. He believed the whole thing was a scheme involving her parents to get him to fail in his walking attempt. The court believed him and dismissed the charges. Sloane reattempted his 2,000 miles in 1,000 hours several months later and succeeded, claiming a world record.

Arrests for Stealing

In 1887, **Thomas Trainor**, a former professional pedestrian, stole a diamond ring from **Thomas Kirk** and was wanted by police. The police spotted him on the streets of Pittsburgh and conducted a foot chase. "But being too fleet-footed for the policeman, he would have escaped had not he been headed off by two other officers."

Getting proper footwear was important to runners. **John Green**, a former professional pedestrian, was boarding with **Thomas White** in Eastleigh, England, in 1887. One day, White noticed Green was wearing a pair of boots and socks that he had stolen from his house. He refused to return them, and

Eastleigh, England

White had Green arrested. At the trial, it came out that the boots, valued at 11 shillings, had been in a box with other things that the landlady had taken from White instead of rent and she had given them to Green. "She said White owed her money, and she detained his box, which after a time she broke open and amongst other things were the boots and socks which she lent to Green,." White dropped the charges, but when investigators looked more closely, it turned out that the boots were military property. The police charged White with unlawful possession and found proof that he had purchased them from Winchester Barracks. He ended up getting a heavy fine for obtaining the articles.

In 1893, the police arrested **Gus Guerrero**, a very successful and wealthy pedestrian from California, in Boston for stealing a bicycle and released him on bail for $300. He had "borrowed" the bike and rode it from Maine to Boston and painted it black.

> **"GUS" GUERRERO HELD IN $300.**
> Champion Pedestrian is Accused of Larceny of a Bicycle.

Arrested for Highway Robbery

In 1892, **Albert Davis** won a six-day race in Atlantic City, New Jersey, and became an instant celebrity. Later, the police arrested Davis for "highway robbery" at May's Landing, New Jersey. He had been wooing a well-known young woman of a prominent family named **Annette Robertson**. Once the arrest became known, her parents forbade her from having any contact with him. "She refused to believe in his guilt and said she would stick to him through thick and thin, and left home."

Robertson visited him in jail, and affectionate interviews have taken place between the two. She brought a clergyman with her to the jail, stating that she was going to marry Davis at once and that she wanted to share his cell with him. The Sheriff refused to allow the marriage until she obtained permission from her parents. The young woman wept terribly, knowing that permission would not come. After two months in jail, Davis was acquitted of all charges. It is unknown if the marriage took place.

Arrested for Drunkenness

It was fairly common for pedestrians to become alcoholics, given the amount of liquor that many of them drank during training and races. In 1883, the English champion, **George Hazael** (1845-1911) from London, England, was in New York City to try to win money racing others and to establish a pub in the city. He said, "I am prepared to run anybody in the world from ten miles to 100 miles. I don't think there will be any more six-day races. There is no money in them. I have run three times more races than any other man. I am well-fixed in regard to finances, and never felt better in my life." Hazael's prediction was wrong. During the next two decades there were nearly 200 six-day races held. And many other pedestrians had run more races than him.

He was soon arrested along with three others in Brooklyn, New York, for drunkenness. "They were found squabbling with a hackman near Broadway and Hazael accused one of them of stealing a buffalo robe, but it was shown that it was dragged off the back in the squabble."

Sunday Lawbreakers

Many cities had laws against holding events on Sundays. In 1879, as six-day races were reaching their height in New York City, the Brooklyn chief of police, **Patrick Campbell** (1827-1908) received complaints about walking matches being held on Sundays at Mozart Garden.

Patrick Campbell

The police chief went to see **Mayor James Howell** (1829-1997), believing that there was a law on the books against the practice and he wondered about the permit that the mayor had issued for the race. The mayor assured the chief that he had not thought about the Sunday problem. "He believed that men should go to church and that the day should be observed according to Christian custom. If such a place as Mozart Garden were kept open on Sunday by virtue of his permission, he wished to revoke the permit." Thus, in Brooklyn, the mayor disallowed races on Sundays.

James Howell

They found an obscure law on the books. "There was no statue in the State on the subject except one, which imposes a fine on a man if he is out walking anywhere on Sunday, unless it be in pursuit of charity, going after medicine or the doctor, or is on his way to church if the church is within a distance of twenty miles." They also found an ordinance against "rope-dancing, an exhibition of animals, puppet shows, or other common shows without a permit signed by the mayor." They knew they needed to pass a specific law against pedestrianism on Sundays and they intended to pursue it.

The mayor pulled the permit for the current female walking match at Mozart Garden. The justification was, "these physical shows on Sundays have become a nuisance to Brooklyn, that residents in the neighborhood are annoyed by them and that adjacent property is depreciated; that the whole thing is foreign to the traditions and habits of Brooklyn; that crowds of idle and loud tonged loiterers are gathered inside and outside the building by them, to the great annoyance of quiet and orderly families who pass on their way to and from church."

Brooklyn took a hard stance and published that week, "Sunday pedestrianism in a public hall to which the public is admitted will not in the future be tolerated in Brooklyn. The morals of the community and the peacefulness of the city on Sunday are of more importance than any 'sacrifice of calves' on the part of any number of pedestrians."

Stapleton, Staten Island

Later that same year, six women were competing in a six-day match at Stapleton, Staten Island, New York. "Two were arrested at night for violation of the Sunday law. The others escaped."

Clergymen Condemn Pedestrianism

Clergymen who were very opposed to the evils of Pedestrianism wished for ways to disrupt the races but usually just

PEDESTRIANISM VIEWED FROM THE PULPIT.
Dr. Newman, of this city, and Rev. Thompson, of Newport, are indignant over the late walking match. In their opinion the exhibition was everything that was horrible, full of all manner of wickedness and evil, and was shameful to our Christian civilization. Rev.

preached hell and damnation the Sunday following an event in their churches, hoping to stir up opposition. In 1884, a prominent clergyman came into Madison Square Garden during a race on a free ticket and sat with the reporters. "He watched the weary men for an hour in thoughtful contemplation and before he went away penciled the following lines from a well-known hymn on the pine writing table: 'Happy the man who ne'er consents by ill advice to walk.'"

Reverend W. Steele of New York used 1 Timothy 4:8 as his sermon text, "For bodily exercise profited little," He claimed that some exercise was good, "but not walking day and night for five or six days together," to which he referred to as abuse. He used it as evidence that walkers were even losing some toenails during their matches. It appalled him to see a bar in Madison Square Garden that was 65 feet long with 21 barkeepers giving out 25,000 drinks during the race, "poisoning the people." But worst of all was the gambling, where over a million dollars changed hands during a match. "A man who takes money he does not earn will steal, and I look at a gambler as a thief."

> **Evils of Pedestrianism.**
> [From the Boston Transcript.]
> "A very fine sermon, Mr. Jones,' said Deacon Brown to the parson at the close of service yesterday. "Several laps ahead of anything you ever gave us before." ": Yes," replied Parson Jones, blushing slightly. "I think myself that I made a pretty good score." Thus doth the virus of the walking match permeate and pervert all classes of society.

Reverend Edward Eggleston (1837-1902), Methodist minister and historian, preached, "When you put men on a racecourse for six mortal days and nights together, it has some elements like the old Roman gladiatorial shows. It is liable to result in the destruction of life and bring an abridgment for life."

Rev Edward Eggleston

Reverend Dr. John Phillip Newman (1826-1899), a Methodist Episcopal minister, added, "The pains of a whole life were endured in a week, and the happiness of a life was sacrificed in the same brief time. Is happiness so cheap? Others will be tempted to try and will suffer in turn. We can applaud the fireman and soldier who suffer in the discharge of their duty, but he who inflicts voluntary suffering upon himself defrauds society."

John Phillip Newman

Davy Crockett

CHAPTER SIXTEEN

George Noremac and Murder

On a summer morning in 1883 in midtown Manhattan, New York City, a young boy ran down 34th Street, getting the attention of a policeman. He cried out, "A man has killed some folks!" Officer **John Hughes** ran with the boy to a new saloon that recently opened. There he saw a man, pale, and trembling. He found out that the man was **George Noremac**, one of the most famous ultrarunners/pedestrians in the country.

Noremac led the officer up two flights of stairs to the apartment where he lived. On the dining room floor lay two dead bodies, Noremac's young wife, Elizabeth, and his longtime friend and trainer, **George Beattie**. A revolver lay on the floor near Beattie's left hand. The murder and suicide occurred while Noremac was downstairs, but his two young children, still crying, had witnessed it all. How could this have happened?

Noremac

George Duncan "Noremac" **Cameron** (1852-1922) was born in Edinburgh, Scotland in 1854. He was the oldest of nine children. His father, **John Cameron** (1834-1902) was a lithographic printer, and George took up the same occupation. Lithography artwork was becoming very popular because it could create many copies of portraits for a reasonable cost.

George Noremac

As a young adult, George became interested in running in 1872 at the age of 20. His first achievement was winning a one-mile race in 5:13 at Powder Hall Grounds, Edinburgh, Scotland. He quickly became recognized as one of the best sprinters in Scotland and would compete in various one-mile races during town fairs, always placing high. He improved his one-mile personal best to 4:21 and won three-mile races too.

In 1875, at the age of twenty-two, George married eighteen-year-old **Elizabeth Edwards** (1855-1883). She was also born in Edinburgh, growing up in a large family of nine children. Her father was a pastry and candy

George Duncan Cameron	
Scotland Marriages, 1561-1910	
Name:	George Duncan Cameron
Event Type:	Marriage
Event Date:	25 Sep 1874
Event Place:	Edinburgh, Edinburghshire, Scotland, United Kingdom
Event Place (Original):	Edinburgh Parish, Edinburgh, Midlothian, Scotland
Sex:	Male
Spouse's Name:	Elizabeth Edwards
Spouse's Sex:	Female

maker. Elizabeth also learned the candy-making business. She gave birth to four children in Scotland, **Alexander Edward Cameron** (1877-1946) and daughter **Jessie Brown Cameron** (1880-1952), and two others who died as infants. Elizabeth was described as "a short, stout woman, with regular features, light complexion and pleasing manners, with blue eyes and brown hair."

Entering Pedestrianism Sport

In 1879, long-distance pedestrianism got intense attention in Scotland as **Edward Payson Weston** barnstormed Great Britain, putting on walking exhibitions and competing in races. With so many others, George entered the sport that year. He was a small man, ideal for long-distance running, standing only 5'3" and weighing about 122 pounds.

He took on the stage name of "Noremac" which is Cameron spelled backwards. He did not originate the idea of using his transposed name as an alias. Other Camerons before him had also used the Noremac alias, both in Scotland and America.

Noremac's earliest known ultra-distance race came in July 1879. He ran in a 26-hour, outdoor six-day running tournament, at the Aberdeen Recreation Grounds in Inches, Scotland. Contestants ran four hours a day and six hours on the last day. It was put on by the 100-mile world record holder, **George Hazael** of London. "By the finish, an immense concourse of people had congregated within the enclosure, who seemed to take on eager interest in the competition, cheering one or other of the competitors whenever a spurt was made." Noremac reached an impressive 156 miles.

Noremac continued to win nearly every race. In January 1880, a two-day (12-hours per day) race was held at Perth, Scotland in Drill Hall. There were 23 starters. The track was very tiny, 31 laps to a mile. Noremac led after the first 12-hours with a remarkable 69 miles. He won by ten miles with a total of 138 miles after the two days.

Noremac's Trainer

As Noremac became serious about being a professional pedestrian, he hired **George Beattie** (1839-1883), of Scotland, age 40, to be his trainer/handler. He met him in London and hired him. He had been a private in the British Army for 22 years, and served 12 years in India where he took part in the Afghanistan war in 1878-79. He belonged to the Fifth Rifle Brigade, where he became a skilled rifleman and took part in competitions. He had recently retired as a sergeant from the service and was living on a soldier's pension, received quarterly. With no living relatives, he went to live with Noremac's family.

Prolific Successful Ultrarunner

During 1880, Noremac became a prolific ultrarunner, competing in races multiple times each month throughout Scotland. His race mileage during 1880 exceeded 4,300 miles, and he won 14 out of his 18 races. He especially found winning success competing in the 72-hour race, which was conducted over six days, 12 hours per day, and he set the distance record in Great Britain of 384 miles for that format. He won five out of eight races of the 72-hour or 74-hour format. Those in the sport took notice, and he progressed from being called a "plucky little

George Noremac

novice" to a "well-known champion."

Newport, Wales, in 1880

With his great success, Noremac competed on the bigger stages outside of Scotland and ran in his first six-day race without a daily limit in hours at the Victoria Hall in Newport, Wales, reaching 459 miles, winning 70 pounds valued at $10,500 today, probably more than he could earn in a year doing his printing job.

His friend Beattie traveled with him, performing attendant duties during his races. Noremac received special recognition by athletic clubs after he broke a British record running 66 miles in 10 hours, outdoors, at Arbroath, Scotland.

Noremac wanted to next compete against **Blower Brown** of Fulham for the six-day long distance championship of England Astley Belt, but terms with Brown could not be reached. With this frustration, he set his sights on competing in America, where there were more opportunities to race for big money.

To America

On May 27, 1881, Noremac and Beattie sailed out of Glasgow, Scotland, for America. He left his wife, **Elizabeth Cameron**, behind in Edinburgh, where she had a candy shop. He had his eyes on competing in a Rose 72-hour contest to be held on Coney Island. He did not know at the time, but with what he found in America, he had left his homeland behind forever. They arrived in New York City on June 10, 1881, and on July 3, 1881, he won the Coney Island race.

SS Circassa

Using his winnings, Noremac opened a saloon called "Walker's Rest" at Prince and Mulberry Streets across from The Basilica of St. Patrick's Cathedral in today's Nolita district in Manhattan. He moved into an apartment above the saloon with Beattie, who worked in the saloon as a bartender. Now settled, he sent Beattie back to Scotland to bring pregnant Elizabeth and his two little children to join him in America. They arrived on October 12, 1881, on the steamship *Circassia*. A daughter, **Jane Cameron**, was born in New York City that year.

Ennis Six-day Race

Noremac next competed in short five and ten-mile races in New York City and did well, but he had his eyes on a bigger prize, a six-day championship put on by **John T. Ennis** (1842-1829) of Chicago, in the American Institute in New York City held on December 26-31, 1881, with fourteen starters. This was the biggest race of his short ultrarunning career.

3,000 people witnessed the start. Noremac started slowly, but each day climbed the leaderboard. Throughout his career, he became known as a slow starter who then ran negative splits later in the week. Competitors learned that no early lead over him was safe. "Noremac aroused the boys in the dull hours long before daylight by performing lively Scotch airs on an accordion while running the race. The other racers fell in behind him, keeping step to the tunes when they were not too fast."

Astley Belt Champion, **Charles Rowell** of England, was watching, not racing. When asked about the new-comer Noremac, he said, "He is a good little man. Now here's a man I think ought to win this race. He's put together well and looks as strong as an ox." In the end, **Patrick Fitzgerald** of Long Island, New York, broke the six-day world record with 582 miles. Noremac finished third with 565 miles, winning $800 valued at $23,000 today. He had quickly established himself as one of the top six-day pedestrians in the world and became convinced that America was the land of his fortunes.

George Noremac

Diamond Whip Six-day Race in Madison Square Garden

Noremac was now accepted to compete against the big boys. His next race was in the historic Madison Square Garden held February 27-March 4, 1882, against a very tough field of ten championship runners who had all before exceeded 500 miles in six days. It was perhaps the greatest six-day race in history. They were competing for a diamond-studded whip. Noremac received help from friends/backers for the required enormous $1,000 entrance fee, each contributing $100. Going into the race, he weighed only 118 pounds, had a 35-inch chest, 13-inch calves, and 18-inch thighs.

BEGINNING THE LONG WALK

OPENING OF THE SIX DAYS' PEDESTRIAN CONTEST.

A GREAT CROWD ASSEMBLED TO SEE THE START—THE PRELUDE OF "SACRED" MUSIC—HART IN THE RACE—HUGHES LEADING ALL THE REST.

Strange Running Tales: When Ultrarunning was a Reality Show

Madison Square Garden was heated by steam and, during the night, was illuminated by 30 electric lights. They boarded certain windows up to keep the gatecrashers out. "The bookmakers were in full force with their tin boxes and sat at little tables near the stand fitted up for newspaper reporters, timekeepers, and scores." **Patrick Gilmore's** 50-piece band played popular songs. The start was witnessed by about 8,000 people. "The great gathering was in an uproar of excitement when at 12 o'clock by the judges' timepiece, Referee Busby gave the word 'Go.' The champions bounded away like deer."

Gilmore's Band

The race initially was highly competitive without drama. "Although the crowd was large, there was less enthusiasm manifested than has been witnessed in previous contests. Except when the band of musicians gave vent to their feelings, the scene was almost funereal. The spectators stared at each other oftener than they did at the champions." The massive bar did good business but ran out of beer and liquors during the first night.

A rumor circulated that the Astley Belt holder, **Charles Rowell**, was using stimulants to stay in the lead. A judge approached his handlers and asked about stimulant used. The reply was, "'Yes, we are stimulating Charley.' 'What are you giving him, beef tea?' 'No, chicken wings and bread.' Just then he handed Rowell a nicely broiled wing and a piece of bread." Meanwhile, "Noremac (age 29), the most boyish-looking of the competitors, plodded along with his stalwart legs close together, his frail trunk erect and his thin arms stiff at his side." Another description read, "Noremac walks or runs with a straightforward

movement, raising his body slightly with each step."

On the third day, he was in last place among the remaining seven champions, some who were on world-record pace. Noremac did not give up and was one of the few that constantly did sprints to increase his pace. At the end of the race, George Hazel broke the six-day world record with 600 miles. Noremac climbed to third place with 555 miles, winning him $3,060, valued at $88,800 today, an incredible fortune for a week's work on the track. "He seemed nearly exhausted at the finish. For some time, he walked painfully, with his mouth open and his lips swollen and discolored."

Noremac's family life had its sadness. On July 20, 1882, their one-year-old daughter, **Jane Cameron**, died at their home at 47 Prince, Manhattan, New York City and was buried in Calvary Cemetery. **Elizabeth Cameron** was pregnant at the time, and a few months later gave birth to another daughter, **Georgina Cameron.**

Championship of the World

Table of the Best Records.

The following are the best records made up to this time:

	M.	L.
Hazael, go-as-you-please	600	1
Vint, go-as-you-please	578	0
Hughes, go-as-you-please	564	0
Rowell, go-as-you-please	566	0
Noremac, go-as-you-please	555	0
Hart, go-as-you-please	565	0
Weston, go-as-you-please	550	0
Harriman, heel-and-toe	530	0
Sullivan, go-as-you-please	525	4
Campana, go-as-you-please	525	0
O'Leary, heel-and-toe	520	0

On October 23, 1882, Noremac started in another big-time six-day race in Madison Square Garden for the "Championship of the World." His entrance fee was $500. Nine champion runners were in the race, all with 550+ mile six-day finishes. "Noremac has trained fine as a thoroughbred. His skin is clear, and his eyes shine like a ferret's." He came out wearing striped drab trunks, a white shirt, and a red and blue cap.

The initial pace was torrid. After 12 hours, **John Hughes** had reached 85 miles and Noremac 75. As usual, he slowed, and reached 100 miles in just over 18 hours. "The band played every fifteen minutes and the colored gas jets were rendered nearly invisible by the brightness of the electric lights." After midnight, a spectator fell headlong out of a gallery box to the floor but did not break any bones.

After three and a half days, the race became very tight, with the top six all within 15 miles of each other. On day five it was reported, "Noremac was wretched in the extreme. His face was wasted and he walked around with his body bent as if he had pains in his stomach." But he climbed into second place with 507 miles.

> **OVER THE SAWDUST TRACK**
>
> NINE MEN IN THE WALKING MATCH
>
> Hazael, Rowell, Fitzgerald, Vint, Hughes, Noremac, Hart, Herty and Panchot Contesting for the Championship of the World—The Start at Midnight.

During the final day, gatecrashers poured into the building from a window where the wire grating had been loosened and pulled back. About fifty boys came in per minute. "Occasionally the hole would come clogged with boys and then there would be a momentary stoppage." This wild influx of attendance made the Garden noisier than it had been for the entire event.

For the final evening, Noremac came out looking like a jockey in bright green cap, brown jacket and white tights. In the end, Fitzgerald won with 577 miles, and Noremac can in second with a lifetime personal best of 567 miles, which was a Scottish record that has lasted through the ages, even to this day. He won about $1,150 and ended out the year a very rich man.

Sadness returned to his family when their one-year-old daughter, **Georgina Cameron**, died. This was Noremac and Elizabeth's fourth child that died in infancy. He refrained from racing for several months and likely concentrated on his saloon business. On June 21, 1883, Noremac became a U.S. citizen. Life looked good in America for Noremac.

> **FITZGERALD THE WINNER.**
>
> THE CLOSE OF A WALK THAT WAS NOT ALTOGETHER SUCCESSFUL.
>
> Very Little Money Left Above Expenses to Divide Among the Pedestrians—Receipts from Admissions Less than $20,000.

Family Strife

In August 1883, Noremac sold his saloon and opened a new one on 466 8th Avenue between 33rd and 34th Street, called "Midlothian Arms," in Midtown Manhattan. A saloon was on the first floor and the basement contained a billiard room and a bowling alley. On the third floor was a nice five-room family apartment with a front parlor, two bedrooms, a dining room, and a kitchen. He spent all his savings on the new place.

The living quarters were crowded. Noremac's trainer, Beattie living with them, slept on a sofa in the parlor. **Peter Campbell**, Noremac's brother-in-law, and **James Barclay**, a Scotsman, lived in one of the bedrooms. Noremac, his wife and children slept on a large folding bed in the dining room. Another boarder had been using the other bedroom, but he had just died from a stroke.

George Beattie had become a changed man since he had been associating and drinking so much with gamblers on the sport. He drank so excessively while working as a bartender in his former place that Noremac fired him as a bartender. He offered to keep him on as a billiard maker, but that made Beattie angry. Things got nasty. Beattie started to drink heavily and annoy everyone working on the new saloon, especially the new bartender. He was also angry at Noremac for not including him in the negotiations for purchasing the new saloon.

When Noremac and Elizabeth returned one evening from a picnic of the Midlothian Society, he discovered that Beattie had been drunk and used abusive language toward the workmen who were putting on the finishing touches for the saloon. "A quarrel between the two men led to blows and Noremac knocked Beattie down and gave him two black eyes. Beattie decided to go to Canada, where he could collect his pension money, but he continued to remain an unwelcome inhabitant of the house."

Beattie thought Noremac had become ungrateful of all his work for him over the years. Elizabeth had become fed up with Beattie, declaring that he was a nuisance in the house. Beattie, probably in a fit of revenge, told Noremac that Elizabeth had been going out secretly at night, implying that she was having an affair with someone. He was obviously causing some serious domestic stress in the family.

It all came to a head on the morning of August 23, 1883. "Noremac threw out some hints of what Beattie had said about her while she was making ready to get breakfast. She was angry and when her husband was going downstairs, she said to him, 'Beattie has been telling you some lies about me.'" Her look was so calm that Noremac made some light reply and went down to the saloon without giving it a further thought. It is believed that after he left, she confronted Beattie about his lies, and they had a terrible argument.

Murder – Suicide

A little of 10 a.m., a boy ran down West 34th Street and got the attention of a patrolman, **John Hughes**, telling him he needed to go to 466 8th Avenue. He asked the boy why. The reply was, "A man has killed some folks." That got Hughes' attention, and he ran to the four-story brick building where Noremac had his new saloon and living quarters on the third floor.

34th Street in 1880

"Noremac met the officer at the door. His face was pale, and he was trembling with excitement. Two or three other men told the policeman that Noremac's wife had been killed by his trainer, **George Beattie**, who had killed himself as well. They led the way up two flights of stairs to the rear dining room, on the floor of which lay two bodies."

"Elizabeth Cameron lay near the door of a small kitchen. She had been killed by a bullet which passed through her head. Beattie's body was in the opposite corner, near a window. He was shot in the left side of the head, near the ear. A large 44-caliber 'British bulldog' revolver lay on the floor near his left hand." On the dinner table were three place settings for breakfast with bread, fried onions, and some newly cooked liver.

"Noremac looked at his wife's body for a moment and then sat down on a chair and buried his face in his hands." The policeman took him out of the room and downstairs and brought to him his six-year-old son, Alexander, who had witnessed the killings.

How it Happened

Here is how it happened. **Alexander Cameron** said that his mother and Beattie had quarreled in the kitchen and that his mother was shot there. "She staggered into the dining room and fell near the door. The boy was too frightened to notice all that happened in the next few seconds, but he heard another shot and saw Beattie fall in the other corner of the room."

The two boarders, **Campbell** and **Barclay**, who had been up late at night bowling in the basement, had been asleep in the middle room when they were awakened by the first gunshot. They quickly dressed and then heard the second shot. Barclay ran downstairs to find Noremac, and Campbell went to investigate.

"Opening the door, he beheld a sight that for several minutes completely overpowered him. Stretched at full length on the floor lay Mrs. **Elizabeth Cameron**, with blood gushing from her mouth, saturating her hair. Kneeling over the dying form of Mrs. Cameron were her two children. The elder boy was trying to stop the flow of blood which came from his mother's mouth. Campbell, who is rather of a timid nature, as soon as he recovered from the shock caused by the sight, hurried downstairs."

Barclay previously ran downstairs to the saloon, where Noremac was behind the bar, waiting until breakfast was ready. They yelled, "Someone is being shot!" Noremac asked where, and they told him it was in the dining room.

MURDER AND SUICIDE

MR. BEATTIE KILLS MRS. CAMERON AND SHOOTS HIMSELF.

THE TRAGEDY WHICH NOREMAC'S FALSE FRIEND CAUSED IN THE HOME OF THE PEDESTRIAN YESTERDAY.

Noremac went upstairs to find his children screaming and his wife dying. She gave a last gasp and died without a word. Little Alexander was crying, "Mamma is killed! Mamma is dead." Noremac  picked up the two children, moved them to another room, and then went back downstairs, staggered, and fell into a chair, pale, hardly able to speak, and asked someone to get a policeman. A boy was sent.

Once the police were through with the investigation after a couple of hours, Noremac said to a friend, "Get his body out of the house. Don't let him stay a moment longer than you can help."

Elizabeth Cameron, who died at the young age of 28, was buried in Evergreens Cemetery, in Brooklyn. Beattie did not leave behind enough to pay for his burial. The shocking news was published all over America and Great Britain. Some  newspapers blamed the whole affair on drinking and the shady gambling sport of pedestrianism.

Noremac stepped aside from racing for eight months to get his life back together and to start training again. He soon married again to "a little Scotch woman."

Running Again

In April 1884, Noremac ran again for six days in Madison Square Garden, where **Patrick Fitzgerald** broke the world record, raising it to 610 miles. Noremac finished 4th place, with 545 miles, winning $1,400, his fifth time going over 500 miles in six days. He was on his way again to compete regularly.

Strange Running Tales: When Ultrarunning was a Reality Show

In July 1884, there were strange happenings at a six-day race in Chicago. On the first day, hot-head **John Hughes** claimed scorers deducted ten miles from his score. Noremac stepped off the track and struck Hughes. Then a runner riot started. **Daniel Burns**, **Frank Hart**, and a backer kept up the disturbance and were arrested. Burns even struck an officer. Noremac quit the race. Hart was told to leave the city. Daniel O'Leary, who put on the race, denounced Hughes' behavior. "He said Hughes was a chronic kicker and had been barred from walking matches all over the country. He started the fight."

5,100 Mile Walk

On November 3, 1884, Noremac started an attempt to walk 51 miles each day for 100 consecutive days (except Sundays), for 5,100 miles, which would break Edward Payson Weston's record of 5,000 miles in 100 days. The terms included that he could not walk for more than 15 hours each day. A wager of $2,000 was made. He walked each day from 9 a.m. to midnight on a tiny indoor sawdust track, 44 laps to a mile, in his own saloon on 8th Street, allowing him to sleep upstairs in his apartment. This was also great marketing for his establishment.

One hundred people could pack into the small hall (70×28 feet) in New York City to watch him make his 8,976 turns each day. Pedestrian **Sammy Day** helped crew him and rubbed him down at stops.

For entertainment, a piano and violin played to spur him on. He ate six meals a day and fell to only 102 pounds at one point. He said his run was "spiritless, and the excitement was wanting, hence the task was monotonous and dreary" He succeeded on February 26, 1884. This was his most famous accomplishment.

However, some sporting authorities said they would not sanction the record for administrative reasons. "He was scored and clocked by competent and reliable people, but he failed to request the assistance of some authority so that the great feat, when accomplished could not be gainsaid as a record. The fact that he failed to have the timing and scoring authenticated debars the performance from taking precedence over Weston's feat." He vowed to do the attempt again with proper scoring, but never did.

Normac was asked why so many pedestrians smoked. He said that he smoked only a little but believed that smoking was stimulating to pedestrians. He liked a good strong smoke, but not when hard pressed by opponents in a race.

Roller skating for Six Days

In 1885, the first six-day roller-skating race was held in Madison Square Garden while Noremac was walking circles in his saloon. The event was popular, but not a financial success and the winner, 18-year-old **William Donovan**, a newsboy from Elmira, New York, who reached

Madison Square Garden

1,092 miles, died a couple months later from pneumonia.

But despite those disappointments, another roller-skating match was scheduled and Noremac entered, in spite of only recently starting to learn how to use the primitive skates at the time. He believed his six-day experience would overcome his inexperience on skates. The event was again held in Madison Square Garden with 15 skaters. It was said, "Poor Noremac could skate very little," and he immediately fell into last place and quit the race after 16 miles in 1:49. **John Alexander Snowden** (1862-1889), a 22-year-old blacksmith of East Boston, won with a world record 1,166 miles and the event was a financial failure. Noremac would continue to practice his skating and occasionally do short exhibitions.

Competitions during 1887-1888

Noremac took six months off, returning in 1886, competing each month in the upper Midwest. He would win in the money but with only few wins. In February 1887, in Easton, Pennsylvania, he broke a 72-hour six-day record by a mile, reaching 415 miles. He would hold that record until broken by **Peter Golden** (1943-1933) in 1888 with 430 miles.

Easton, Pennsylvania

Noremac, now trained by a very competent trainer, **Joseph Miller**, continued his prolific racing in 1887. He was highly competitive. At a six-day race in Philadelphia, where he placed fourth, with 501 miles, it was commented, "Noremac is very cross and whimsical. The feeling between Noremac and **Peter Panchot** is very bitter and they call each other names every time they get close enough. There is some fear that Noremac may lose his temper and get into a personal encounter."

Noremac

In February 1888, he competed in a major six-day race in Madison Square Garden with 24 runners. "The buxom wife of George Noremac, who has been in attendance on her plucky husband all through the race, has established herself at housekeeping in a sort of front wing to his booth." When a bagpiper played, Noremac ran with a smile on his face. **James Albert (Cathcart)** (1856-1912) broke the six-day world record in 621 miles. Noremac reached 525 miles, finishing in eighth place, and winning $240 for all his work.

Runners Against Cyclist

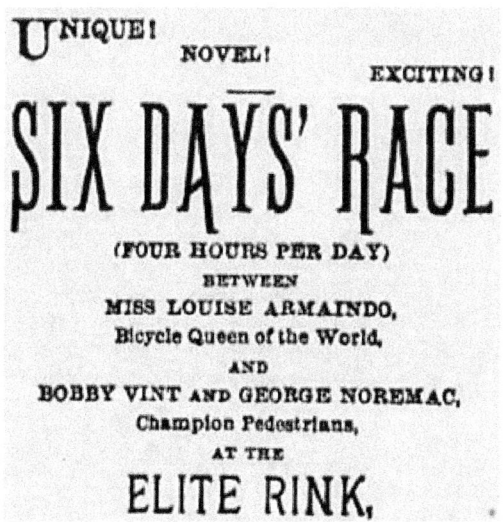

Louise Armaindo

In March 1888, Noremac and **Robert Vint** competed in a novel competition against a female champion Canadian cyclist, **Louise Armaindo** (1861-1900), at Elite Rink in Philadelphia, Pennsylvania. The race was for six days, four hours per day. Noremac's and Vint's running miles were added together against Armaindo's biking miles. Thousands came each night to watch. "Noremac showed some of the remarkable speed for which he is noted, and in several spurts down the side stretches of the track he held his own against the wheel. Miss Armaindo received more bouquets, baskets and horseshoe arrangements than they could carry away." In the end, the ultrarunners won in a very close race all week, 328 miles to 326 miles.

George Littlewood's Historic World Record

Noremac competed in the historic Fox Championship Belt race in November/December 1888, in Madison Square Garden, when **George Littlewood** (1859-1912) of England broke the six-day world record with 623 miles, a record that would stand for nearly a century. Noremac finished

The following was the final score in miles:

Littlewood	623 0	Golden	534 0
Herty	605 0	Mason	528 0
Moore	553 0	Taylor	450 0
Cartwright	546 0	Campana	450 0
Noremac	542 0	Elson	421 0
Hart	539 0	C. Smith	301 0
Howarth	536 0	Peach	262 0
Connor	536 0		

in fifth place, covering 542 miles, winning $573. Ten runners covered at least 500 miles in the most competitive six-day race in history. Five of them had first names of "George."

Moved to Philadelphia

In 1888, he moved to Philadelphia, Pennsylvania, where many pedestrian races were being held, and he opened a cigar store. In April 1889, he won a major six-day race in Pittsburgh with 501 miles, but after that he raced less often and fell out of shape.

1889 race in Pittsburgh

By late 1889, he discovered that maintaining the championship form was becoming harder. He admitted he was not in top condition, and it showed when he finished last with only 212 miles in 72-hour six-day race in Pittsburgh. Any winnings earned were far less than in prior years and his backers lost large amounts of money.

But Noremac did not give up. His wife helped crewed him in at his races, watching her plodding husband with constant and anxious eyes. "His wife, a large, buxom woman, is his trainer and attendant, and there is no more faithful or skillful one in the business." Finally, in March 1890, in Detroit, he got back into his groove and placed second in a six-day race with 500 miles winning $424.

But at age 37, he was a mid-pack runner and just couldn't break into winning the big races again. He battled injury, causing him to skip months of races. It was said of him, "He can be depended upon to stay on the track

Mrs Noremac

until the walk is over, but not as a rule a first prize winner, but he usually wins some prize."

Noremac

In March 1891, he ran in a six-day race in Madison Square Garden with 43 entrants. It was billed as, "A determined attempt to revive the interest in pedestrianism." He reached 525 miles, qualifying him for a share of the profits. It was at least the 12th time in his career that he exceeded 500 miles in a six-day race. After the race, it was called, "The greatest fizzle of a six day walk that was ever held. It has been a most dismal failure from the standpoint of sport, and its promoters and everybody connected with the affair have lost money."

Comeback Attempt

Noremac's last truly competitive six-day race was in May 1891 in Madison Square Garden, when at the age of 39, he finished in sixth, with 525 miles. Finding it difficult to win money, Noremac went into retirement as fewer six-day races were being held. In 1896, he married for the third time, **Delia (Cobey) Miller** (1859-) in Philadelphia. She had recently divorced her husband. They stayed together for the rest of his life.

In May 1899, at the age of 47, Noremac was determined to compete again as six-day races were trying to make a comeback. He competed in a 72-hour, six-day race in New York City at the Grand Central Palace on a track 13 laps to a mile. He was the old-timer in the race. He came in last place. Two doctors with the Board of Health visited and threatened

Original Grand Central Palace

to take all the old runners off the track. He continued to try to compete but always finished in the back. The new Mrs. Noremac would help during the races. His comeback attempt was partially successful in 1901 at the age of 49 when he finished fourth at a six-day race in Pittsburgh, Pennsylvania with 414 miles, winning him "an immense bouquet of chrysanthemums."

It can be said that Noremac never fully retired from Pedestrianism, the sport retired on him. He kept competing to the bitter end in 1903 until most competitions were discontinued due to lack of interest and local laws put in against such events. His last known true race was a relay race in November 1903, when he was 51 years old. He teamed up with fellow old-timer, **Sammy Day,** in a six-day race at the Industrial Hall in Philadelphia, Pennsylvania on a track measuring 17 laps to a mile. They dropped out on the second day.

Running Finally Over

In January 1908, when Noremac was 56, Akron, Ohio, thought it would be fun to put on a six-day race and invited many of the aging pedestrians for a nostalgic race. Enormous crowds came out. "Noremac appears periodically on the track and adds to the amusement of the crowds. The shrewd little Scotsman's observations on his competitors have proved an unfailing source of amusement to the watchers." He came in last with 73 miles, only able to walk a few days and not truly trying.

In 1910 it was written, "The six-day go-as-you-please foot races seem to be a thing of the past, although one or two feeble attempts have been made in recent years to revive the sport. We no longer hear of men who have international reputations as six-day runners and the deeds of old-timers seem destined to remain on record."

Noremac spent his final years operating a small hotel and saloon in Philadelphia and still selling cigars. On February 15, 1922, George D Cameron, "Noremac," died, at the age of 69, because of pneumonia and contributing heart disease. "The class of Noremac in his chosen field may be judged from the fact that he finished in the money in

AN OLD-TIME SPORT DYING OUT.

Six-Day-Go-as-You-Please Races Almost a Thing of the Past.

VETERAN RUNNER'S FUNERAL TOMORROW

George D. Noremac, Noted Scotch Athlete, Succumbs to Pneumonia at 69 nearly every race in which he took part." It was also impressive how he perfected the strategy of negatives splits, more miles during the final three days compared to the first they days of a six-day race.

George Noremac was perhaps the most prolific six-day ultrarunner in history. It is estimated that he finished about 80 six-day races, reaching more than 300 miles in nearly all of them, and exceeding 500 miles in sixteen of them. In all, his career miles in races exceeded 30,000 miles, spanning 25 years.

Noremac was buried in Arlington Cemetery in Philadelphia, not next to his murdered first wife, Elizabeth, buried and forgotten in New York City.

Left to Right - Fitzgerald, Rowell, and Noremac

Davy Crockett

CHAPTER SEVENTEEN

The Strange and Tragic

In 1882, it was declared, "The six-day walking matches are the sickest swindles gamblers have yet invented for defrauding a virtuous public." Well, many of both the public and the running participants were not the most virtuous people on the planet at that time, contributing to the wild strange stories that continually occurred related to the sport of ultrarunning/pedestrianism.

Also, this opinion expressed in the New York Herald was common: "A six-day walking match is a more brutal exhibition than a prize fight or a gladiatorial contest. In the last half of a six-day walk, nearly every contestant is vacant minded or literally crazy. He becomes an unreasoning animal, whom his keepers find sometimes sullen, sometimes savage, but never sensible." During this era, from 1875 to 1909, competitors worldwide raced in at least 400 six-day events, and millions of people paid to watch. The stranger things that occurred related to the sport of that age were a collection of surprises and tragedies.

John Dermody Joins a Women's Six-day Race

In December 1879, **John Dermody**, age 45, was a homeless lemon peddler in Brooklyn, New York. The six-day race ultrarunning/pedestrian fever was raging in America. He believed that his business had hardened his leg muscles with great strength and that he would make an excellent professional pedestrian, and he longed to compete in one of the dozens of races that were being held in the New York City area that year.

Dermody could find no one to back him financially and help him pay an entrance fee to a race.

Brooklyn, 1880

A Women's International Six-Day Tournament was scheduled for December 15-20, 1879, in Madison Square Garden with 26 entrants. As it approached, Dermody became so interested in it that he had been unable to think or talk of anything else.

On the Sunday afternoon before the start, Dermody entered the Darwin & Kindelon saloon at 507 Third Avenue,

drinking perhaps too much and jabbering about the sport of walking, wishing that he could see the start of the women's tournament. Darwin, a known practical joker, asked Dermody how he would like to enter this contest. "Dermody seemed perfectly delighted. His acceptance of the proposition was hailed by some practical jokers as a good chance for amusement, and they at once began to improvise a female wardrobe which would conceal his sex. His flowing reddish beard was shaved off in a neighboring barber shop, and he was dressed in a calico skirt and spotted jacket."

They added a pair of long stockings, a handkerchief around his head, a blue veil around his neck, and three yards of white gauze to make a sash to hide his face. They made a bib number with "32" to be suspended from his neck. Ready to go, his new backers took him to Madison Square Garden, where the race was about to start.

Out on the Track

"The party hid his raiment under an overcoat as they entered and unshrouding him in a sequestered part of the place. That done, they slipped him under the railing out on the track and away he sped, with his arms going like windmills and his raiment flying out behind him like a comet. A batch of the authentic contestants had just passed, and the counterfeit put on a spurt to overhaul them."

A roar of laughter arose as the audience began to discover what was going on. Around the track he went in a happy-go-lucky style, trying to catch up to the leader. Just as he was finishing the first lap, Sergeant Keating of the 29th precinct, observant that the bib number 32 made no sense because there were only 26 starters, stepped on the track to arrest Dermody.

A Man in Woman's Clothing on the Track.

Arrest

"It was no easy matter catching up with the phenomenal contestant, but the Sergeant at length brought Dermody's pace down to a walk and made a circuit of the track in his captor's custody." He locked him up for the night at the precinct.

The next day they arraigned him at the Jefferson Market Police Court with the charge of being intoxicated. He was still wearing his costume from the previous evening. "When Sergeant Keating told his story, the stranger's real character was afforded by a person in the court, who, it appears, was responsible for the masquerade in pursuance of a practical joke."

Justice Bixby, probably laughing, decided that Dermody had been sufficiently punished and set him free. He went off "at an orthodox pedestrian pace," probably still happy that he had been able to participate in a pedestrian race.

Jefferson Market Courthouse

George Cartwright – Scoundrel

Too often, nineteen century ultrarunners put the sport ahead of their families and some could be referred to as scoundrels or cads. **George Cartwright** (1848-1925+) was a laborer of Caxton, near Walsall, England and became one of the most famous and accomplished British long-distance runners of the time. He entered the sport in the early 1880s competing successfully at the shorter distance ultras, such as the six-hour race. He was a true runner, with great speed, and started to be referred to as "the champion of England."

In February 1880, at the age of 32, Cartwright ran in his first multi-day race, a seven-day contest in Nottingham, England, six hours per day and won with 270 miles. Seven months later, in September 1880, he competed in a major six-day, 12-hours per day race in London, at the massive Agricultural Hall. There were 29 starters, and he went out fast with the more experienced front-runners, reaching 76 miles in the first 12 hours. But after day two, he quit the race after reaching 138 miles with a foot injury. He healed up and continued to compete in six-day, six hours per day races for the next couple of years.

Arrested for Deserting Family

But then Cartwright got into legal trouble. On April 24, 1882, he started in a six-day race for the Astley Championship Belt held at Drill Hall in Sheffield, England with 25 starters. As usual, he went out very fast, cheered by 2,000 spectators. He finished the first 12-hour day in the lead with 76 miles.

On the third day, he fell well behind the leaders, and he decided to quit the race. As he started his journey to his room at midnight, an officer arrested him. The warrant charged him for deserting his wife and five children, who became wards of the Lichfield Guardians. News reports of the race helped authorities locate him. "He was taken to a police cell instead of to the comfortable training quarters to which he had been no doubt looking forward after his pedestrian exertions."

Drill Hall, Sheffield, England

When he was brought before the court, instead of showing concern and going to help his family, he wanted to pay the costs incurred by the Guardians, so that he could stay in Sheffield. The court stated that they had no authority to accept his payoff money, and assigned an officer to take him to Lichfield, Staffordshire, England. 70 miles away, to be dealt with. Evidently, he settled the complaint and just two weeks later was again racing in Dundee, Scotland, far from his family, in a 26-hour race which he quit after 71 miles because of a sore ankle.

Cartwright Attacked During Race

In October 1882, while competing for the Astley Champion Long Distance Belt at Bingley Hall in Birmingham, England, a strange incident occurred. He was leading the 12-hours per day six-day race, reaching 82 miles on the first day. Large wagers had been bet on the results. "On day two, Cartwright was attacked upon the course by one of the spectators who dealt him a violent blow across the head, with a heavy bludgeon, causing the blood to flow copiously for several minutes."

"It was thought that the injury would necessitate the removal of the competitor from the course, but encouraged by his friends, Cartwright resumed his journey soon after, wiping the blood from his face as he went along. The police arrested one man, but it is considered doubtful whether he was the actual assailant." Cartwright later broke down on day three and quit the race George Littlewood won with 415 miles, breaking the world record for that six-day format.

Over the next few years, Cartwright established himself as one of the best six-day pedestrians in the world, achieving a personal best of 570 miles at Sharonen, England. During that race, he reached an astonishing 152 miles on the first day. If true, it was a world record for 24-hours. On February 23, 1887, he broke the 50-mile world record at Westminster Aquarium in London with an amazing time of 5:55:04. That mark would stand for decades.

To America

With all his success in Great Britain, it was time for Cartwright to take his talents to America. He sailed for America on January 4, 1888, on the steamship *Ohio* to compete in the Six Day's International Go-

SS Ohio

as-you-please Race at Madison Square Garden on February 6-11, 1888. After a two-week ocean voyage, he arrived in New York City. He was brash in his predictions. "Records don't frighten me. Anybody who beats me in this race will have to beat 625 miles." The current world record for six days was 610 miles, held by **Patrick Fitzgerald** of Long Island City, New York.

The big race started with 47 runners. Unfortunately, Cartwright had caught a cold while training on Coney Island, and during the race was seized with "inflammation of the lungs." He quit after reaching only 105 miles. Later that night outside his hut, several of the trainers got in a wild fight, smashing sticks and chairs over each other's heads. Yes, these six-day race sideshows were always unpredictable. **James Albert** of Philadelphia, Pennsylvania, went on to break the world record with 621 miles.

THE START.

After competing in a couple more races, he returned to England to take care of some business, but then quickly returned to America for an extended stay on the steamship *Servia*. "On the journey, he took practice runs three times a day on the deck of the steamer. An eight-lap to a mile track was measured off and some days he covered as much as 45 miles. His work was watched with interest by other passengers." He was eager to establish himself firmly as the champion of England, hoping to beat the new sensation, young George Littlewood. Cartwright went into training on Staten Island for another six-day race at Madison Square Garden.

The race began on May 7, 1888, with 42 starters, including most of the world's best six-day ultrarunners.

START OF THE SIX-DAY WALK.

Madison Square Crowded to See the Pedestrians Get Away.

5,000 people viewed the start, including 100 police officers who kept the peace. Cartwright, for some reason, despised his fellow countryman George Littlewood and wanted to see him defeated. Well, Cartwright's race was another bust. Once Littlewood seemed to break down, Cartwright's motivation went away, and he quit on the third day with 202 miles. "He lacked the grit to stand punishment. He had satisfied himself and everybody else that he was not a six-day pedestrian." With his speed, everyone thought he was better suited for lower distances of 50 or 100 miles. Littlewood recovered and won with 611 miles, just ten miles short of the world record.

Cartwright in Trouble Again

Cartwright continued to compete in American races throughout 1888 and did win at times. But his secret scoundrel ways surfaced. In September 1888, at Saratoga Springs, New York, he won a six-day, four hours per day race with a world best of 185 miles. He then made Saratoga his training headquarters. It was soon revealed why he enjoyed being in this remote resort town in Upstate New York, home of horse racing, gambling, and luxury hotels.

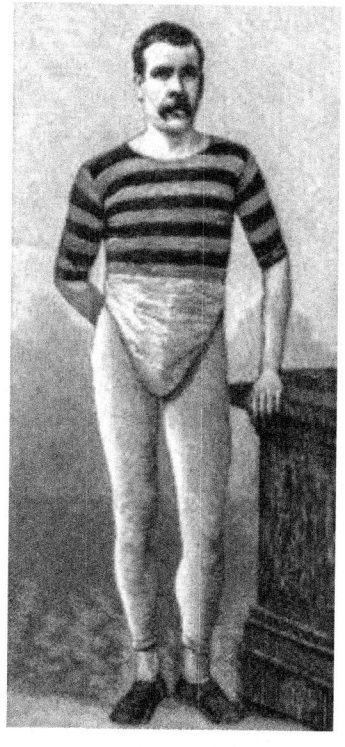

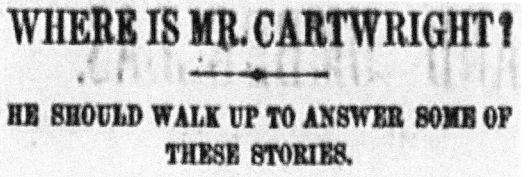

In late 1888, Cartwright, age 40, proposed marriage to Mary Hawkins, age 26, of Staffords Bridge, New York. The marriage was going to take place in Saratoga. But Cartwright still had a wife and children back in England, who he certainly was still neglecting. Word got out a few days before the wedding that he was entering a bigamist marriage. He denied being married and even made arrangements for an apartment to live in with his new young bride.

When the marriage ceremony was to take place on December 6, 1888, Cartwright

GEORGE CARTWRIGHT RUNS AWAY.
The Pedestrian Accused of Trying to Commit Bigamy.

was a no-show. He left his bride at the altar and was going to flee back to England. This infuriated her brother, who vowed to wreak vengeance if he found him anywhere in America. A reporter searched Saratoga unsuccessfully trying to find him. Even his sporting friends did not know where he was.

Billy O'Brien, the manager of the recently concluded Fox Diamond Belt six-day race at Madison Square Garden said, "He acted very shabbily towards the management of the race. I paid his entrance fee, his training expenses, other bills during the race, and also advance him some money in cash. He promised to settle everything but has not kept his promise." Cartwright finished sixth in this race with 546 miles. This was the race where his nemesis, **George Littlewood**, broke the six-day world record with 623 miles, a record that would stand for nearly a century.

George Cartwright

SILENTLY SAILED AWAY.

Cartwright's Saratoga Fiancee was not Seen When the Pedestrian Took Passage.

The day after the jilted wedding, it was reported that he was at Putnam House in New York City, but left early in the morning with his baggage, and went to board steamer *Umbria* for England. No one saw him off, so it appeared to be a secret rushed departure. Someone found him before he left, and he denied ever proposing marriage to Miss Hawkins.

Once the heat was off, Cartwright returned to America about a month later, apparently with his wife, with plans to stay. He claimed he was looking for the man who originated what he said was the false story about his attempted marriage. But he quickly resumed racing in California, far away from Saratoga Springs, New York. In June 1889, it was reported that he was suffering from malaria, staying with his wife in New York City.

As six-day races became fewer in the mid-1890s, Cartwright took up long-distance bicycle racing in 1894 and competed in his first six-day riding race in Chicago's Tattersall's in February 1897. At age 48, he was over-the-top confident, with his experience running six-day races and his ability to stay out on the track without sleep. "I do not like to boast, but I am going to beat the record." For some reason he falsely stated that he was 42 years old. He only lasted one day and about 300 miles. The winner rode 1,788 miles in six days. In 1898, he claimed he had been testing bikes

for a manufacturer in Syracuse, New York, and covered 25,000 miles, which is highly unlikely. In 1899, he returned to six-day running races competing during the waning years through 1908.

On June 29, 1901, at the age of 52, Cartwright became a U.S. citizen at Syracuse, New York and lived out his years there. He died after 1925.

Weary Pedestrian Shot his Wife

Way back in November 1850, **Robert Harriett "Mickey Free"** (1813-) of Liverpool, England finished a walk of 1,100 miles in 1,100 consecutive hours, one mile each hour, which is a variation of the standard **1,000×1,000 Barclay Match** that was a rage for years. He was a noted British runner of that era, who had success winning races of distances of a mile or more. His every-hour walk lasted for 44 days and was accomplished outdoors at Strawberry Gardens in Everson, England despite some severe weather along the way.

On November 20, 1850, a week after completing his walking task, he and his wife, **Mary Harriett**, a seamstress, went into the pub "Jamaica Vaults." He ordered a beer for himself and some whiskey for his wife. "In his hand, he held a pistol, with which he said he would blow someone's brains out before he slept that night. The boy who served the liquor asked him for payment, upon which Harriett said he would shoot the boy if he said another word."

He then placed the pistol on the counter, left the pub, went to a store, and purchased ignition caps for his gun. He told the store clerk that he was going out to shoot. Returning to the pub, he called for another beer. His wife came back in and asked him to go home with her. "He replied, 'Go from my presence, or I'll shoot you.' He then took aim with the pistol at his wife, upon which she rushed forward, but he pulled the trigger, and shot her through the right hand. After making an inquiry as to whether he had killed his wife, he gave up the pistol, and was taken into custody."

His poor wife was rushed to the hospital, and it was necessary to amputate two of her fingers. She was in serious condition. When police interrogated Harriett, he told them about his weary 1,100 miles that he had recently walked. He had bought the pistol from the landlord of Strawberry Gardens that was used to shoot off during the night to wake him up each hour. "Since completing his pedestrian feat, whenever he got any drink, he did not know what he was doing, and as to his wife and children, he loved them most dearly. He then wept bitterly and was committed for trial." His wife remained in the hospital for many days.

At the trial, he defended himself and couldn't understand how it happened, that he could not remember that night. The jury returned a verdict of guilt, but strongly recommended mercy for him. The judge said it did not surprise him that the great exertion of his walk, and the lack of rest, caused Harriett to experience "considerable nervous excitement and irritability." Combined with the vice of intoxication, it produced a most brutalizing effect on him. But that didn't excuse him for his actions. He was sentenced to prison with hard labor for nine months.

Baltimore City Prison

Race with a Wooden Leg

During that same month, in 1850, another pedestrian event grabbed the attention of London newspaper readers. Two men engaged in a 13-mile walking match from Plymouth to Ivybridge, England. One man was a tailor who had a wooden leg, and the other man was known as "Giant Grumbo." The race started at midnight. "They left at that hour and the tailor kept well up 'till within two miles of Ivybridge, when his stump broke in two and his competitor came off victorious.

Pedestrian's Wife Burned to Death

Tragedies that came into the lives of these famous pedestrians were often noted in the newspapers.

Thomas Howarth (1860-1932) was from Lancashire, England. He started running at the age of 12 when he ran a mile in less than six minutes.

Strange Running Tales: When Ultrarunning was a Reality Show

A few years later, he emigrated to America to Atlantic City, New Jersey, and Philadelphia, Pennsylvania. He was a runner, not a walker. He set an American record for 25 miles, with 2:41 and clocked 50 miles in 6:21. He started participating in six-day races in 1887 and quickly progressed to be one of the top pedestrians in America and was thought to be the youngest runner to reach over 500 miles. During the later 1800s, he competed in at least 23 six-day races and regularly won them. In 1891, he retired and raised some of the finest game cocks in the country and was involved in cockfighting.

Thomas Howarth had married **Sarah Howarth** in 1889, and they had a daughter, **Gertrude Howath.** But in 1903, the Howarths became separated. On September 7, 1903, tragedy struck. "About 4:00 in the afternoon, Sarah retired to her room. Fifteen minutes later, Policemen Wright and Lint, who were watching a ball game on a lot close by, saw smoke issuing from the second-story windows of the Elser Street dwelling. Hurrying to investigate, they learned that the smoke was coming from the room occupied by Mrs. Howarth. The door of the apartment was quickly forced and the woman was found lying on the bed, dead."

> **WOMAN BURNED TO DEATH IN BED**
>
> Charred Body of Professional Pedestrian's Wife Found—Cigarette Ignited Clothing

"She had been burned to death. The stump of a cigarette was found beside the bed. The police believe that the woman fell asleep with the lighted cigarette in her hand and that the sparks set fire to the bed clothing."

Howarth went on to marry again to Mary and worked as a groundskeeper at an athletic field. He later found employment at the Electric Storage Battery Company. He died on March 1, 1932, at the age of 71 in Philadelphia, from Bronchial Pneumonia contributed by alcoholism.

A Mother's Tragedy

At a six-day race in Baltimore, at Kernan's Summer Garden, in August 1879, a Mrs. Power left a sick child at home to try hard to

> **Kernan's Central Summer Garden.**
> Now Going On,
> THE GREAT SIX-DAYS'
> FEMALE WALKING MATCH,
> Between the following well-known Female Pedestriennes:
> CORA CUSHING, LITTLE LIGHTFOOT, CARRIE LEE, MAID OF THE WATER-WORKS,
> For a Purse of $600.
> Admission 25 cents.

obtain a share of the winnings to provide for her family. "Although the child was failing daily, she was deceived in regard to its condition in order not to interfere with her chance of winning. On the fifth day, it died, when the heartless friends dared no longer to conceal the truth, and the wretched mother was overwhelmed by the intelligence and immediately went to mourn over the remains of her darling." The mother had reached 238 miles and likely would have finished in second place. The race management had a heart and generously gave her $250.

Mother Tries to get Daughter to Stop

Finishing this chapter on a lighter note, a young woman, **Hattie Williams**, age 16, was competing in a six-day, four hours per day race in 1893 in Rochester, New York. Her mother showed up on the second day and "raised a row" demanding that they stop her daughter. The girl wanted to continue, and the race manager was fine to allow her to go on. The next night, the mother, with a friend, pulled her away from the race and took her to the police station to have them talk some sense into her. But Williams rudely declared to the police that she would not go home if they did not allow her to continue in the walking match.

> WOULD NOT GO HOME
> Female Walking Match in Rochester Nearly Brought to Close.

The Brooklyn Citizen wrote, "It is difficult to see what great magnet of attraction a woman can see in such a line of amusement, but there remains still a possibility that ere the six days are over, the obstreperous miss may be only too glad to seek the shelter of her home and there rest her weary body and aching joints, probably with a full sense of her own folly impressed on her weakened intellect."

Conclusion

This book was about many of the outliers in the sport. It told about the good, bad, and ugly, with emphasis on the bad and ugly. Most of the ultrarunners/pedestrians were very good people, who went on to work if respectable occupations.

By 1906, when nearly all the indoor pedestrian events ceased, most of old-time pedestrians had also retired from the sport. Many had lost their fortunes due to the financial downturn of the late 1800s and mismanagement of finances. Where were many of these old-time pedestrians in 1906?

Frank Hart (1856-1908) had been a professional trainer of long-distance cyclists and runners during his final years. **Napoleon "Old Sport" Campana** (1836-1906) was selling chewing gum on the streets of Chicago and was seriously ill. **Gus Guerrero** was a gate-tender on the Broadway subway in New York City and trainer for the New York Giants baseball team. **Henry O. Messier** (1862-1945), the sport's historian, was a book salesman. **James Albert** (1856-1912), the American six-day record holder (still holds the record with 621 miles), was operating a cattle ranch in Texas. **Patrick Fitzgerald** (1846-1900), former world record holder and alderman in New York, had recently died. **Stephen Barnes "Old Soldier"** (1846-1916), age 60 was retired, but still made plenty of public appearances, carrying an American flag at marathons and other shorter races. The former six-day world record holder, **Robert Vint** (1846-1917), the shoemaker, lived in California. **George D. Noremac** (1852-1922) was operating a hotel in Philadelphia. **Peter Golden** (1943-1933), and **Peter Hegelman** (1864-1944), were clerks in New York City. **John Glick** (1869-1929) was working in the cotton mills in Philadelphia. **Edward C. Moore** (1860-1927) was in Europe working for the Standard Oil company. **Richard Lacouse** (1848-1923) was a bricklayer in Montana. **George W. Guyon** (1853-1933) was a "tinker" in Oklahoma City. **Charles A. Harriman** (1853-1919) was a farmer and pastor in Rockport, Maine. **John "Lepper" Hughes** (1850-1921) of New York City, was operating a saloon. Former six-day world record holder from England, **Charles Rowell** (1852-1902) had recently died. Another former world record holder, **Henry "Blower" Brown** (1843-1900) of England, had also died. The six-day world record holder, **George Littlewood** (1859-1912) was in business in England. **Daniel O'Leary** (1846-1933), was still walking, and the next year at the age of 61 would conquer the Barclay Match by walking 1,000 miles, one mile each hour, for 1,000 consecutive hours in Cincinnati, Ohio. **Edward Payson Weston** (1839-1929) was still a professional walker, and that year, at age 67 walked from Philadelphia's city hall to the Fifth Avenue Hotel in lower Manhattan in 24 hours. **Thomas Howarth** (1860-1932) was working as a groundskeeper in Philadelphia, Pennsylvania. **George Cartwright** (1848-1925+) was working for a bicycle manufacturing company in Syracuse, New York. **Patrick Cavanaugh** (1863-1908) was working construction in New Jersey. **Richard Lacouse** (1848-1923), was working for a mining company in Anaconda, Montana. Trainer **John D. Oliver "Happy Jack Smith"** (1860-1914) was still training athletes in Massachusetts.

Sources

Chapters One and Two

- Peter Radford, *The Celebrated Captain Barclay: Sport, Gambling and Adventure in Regency Times.*
- Andy Milroy, *"The History of the 1,000 Mile Race"*
- P. S. Marshall: *Richard Manks and the Pedestrians*
- Walking 1100 Miles in 1100 Hours
- Derek Martin "A Short History of the Barclay Match: 1809-1909"
- The Ipswich Journal (England), Jul 22, 1809, Oct 1, 1808, Nov 5, 1808
- The Observer (London), Oct 30, 1808
- The Morning Post (London), Jun 5, Dec 27, 1808
- The Bury and Norwich Post (England) Dec 21, 1808
- The Lancaster Gazette (England), Jul 22, 1809
- The Evening Post (New York), Sep 19, 1809
- The Freeman's Journal (Ireland), Aug 16, 1809, Aug 19, 1813
- Hampshire Telegraph and Navel Chronicle (England), Jul 31, 1809
- The Caledonian Mercury (Scotland), Aug 25, 1814
- The Exeter Flying Post (England), Nov 16, 1815
- The Champion and Weekly Herald (England), Nov 4, 1838
- The Preston Chronicle and Lancashire Advertiser, Dec 1, 1838
- Jackson's Oxford Journal, Oct 27, 1838
- Brooklyn Evening Star, Aug 26, 1842
- New York Daily Herald, Jun 1, 1845
- The Times-Picayune (Louisiana) Apr 20, 1845
- Buffalo Morning Express, Jul 25, 1846
- The Weekly Standard and Express (Blackburn, England) Dec 12, 1838
- The Era (London, England), Aug 3, 24, 1851
- The Portsmouth Inquirer (Ohio), Nov 7, 1851
- Liverpool Mercury, Sep 24, Oct 12,19, 29, Nov 2, 1852, 21 Sep 1864
- The Brooklyn Daily Eagle, Sep 10, 1857
- Buffalo Courier, Sept 27, 1858
- The Leeds Mercury, 20 Nov 1877
- The Bristol Mercury and Daily Post, (England) 17 Nov 1877
- The Marion Star (Ohio), Sep 7, Oct 19, 1907
- The Cincinnati Enquirer, Sep 23, Oct 22, 1907
- The Dayton Herald (Oho), Oct 17, 1907
- The Sun (New York), Oct 21, 1907
- Harrisburg Telegraph, Nov 13, 1946

- The Observer (London), April 13, 2003
- The Guardian (London), Apr 7, 2003

Chapters Three and Four

- The Buffalo Commercial (New York), Jan 28, 1879
- The New York Times (New York), Feb 2, 10, Mar 24, 1879
- The Inter Ocean (Chicago, Illinois), Jan 18, May 1, 1887, Feb 15, 1879
- The Saint Paul Globe (Minnesota), Feb 24, 1879
- The Philadelphia Inquirer (Pennsylvania), Feb 24, 1879
- The Sun (New York City, New York), Mar 4, 1879
- The Boston Globe (Massachusetts), Mar 4, 1879
- New York Daily Herald (New York), Mar 4, 1879
- The Gazette (Montreal, Quebec, Canada), Aug 19, 1885
- The Indianapolis News (Indiana), Aug 7, 1885, Dec 18, 1885
- Winfield Daily Courier (Kansas), Feb 17, 1886
- The Post-Star (Glens Falls, New York), Jul 8, 1886
- The Indianapolis Journal (Indiana), Nov 23, Dec 12, 1886, Apr 10-11, Jul 28, 1887
- The Muncie Morning News (Indiana), Jan 8, 1887
- The Dayton Herald (Ohio), Jan 21, 1887
- The Fort Wayne Sentinel (Indiana), Mar 21, 1887
- The Indianapolis Journal (Indiana), Apr 17, 1887
- Chicago Tribune (Illinois), Oct 29, 1887
- The Jasper Weekly Courier (Indiana), Nov 11, 1887
- The Advance (Soldiers Grove, Wisconsin) Dec 12, 1887
- The Huntington Democrat (Indiana), Dec 15, 1887
- The News (Quincy, Illinois), Dec 6, 1887
- The Cincinnati Enquirer (Ohio), Dec 6, 1887
- The Boston Globe (Massachusetts), Dec 7, 1887
- Manitoba Weekly Free Press (Winnipeg, Canada), Dec 8, 1887
- Democrat and Chronicle (Rochester, New York), Apr 15, 1900

Chapters Five and Six

- Tom Osler and Ed Dodd, *Ultra-marathoning: The Next Challenge*
- P. S. Marshall, *King of the Peds*
- Evening Star (Washington, D. C.), Nov 21, 1876
- The Ottawa Free Trader (Illinois), Jun 23, 1877
- The New Orleans Weekly Democrat (Louisiana), Mar 15, 1879

- The Selinsgrove Times-Tribune (Pennsylvania), Mar 19, 1879
- Hartford Courant (Connecticut), Sep 26, 1879
- The San Francisco Examiner (California), Oct 16, 1879
- The Cincinnati Enquirer (Ohio), Feb 22, 1881
- The Boston Globe (Massachusetts), Mar 1, 1881
- Columbus Daily Telegram (Nebraska), Mar 26, 1891
- Birmingham Daily Post (England), Sep 26, 1882
- The Birmingham Daily Mail (England), Sep 26, 1882
- The Evening World (New York, New York), Feb 6, 1888
- The Union Leader (Wilkes-Barre, Pennsylvania), Feb 24, 1888
- The Minneapolis Times (Minnesota), Feb 8, 1891
- Altoona Tribune (Pennsylvania), Feb 24, 1891
- The Brooklyn Citizen (New York), Mar 24, 1891
- Pittsburgh Daily Post (Pennsylvania), Nov 13, 17-18, 1901
- Louis Post-Dispatch (Missouri), Feb 11, 1902
- The San Francisco Call (California), Feb 11, 1902
- The New York Times (New York), Feb 14, 1902
- Buffalo Evening News (New York), Feb 28, 1903
- Sun-Journal (Lewiston, Maine), Dec 29, 1906

Chapter Seven

- Tom Osler and Ed Dodd, *Ultra-marathoning: The Next Challenge*
- P. S. Marshall, *King of the Peds*
- The Ottawa Free Trader (Illinois), Jun 23, 1877
- The Stark County Democrat (Canton, Ohio), Nov 14, 1878
- Chicago Daily Telegraph (Illinois), Mar 4, 1879
- Chicago Tribune, Apr 4, May 23, 1879
- The Philadelphia Times (Pennsylvania), Apr 15, Sep 23, Nov 1-15. 1879
- San Francisco Chronicle (California), Oct 8, 1879
- Selma Dollar Times (Alabama), Oct 15, 1879
- Richmond Dispatch (Virginia), Nov 14, 1879
- Boston Globe (Massachusetts), Mar 1, 1880
- Burlington Free Press (Vermont), April 1, 1880
- New York Tribune (New York), Apr 15, 1880
- The Valley Sentinel (Carlisle, Pennsylvania), Jul 16, 1880
- The Boston Globe (Massachusetts), May 28, 1883
- The Macon Telegraph (Georgia), Sep 24. 1884
- The Illustrated London News (England), Nov 29, 1884
- The Evening World (New York, New York), Feb 8, 1888
- The Evening Mail (Stockton, California), May 19, 1888

- The Kansas City Star (Missouri), Feb 23, 1891
- The Evening World (New York, New York), Mar 19, 1891
- The Standard Union (Brooklyn, New York), Mar 19, 1891
- The Brooklyn Daily Eagle (New York), May 13, 1879, Mar 22, 1880, Mar 20, 1891
- Interstate News-Record (Ironwood, Michigan), Apr 18, 1891
- St. Louis Globe-Democrat (Missouri), Mar 31, 1892
- The Age (Melbourne, Australia), Apr 25, 1895
- The Philadelphia Inquirer (Pennsylvania), Nov 14, 1879, Mar 14, 1902
- The Indianapolis Star (Indiana), Aug 26, 1903
- The Philadelphia Inquirer (Pennsylvania), Nov 10, 1902, Feb 10, 1908
- The Journal (Meriden, Connecticut), Mar 19, 1908

Chapter Eight

- Chicago Daily Telegraph (Illinois), Mar 17, 1879
- The Brooklyn Daily Eagle (New York), Mar 17, Sep 26, 1879
- The Sun (New York, New York), Mar 25, 1879, May 25, 28, 1881, May 2, 4, 1884
- Star Tribune (Minneapolis, Minnesota), Mar 19, 22, 1879
- The Raleigh News (North Carolina), Sep 30, 1879
- The Brooklyn Daily Eagle (New York), Oct 11, 1879
- New York Daily Herald (New York), Oct 9, 1879
- Philadelphia Times (Pennsylvania), May 3, 1879
- The Philadelphia Inquirer (Pennsylvania), May 3, 5, 1879
- The New York Times (New York), Mar 2, 5, 1879, May 3, 1884
- Sporting Life (London, England), Nov 10, 1880
- The Boston Globe (Massachusetts), Mar 15, 1879, Dec 5, 1880
- The Evening Review (East Liverpool, Ohio), Nov 23, 1887
- The Cincinnati Enquirer (Ohio), Nov 24, 1887
- The Evening World (New York, New York), Feb 7, 1888
- Brooklyn Times Union, Mar 20, 1891

Sources for Chapter Nine, Ten, and Fifteen

- Tom Osler and Ed Dodd, *Ultra-marathoning: The Next Challenge*
- P. S. Marshall, *King of the Peds*
- Steve Brodie (bridge jumper)
- That daredevil Steve Brodie!
- The Daily Record of Times (Wilkes-Barre, Pennsylvania), Aug 3, 1875

Strange Running Tales: When Ultrarunning was a Reality Show

- Pittsburgh Daily Post (Pennsylvania), Jul 29, 1875
- The Courier and Argus (Dundee, Scotland), Dec 14, 1876
- New York Daily Herald (New York), Mar 31, 1879, Feb 15, 1879
- New York Tribune (New York), Apr 15, 1879
- The Buffalo Commercial (New York), Apr 16, 1879
- Intelligencer Journal (Lancaster, Pennsylvania), Apr 17, 1879
- The Sun (New York, New York), Apr 18, 1879, Sep 8-17, 25, 1880
- Buffalo Weekly Courier (New York), Apr 23, 1879, Sep 10, 1889
- Brooklyn Times Union (New York), Apr 25, 29, 1879, Sep 17, 1895
- The Philadelphia Times (Pennsylvania), Mar 4, 1879, Apr 29, May 1, 16-17, 24, 1879
- The Times (Philadelphia, Pennsylvania), May 3, 1879
- The Daily News (Lebanon, Pennsylvania), May 5, 1879
- Harrisburg Daily Independent (Pennsylvania), May 15, 1879
- The Brooklyn Daily Eagle (New York), Feb 6, Mar 22, 24, 1879, Sep 16, 24, 1880, Feb 24, 1881, May 17, 1886, Jun 17, 1915
- The Norfolk Virginian (Virginia), Jul 8, 1879
- The Topeka State Journal (Kansas), Sep 13, 1879
- Harrisburg Daily Independent (Pennsylvania), Sep 18, 1879
- The San Francisco Examiner (California), Oct 15-22, 1879
- San Francisco Chronicle (California), Oct 18, 19, 1879
- The York Daily (Pennsylvania), Sept 3, 1879, Jul 3, 1885
- The Daily Telegraph (London, England), Apr 29, 1880, Jun 4, 1881
- The Brooklyn Union (New York), Mar 5, 1881
- The New York Times (New York), Mar 7, Apr 15, 20, 1879, Sep 16, 1880, Mar 6, Oct 3, 1881, Mar 27, Dec 15, 1883, Mar 8, 1886, Mar 6, 1892, Feb 1, 1901
- The Baltimore Sun (Maryland), Feb 23, Mar 7, 1881
- Edinburgh Evening News (Scotland), Jun 6, 1881
- The Boston Globe (Massachusetts), Apr 14, 17, 19, 22, 1879, Feb 18, 1880, Jun 5, Jul 10, 1881, Feb 25, 1883, Nov 9-10, 28, 1886
- The Cincinnati Enquirer (Ohio), Jun 22, 1881
- Nottingham Journal (England), Jan 8, 1881
- Sheffield Daily Telegraph (Yorkshire, England), Nov 16, 1881
- Derby Mercury (Derbyshire, England), Jul 9, 1881, Nov 16, 1881
- The Merthy Express (Wales), Nov 7, 1885
- The Hampshire Advertiser (Southampton, England), Dec 17, 21, 1887
- Buffalo Evening News (New York), Sep 9, 13, 1889
- The Shore Press (Asbury Park, New Jersey), Jul 8, 1892
- The Inter Ocean (Chicago, Illinois), Jul 19, 1879, Jun 29, 1893
- The Philadelphia Inquirer (Pennsylvania), Apr 28, May 1, 31, 1879, Jul 1-2, 1885, Sep 11, 1894

- The Atlanta Constitution (Georgia), May 17, 1898, Dec 9, 1899, Feb 19, 1904
- The Troy Messenger (Alabama), Mar 14, 1900
- The Buffalo Enquirer (New York), Feb 2, Aug 23, Dec 3, 1900
- The Buffalo Review (New York), Feb 24, 1900
- The Buffalo Times (New York), Nov 22, 1900, Jan 26, 1901
- Miners Journal (Pottsville, Pennsylvania), Feb 6, 1901
- Passaic Daily Herald (New Jersey), May 3, 1902
- The Weekly Dispatch (London, England), Jun 12, 1904
- The Macon Telegraph (Georgia), Feb 19, 1904
- The Nottingham Evening Post (England), Jan 16, 1905
- The Minneapolis Journal (Minnesota), Apr 9, 1906
- Ashbourne News (Derbyshire, England), Aug 23, 1907
- Manchester Courier (England), Sep 11, 1907
- The Tacoma Daily Ledger (Tacoma, Washington), Jun 10, 1908
- Lancaster New Era (Pennsylvania), May 13, 1912
- Leicester Evening Mail (England), Jul 4, 1913
- The Morning Call (Paterson, New Jersey), Jun 16, 1915
- Brooklyn Times Union, Mar 20, 1891
- The Ashbourne News (Derbyshire, England), Feb 2, 1906
- The Staffordshire Sentinel Daily and Weekly (England), Sep 2, 1905
- Midland Daily Telegraph (Coventry, England), Sep 23, 1905
- The Gloucestershire Echo (England), Jan 1, 1907

Sources for Chapter Eleven

- The Evening Mail (Stockton, California), Dec 7, 1887
- The Boston Globe (Massachusetts), Nov 27, Dec 28, 1887
- Pittsburgh Dispatch (Pennsylvania), Feb 17, 21-23, 1889, Apr 10, Jun 9, 1891
- The Morning Journal-Courier (New Haven, Connecticut), Oct 2, 1889
- Miners Journal (Pottsville, Pennsylvania), Dec 2, 1890
- Wyoming Democrat (Tunkhannock, Pennsylvania), Dec 5, 1890
- The Times Leader (Wilkes-Barre, Pennsylvania), Dec 2-3, 5, 1890
- Sunday News (Wilkes-Barre, Pennsylvania), Dec 7, 1890
- The Anaconda Standard (Montana), Sep 6, 1891
- Minneapolis Daily Times (Minnesota), Apr 5, 1892
- The Pittsburgh Press (Pennsylvania), Aug 13, 1891, Apr 25, 1897
- The Evening Review (East Liverpool, Ohio), Apr 17, 26-27, Jun 15-28, Jul 7, 19, 21, 24, Aug 17, Sep 1, 29, Oct 5, 20, 1897, Sep 13, 1900, Nov 13, 1901, Jul 25, 1902, Mar 6, Dec 2, 1903, Jul 14-15, 1904
- Pittsburgh Daily Post (Pennsylvania), May 5, 1887, Apr 25, Jun 15, 1897, Aug 30, 1906

Sources for Chapter Twelve

- Harry Hall, *The Pedestriennes: America's Forgotten Superstars*
- The Norfolk Virginian (Virginia), Apr 1, 1879
- The Boston Globe (Massachusetts), Jul 14, 1879, May 7, 1884, Mar 15, 1919
- Louis Globe (Missouri), Jul 14, 1879
- The Cincinnati Enquirer (Ohio), Jul 15, 1879
- Evening Star (Washington, D.C), Jul 15, Oct 20, 1879
- Democrat and Chronicle (Rochester, New York), Jul 23, 1879
- Louis Globe-Democrat (Missouri), Nov 19, 1880
- The Brooklyn Daily Eagle (New York), Nov 18, 1880, Jan 21, 1881
- The Brooklyn Union (New York), Feb 6, Nov 29, 1880
- The Sun (New York), Mar 20, 1881
- The New York Times (New York), Mar 28, 1879, Jun 28, 1884
- Tulare County Times (Visalia, California), May 17, 1879
- The Highland Weekly News (Hillsboro, Ohio), Jul 3, 17, 1879
- Fayette County Herald (Washington, Ohio), Jul 17, 1879
- The Evening Mail (Stockton, California), Dec 14, 1880
- The Times-Democrat (Lima, Ohio), Apr 22, 1880
- The Spirit of the Times (New York, New York), Feb 16, 1884
- Savannah Morning News (Georgia), Jun 26, 1884
- The Atlanta Constitution (Georgia), Jul 10, 26, 1884
- The Macon Telegraph (Georgia), Jan 13, 1887
- The Cincinnati Enquirer (Ohio), Feb 3, 1889
- The Dayton Herald (Ohio), Feb 2, 7, 1889
- Sun-Journal (Lewiston, Maine), Jan 8, 1907
- The York Dispatch (Pennsylvania), Jun 6, 1935

Sources for Chapter Thirteen

- Mike Huggins, "Match-fixing: a historical perspective."
- Reading Times (Pennsylvania), May 13, 1879
- New York Daily Herald (New York), Oct 11, 1879
- The San Francisco Examiner (California), Nov 24, 1879
- Sacramento Bee (California), Jan 17, 1880
- The New York Times (New York), Jan 24, Mar 6, 1881, May 4, 1884
- The Boston Globe (Massachusetts), Mar 6, 20, May 28, 1881, Feb 12, 1888, Dec 4, 1891, Nov 27, 1914
- Arkansas Democrat (Little Rock, Arkansas), May 28, 1881
- The Macon Telegraph (Georgia), May 5, 1885
- The Atlanta Constitution (Georgia), May 4, 1885

- The Daily News (Lebanon, Pennsylvania), May 4, 1885
- The Evening World (New York, New York), Feb 8, 1888
- The Philadelphia Times (Pennsylvania), Feb 12, 1888
- The Sun (New York, New York), Sep 5, 1883, Feb 12, 1888
- Waterbury Evening Democrat (Connecticut), Feb 23, 1888
- The San Francisco Examiner (California), Apr 22, 1889
- The Daily Courier (San Bernardino, California), May 16, 1889
- The Yonkers Herald (New York), Aug 22, 1894
- Asbury Park Press (New Jersey), Nov 5, 1898
- The Evening Mail (Stockton, California), Oct 14, 1901
- Evening Sentinel (Santa Cruz, California) Oct 9, 1902
- Buffalo Evening News (New York), Feb 14, 1903
- Star-Gazette (Elmira, New York), May 13, 1914

Sources for Chapter Fourteen

- Boston Globe (Massachusetts), Oct 29, 1875, May 5, 14-18, 31, Jun 1, Jul 24, Aug 4, 14, Jul 27, 1879, Oct 25-26, 1879, May 31, Dec 26, 1880, Mar 7, 20, 1881, Aug 20-21, Sep 6, 1884, Jun 20, Dec 30, 1884, Apr 2-3, 7, Aug 3, 17, Sep 15-16, 1885, May 14, Jun 3-4, 1886, Oct 12, 1888, Jul 25, 1906
- Fall River Daily Evening News (Massachusetts), May 27, Oct 27, 1879
- The News Journal (Wilmington, Delaware), Jun 2, 1879
- Hartford Courant (Connecticut), Jul 28, 1879
- New York Daily Herald (New York, New York), Aug 16, 1879
- Fort Scott Daily Monitor (Kansas), Sep 7, 1879
- New York Times (New York), Jan 28, Mar 2, 1881
- The Galveston Daily News (Texas), May 19, Jun 3,5. 8, 26. Jul 1, 1886
- Louis Globe-Democrat (Missouri), Jun 3, 1886
- The Saint Paul Globe (Minnesota), Jun 4, 1886
- The Sunday Leader (Wilkes-Barre, Pennsylvania), Jun 6, 1866
- The Anaconda Standard (Montana), Feb 12, 16, 1892
- The Butte Miner (Montana), Jun 21, 1921, Nov 6-15, 1923

Sources for Chapter Sixteen

- P.S. Marshal, *King of the Peds*
- P.S. Marshal, *GEORGE NOREMAC: The Original "Flying Scotsman!"*
- New York Daily Herald (New York), Feb 24, 1865
- North British Daily Mail (Lanarkshire, Scotland), Aug 20, 1877
- New York Times (New York), Jun 16, 1879, Feb 27, 1882, Mar 2, Oct 29, 1882, Aug 24, 1883, May 11, 1885

Strange Running Tales: When Ultrarunning was a Reality Show

- New-York Tribune (New York), Mar 5, 1882, Oct 23-28, 1882, Aug 24, 1883, Dec 2, 1888
- The Brooklyn Daily Eagle (New York), Jul 22, 1881, May 11, 1885
- The Brooklyn Union (Jun 16, 1879)
- The Sun (New York, New York), Dec 26, 28, 1881, Mar 1, Oct 29, 1882, Aug 24, 1883
- Aberdeen Journal (Scotland), Jul 8, 1879
- The Courier and Argus (Dundee, Scotland), Jul 15, 1879
- Sporting Life (London, England), Jan 3, 1880
- Aberdeen Herald (Scotland), May 29, 1880
- Sporting Life (London, England), Oct 6, 1880, May 31, 1881
- Glasgow Herald (Scotland), Dec 20, 1880
- North Star (Darlington, England), Jan 6, 1881
- The Evansville Journal (Indiana), May 14, 1882
- The Boston Globe (Massachusetts), Aug 1-5, 1882
- The Penny Pater (Cincinnati, Ohio), Oct 12, 1882
- Chicago Tribune (Illinois), Aug 24, 1883
- The Daily News (Lebanon, Pennsylvania), May 28, 1883
- The Fall River Daily Herald (Massachusetts), Aug 27, 1883
- The Daily Deadwood Pioneer-Times (South Dakota), Aug 28, 1883
- The Baltimore Sun (Maryland), Nov 4, 1884
- Lancaster New Era (Pennsylvania), Nov 4, 1884
- The Philadelphia Times (Pennsylvania), Mar 25, 1888
- Waterbury Evening Democrat (Connecticut), Oct 14, 1889
- Pittsburgh Dispatch (Pennsylvania), Dec 3, 28, 1889
- Louis Post-Dispatch (Missouri), Dec 23, 1890
- Star Tribune (Minneapolis, Minnesota), Jan 11, 1891
- The Evening World (New York, New York), Mar 21, 1891
- The Los Angeles Times (California), May 13, 1899
- The Pittsburgh Press (Pennsylvania), Nov 17, 1901
- The Philadelphia Inquirer (Pennsylvania), Feb 18, 1922

Sources for Chapter Seventeen

- Liverpool Mercury (England), Nov 1, 8, 1850
- The Guardian (London, England), Nov 9, 1850
- Liverpool Mercury (England), Nov 22, 1850
- The Morning Chronicle (London, England), Dec 16, 1850
- The North Alabamian (Tuscumbia, Alabama), Sep 5, 1879.
- The Brooklyn Daily Eagle (New York), Dec 15, 1879
- The New York Times (New York), Dec 15, 1879

Davy Crockett

- New York Daily Herald (New York), Dec 16, 1879
- Sheffield Independent (England), Apr 25, 1882
- Manchester Evening News (England), Apr 27, 1882
- Sheffield Independent (England), Apr 28, 1882
- Dundee Advertiser (Scotland), May 15, 1882
- Illustrated Police News (London, England), Oct 7, 1882
- The Leavenworth Standard (Kansas), May 1, 1884
- York Herald (England), Jan 7, 1888
- The Boston Globe (Massachusetts), Mar 11, Dec 8, 1888
- The Evening Bulletin (Maysville, Kentucky), Apr 16, 1888
- The New York Times (New York), Apr 17, 1888
- Chicago Tribune, (Illinois) May 7, 1888
- The Post-Star, (Glens Falls, New York), Sep 25, 1888
- Fall River Daily Evening News (Massachusetts), Dec 7, 1888
- The Evening World (New York, New York), Dec 7, 1888, Jun 29, 1889
- The Times Leader (Wilkes-Barre, Pennsylvania), Dec 10, 1888
- The Record-Union (Sacramento, California), Dec 7, 1888, Mar 29, 1889
- Toronto Daily Mail (Ontario, Canada), Jan 18, 1889
- The Brooklyn Citizen (New York), May 11, 1893
- Louis Globe-Democrat (Missouri), Feb 9, 1897
- The Philadelphia Inquirer (Pennsylvania), Sep 8, 1903

About the Author

David "Davy" R. Crockett is a veteran ultrarunner and historian. He began serious running in 2004 and finished more than one hundred 100-mile races during the next fourteen years. In 2005, he combined his love for running and history by organizing the "Pony Express Trail 50 and 100" held on the historic Pony Express Trail in the west desert of Utah.

In 2018, he established ultrarunninghistory.com and the Ultrarunning History Podcast, authoring long articles and episodes every two weeks, documenting long-forgotten stories of the sport.

In 2020, he became the new Director of the American Ultrarunning Hall of Fame, which is hosted on ultrarunninghistory.com.

Davy Crockett is the author of four previous books on the American 19th-century westward migration, and two previous books in the Ultrarunning History Series, *Frank Hart: The First Black Ultrarunning Star* and *Grand Canyon Rim to Rim History*. He has also published numerous articles in magazines and newspapers, and two online books on ultrarunning.

He and his wife Linda are the parents of six children and twelve grandchildren, all living in Utah.

Ultrarunninghistory.com

Crockettclan.org/blog

Acknowledgments

Thanks to **Andy Milroy** of England for inspiring and guiding me in my quest to learn and understand the history of ultrarunning. Thanks to **P.S. Marshall** for his exhaustive collection of early pedestrianism, including photos, and outstanding reference book, *King of the Peds*. Thanks to ultrarunning legendary **Ed Dodd** for reintroducing the American ultrarunning sport to pedestrianism history in 1979 and was instrumental in bringing back the six-day race after more than 70 years of absence. Thanks to **Harry Hall** for bringing the spotlight on women pedestrians with his excellent research documented in *The Pedestriennes: America's Forgotten Superstars*. I am also thankful for my dedicated audience of Ultrarunning History Podcast, who have encouraged me to collect my writings into books so they can be preserved.

Listen to the Ultrarunning History Podcast in your favorite podcast app or on ultrarunninghistory.com. You can also watch the episodes on the Ultrarunning History YouTube Channel.

Index

Adams, Harriet "Hattie", 98, 99, 103, 105
Adams, Henry, 98
Albert, James, 43, 150, 156, 157, 158, 160, 211, 226, 233
Alexandria, Martha, 110
All, Mark, 183, 184, 185, 186
Allen, Joseph, 62
Alvina Wurms, Frances, 132
Anderson, Ada, 43
Anderson, Hans, 102
Anderson, Lillian, 102
Apgar, Melville B., 66
Armaindo, Louise, 213
Atkinson, George W., 73
Avery, George F., 134, 135
Barclay, Captain Robert, 2-9,
Barnam, P.T., 134
Barnes, Old Soldier Stephen, 39
Barnet, N. B., 15
Barnum, P.T., viii, 164
Barrett, Joseph M, 137
Beachmont, Tom, 40
Beattie, George, 195, 196, 197, 198, 199, 204, 205, 206, 208
Belden, Edward, 21, 22
Bennett, Emily, 188
Bibbins, Charles, 150
Blodin, Charles, 164
Brodie, Bridget Breen, 89
Brodie, Dan, 90
Brodie, Richard, 80
Brodie, Steve, v, 79-96, 168, 238
Brown, Henry "Blower", 198, 233
Buckler, William, 107
Bunny, Bugs, 95
Burgoine, Joseph, 21, 23
Burns, Daniel, 155, 156, 209
Burrows, Captain C., 176
Butler, Dennis F., 94

Cameron, Alexander, 206
Cameron, Alexander Edward, 196
Cameron, Elizabeth Edwards, 196, 199, 202, 205, 207, 208, 217
Cameron, Georgina, 203
Cameron, Jane, 199, 202
Cameron, Jessie Brown, 196
Cameron, John, 196
Campana, Peter Napoleon, 149, 151
Campbell, Patrick, 191
Campbell, Peter, 204
Carr, Elizabeth, 181, 182
Cartwright, George, 41, 51, 223-229
Cavanaugh, Patrick, 51, 58
Chenowith, William, 57
Clow, Ephraim, 151
Clute, John, 76
Comber, John, 67
Cousins, William, 131, 132, 133
Cox, Tom, 43, 61
Crawford, James "Hoppy", 61
Creamer, Frank, 71
Crockett, Davy, 245
Cross, William, 6
Curran, Ben, 74, 152-155, 160, 169
Daly, Bill, 148, 149, 150
Davis, Albert, 190
Davis, Dean, 46
Day, Sammy, 40, 97, 154, 209, 216
Dean, James, 38
Dermody, John, 220, 222
Dickinson, John J., 85
Dillon, John, 59
Dobler, James, 56
Dodd, Ed, 246
Donaldson, Robert, 120
Donovan, William, 210
Doran, Joseph, 179
Drake, Clinton, 65
Dutcher, William, 58

247

Dwyer, John, 100
Eaton, Josiah, 10-15
Edson, Maud, 170-176
Edwards, Fannie, 129, 130, 131, 132, 133
Edwards, Frank, 86, 131
Eggleston, Reverend Edward, 193
Ellsworth, Captain Thomas, 19
Ennis, John T., 199
Fahey, Martin, 37
Fields, Thomas, 102
Finerty, Tom, 45
Finley, Julie, 55
Fisher, Aleck, 65
Fitzgerald, Patrick, 77, 157, 161, 162, 169, 200, 203, 208, 226, 233
Flemming, Frankie, 112
Floyd, George, 90
Ford, James Willliam, 135
Foster, Annie, 115
Fowler, Benjamin, 61
Frazier, Emma, 181
Fulton, Dr. Justin D., 98
Gale, William, 20
Geon, Joseph, 120
Gillespie, Grace, 145
Gilmore, Patrick, 201
Glick, John, 46, 233
Golden, Peter, 74, 211, 233
Gowan, John, 54, 55
Green, John, 189
Grotenthaler, J. L., 182
Guerrero, Gus, 45, 59, 87, 88, 189, 233
Gully, John, 5
Guyon, George W., 233
Hager, Harry, 134
Hall, Frank W., 75
Hall, Harry, 246
Halleck, T. E., 167
Harriett, Mary, 229
Harriett, Robert "Mikey Free", 229, 230

Harriman, Charles, 40, 41, 42, 140, 141, 142, 143, 233
Harris, Charles, 16
Harris, William, 59
Hart, Frank, iv, 39, 47, 48, 52, 166, 168, 209, 233, 245
Harvey, Aggie, 117
Hayes, Rutherford B, 71
Hazael, George, 71, 161, 190, 191, 197
Healy, M. J., 173
Hegelman, Peter, 233
Herrick, Myron Timothy, 127
Hershey, E. A., 127
Hibberd, Jack, 73
Hinman, J. W., 138
Hoag, David, 60
Holland, Ephraim, 71, 72
Holske, Charles Edward, 86
Hooker, General Joseph, 50
Houlett, John, 171
Howard, Amy, 25
Howard, Clarence, 61
Howarth, Thomas, 230, 231
Howath, Gertrude, 231
Howell, James, 191, 192
Huggins, Mike, 147
Hughes, John "Lepper", 47, 48, 77, 151, 168, 195, 203, 205, 209, 233
Jackson, John W., 145
Jamison, James B., 182
Jarbeau, Happy, 114, 115, 187
Jarrold, Ernest Justin, 93
Jones, Agnes Jane, 110
Kelly, James E., 154
Kerr, Mollie, 135, 136, 137, 138, 139
Kilbury, Bella, 49, 50, 113
Kirk, Thomas, 189
La Chapelle, Exilda, 49
Lacourse, Annie Lawnson, 177
Lacourse, Emelie Guilbert, 164
Lacourse, Helen, 177, 179
Lacourse, Joseph Octave, 164
Lacourse, Octave "Otto", 177, 179

Strange Running Tales: When Ultrarunning was a Reality Show

Lacouse, Catherine Buckley, 164, 167, 170
Lacouse, Joseph Richard, 170
Lacouse, Joseph, 178
Lacouse, Richard, v, 154, 160-178, 233
Lacouse, Winfred, 178
Lecher, Otto, 71
Leck, George, 61
LeFranc, Bertha "Bertie", 134
Leonardson, Delia, 130
Leonardson, Frank, 130
Levy, Simon, 21
Lipsey, Thomas, 133
Lipsey, Tryphena (Curtis), 133
Littlewood, George, 159, 213, 233
Livingston, Charles, 99, 100, 101, 102, 103
Loeslein, Tony, 38
Love, James Henry, 148
Lyons, Henry, 84
Mahoney, Patrick, 170
Manks, Richard, 17
Marshall, Mary/May, 99, 133, 134, 135, 235, 236, 237, 238
Marshall, P.S., 246
Martin, Emma, 145
McCullough, David, 92
Merritt, Sam, 71
Messier, Henry O., 116, 233
Miller, Burt, 144
Miller, Delia Cobey, 215
Milroy, Andy, 246
Mishler, Samuel F., 186
Mitchell, Charles, 62
Moorcroft, Walter B., 102, 103, 104
Moore, Edward C., 233
Moore, Orain, 41
Moore, Walter, 98, 99, 103
Morgan, Walter B., 103
Muldoon, "Tricks", 67
Murphy, T. J., 100
Newman, Dr. John Phillip, 193
Nichols, Richard, 60
Nolan, William, 41
Noon, James, 56
Noremac, George, v, 48, 195-217, 233
O'Leary, Daniel, 42, 55, 59, 97, 106, 151-153, 160, 169, 177, 188, 209, 233
O'Reilly, Daniel, 100
Odlum, Robert Emmet, 90
Panchot, Peter, 59, 211
Parker, Carrie, 55
Parsons, John S., 172
Pegge, George, 186
Perry, George, 120
Plummer, Edward F., 49
Potts, 62, 63, 64
Powell, Foster, vii
Prater, James Alfred, 105, 106, 135, 136, 139
Raft, George, 95
Remer, Isabella M., 131, 132
Rich, Fannie, 49
Robertson, Annette, 190
Robinson, James, 168
Robison, Alice, v, 109-127, 187, 188
Robison, David, 122
Robison, David S., 111
Robison, Georgia, 110
Robison, Robert, 110
Robison, Susan, 110
Robison, Thomas, 116, 122, 126
Robison, Zachariah, 110-127, 187
Roosevelt, Caroline, 145
Rose, Millie, 55
Rowell, Charles, 55, 66, 77, 161, 200, 201, 233
Sam, Rocky Mountain, 149, 150
Schneider, Joseph, 132, 133
Searles, James, 17
Sessions, Petty, 13
Sharp, Emma, 18, 19
Sheldon, Frank, 39

Sherlock, Robert, 54
Skipper, Robert, 15
Smith, "Happy Jack", 161, 233
Smith, Thomas Jr., 187
Smith, Thomas Sr., 187
Snowden, John Alexander, 210
Snyder, John Owen, 27, 28, 29, 31, 32, 33, 34, 35
Stackhouse, George, 140, 141
Stackhouse, Katie, 140, 142
Stackhouse, Willaim, 142
Stackhouse, William, 142
Standen, Thomas, 10
Stewart, Charles "Chuck", 116, 117, 118, 119, 122, 124, 125
Stewart, Hattie, 111
Stonewall, Lipsey/Curtis, 134
Strokel, Antoine, 43
Sullivan, Joseph Romeo, 58
Tanner, Dr. Henry S., 100
Thall, Mark, 148, 150
Thompson, Charles H., 77
Thompson, John, 155
Thorpe, Henry, 186
Tobias, Sarah, 113
Todd, Tony, 188
Trainor, Thomas, 189
Van Houten, William, 65
Van Keuren, Elijah, 61
Van Ness, Peter, 21-26, 86
Vaughn, Henry, 75
Vinson, Samuel, 145
Vint, Robert, 46, 73, 97, 213, 233
Von Berg, Bertha, 49
Von Blumen, Elsa, 143, 144, 145
Waldron, Madame, 98, 99, 103, 105
Wall, Albert, 62
Wallace, Ada, 49, 50
Waters, Mary Jane, 114
Weigand, Agnes "Maggie", 117, 119, 120, 125
Weigand, George, 119, 120
West, Kid, 39
Weston, Edward Payson, viii, 52, 55, 59, 80, 106, 197, 209, 210
White, "Fannie" Augustus, 136, 137
White, J. M., 62
White, Jabez, 137
White, Jabez M, 137
White, Thomas, 189
William, Richard, 179
Williams, Alexander "Clubber", 70, 75
Williams, Hattie, 232
Wilson, Edward G., 119
Wilson, John, 65
Wilson, Josie, 67

Printed in Great Britain
by Amazon